S0-AWC-881

THE BOOK OF GIRLS' NAMES

Uniform with this volume

THE BOOK OF
BOYS' NAMES

THE BOOK OF GIRLS' NAMES

by

LINWOOD SLEIGH

and

CHARLES JOHNSON

THOMAS Y. CROWELL COMPANY

NEW YORK · ESTABLISHED 1834

Printed in Great Britain

Library of Congress Catalog Card No. 63–8046

How to use this Book

The first part of this book, after the Introduction and Calendar of Saints, is devoted to the girls' names principally used in English-speaking countries. Their origins and meanings are fully given, together with many fascinating facts that have affected their popularity in different periods.

The Main Index, containing over 1400 names, is an index to this first part; you will find listed there all the main names and the varying forms they have taken.

The Supplementary List contains 1300 more names—the rarer, the fanciful, the recent—with an indication of their sources and meanings.

Thus by using both lists you have a choice of 2700 girls' names. Whatever is not in one list should be in the other. Remember, though, that new variants of old names and newly invented names are appearing every day. Omissions are inevitable, but we believe these lists are as comprehensive as any such lists can be at any given moment.

Each name, with its related details, is like a small piece of jigsaw, but the introduction gives you the complete picture which emerges when all these names are surveyed together. The interlocking elements of history, fashion, law, and language then become visible. When you have seen your name in close-up, as it were, read the Introduction, for this shows you it in perspective.

CONTENTS

INTRODUCTION

NAMES are as old as human speech. We read in Genesis how
Adam named all the birds and beasts, and, at first, called his
wife 'woman'; but when the children arrived she became Eve,
which means 'life'—an appropriate name for the first of all
mothers. It distinguished her from her children, Cain, which
means 'begotten,' and Abel, which means 'fleeting.'

This allegorical story gives a key to the origin of names.
To begin with, like nicknames, they were purely descriptive,
to prevent one person being confused with another. But names
soon took on a greater significance, and naming a child became
a serious business. The Israelites, for example, believed that a
child's future was closely linked with its name. Many names
contained the Hebrew word for 'God' with the idea that the
child would thereby live under divine protection. Johanna,
for instance, means 'grace of God.' The same principle
inspires the Catholic custom of naming a child after a saint,
who becomes his or her patron; hence the numerous references
to saints in this book, and the inclusion of a 'Saints' Calendar.'

Early names nearly always had a religious or magical inten-
tion. Parents named a child after a venerated character of the
past, in the hope that it would inherit the qualities of the
namesake. Animals and birds, often connected with pagan
rites, were another source of names thought to confer special
qualities. Some ancient peoples believed in reincarnation. Life
was short, and since it was rare for three generations to be alive

at the same time a child was thought to be his grandparent reborn, and was given the same name. The Red Indians adopted an interesting variant. The squaw called the child after the first thing she particularly noticed after the birth. This resulted in such odd names as Minnehaha ('Laughing Water').

Girls were often given magical names with beautiful associa/ tions, in the hope that they would be transferred to the child. Both the ancient Greeks and the Celts were fond of names con/ nected with flowers and trees. The Welsh Gwenonwy, mean/ ing 'lily of the valley,' is an example. The matter/of/fact Romans were, at first, less imaginative. The girl's name was merely the feminine form of the boy's, so that Claudius became Claudia, and Octavius became Octavia. Greek influence later enlivened this system with the names of goddesses, nymphs, and other mythical figures.

Most of these elements appear in the history of English names. The Romans brought their names to Celtic Britain. The Anglo/Saxons, when they came, added theirs. Like almost every one else at the time, they chose names suggesting desirable qualities; later it became usual to add a second word to the first to form a compound name, both parts of which presumably made sense in relation to each other (e.g., Elfrida, 'elf/strength'). As time went by meanings were ignored and any two elements were combined, resulting in an extraordinary variety of pre/ Conquest names in England.

The Normans, a much travelled people, brought names to this country from four sources: those of their Scandinavian ancestors—e.g., Gunnora, from Old Norse 'gunnr,' 'war'— Germanic names, such as Aaliz (Alice), brought across the Rhine by the Frankish invaders; old Celtic names, such as Muriel, which had disappeared in Britain during the Roman and Anglo-Saxon occupations except in the remote north and west, but were revived by the troops from Celtic Brittany who accompanied William the Conqueror; and, fourthly, the names of saints of the East brought back by the Crusaders.

The Normans ruthlessly discouraged the use of English for official documents, and names that survived the Conquest were written in Latin and French versions; but it is unlikely that they were spoken in these forms in everyday life.

Many influences can be traced in the Christian names which have been used since the Norman Conquest. The Bible in the Latin Vulgate version and the Saints' Calendar made many contributions in the Middle Ages. The Renaissance brought a flood of classical names, mostly Greek. Cora, for example, meaning 'maiden,' was much favoured by seventeenth-century lyric poets, and its delightful diminutive Corinna was also popular. Saintly names went out of fashion after the Reformation, and Old Testament ones—some of them very odd indeed—became popular. The Puritans added the names of virtues, such as Charity and Prudence.

Fashions in names change. In the eighteenth century there was a return to Anglo-Saxon and medieval names on the one hand, and the adoption of Latin forms—such as Maria for Mary—on the other. Early Victorian names tended to be high-flown, even pompous, but good sense prevailed, and girls' names were chosen, even invented, for their prettiness. Flower and jewel names, for example, first became popular here in the 1880's. The influence of the Romantic writers of the 1800's resulted in a revival of many long-neglected ancient names—for example, Amy and Edith.

The twentieth century has enormously increased the number of names, and often shortened them, usually down to the first syllable. In other periods, among the leisured classes there was time for long words and long, elaborate names. To-day, in the age of speed, names are streamlined to match our hurried life. The rise in population has probably made recent genera-tions more ingenious than any before in the creating of new names—and the perpetual search by stars of stage, screen, and television for something distinctive has helped this process.

But there are wonderful sources for new forms of names among the foreign ones that are met with every day; foreign-speaking members of the British Commonwealth, as well as other nationals, make their homes in Britain. Their names, if not assimilated, are not included in this book. But some, like Ingrid, we have already made our own; others, like Hanele, have inspired an anglicized variant, Hanella.

Africa and India (Aïssa and Santha have already appeared) may one day enrich our store of names as Scotland, Wales, Ireland, and Hollywood have done already. These Celtic and American borrowings—a feature of this century—are more fully represented in this book than ever before.

Whether a name is old or new, whether it is chosen for its associations, its pretty sound, or as a compliment to a god-mother, one thing is certain: it is chosen with care and love, like the wishes the good fairies chose for Princess Briar Rose. One little word has to epitomize all the wishes and hopes of the parents and express their ideals and traditions. There are no words in any language so packed with significance (private though it be) as names are. This is what is meant by the 'magic' of a name; and the importance attached to name-giving suggests that still to this day in the modern world the belief in this 'magic' is as strong as ever.

B.L.S.
C.B.J.

ACKNOWLEDGMENTS

THE authors are deeply indebted to Mr Trefor Rendall Davies for his valuable assistance with regard to the Welsh names figuring in this book; to Dr Tomás de Bhaldraithe for his useful advice on Irish names; and to the Rev. Paul Browne, O.S.B.

CALENDAR OF SAINTS

THE list of saints' days which follows is taken from various sources. The most extensive and reliable English work on the subject, giving a short biography of every officially recognized saint in every country and of every century, is Butler's *Lives of the Saints* (1756–59), revised (1956) by H. Thurston, S. J., and D. Attwater, which should be available in every public library. Another useful work is S. Baring-Gould's *The Lives of the Saints* (1898). This is not as reliable as Butler's work, but contains a practically complete account of every saint, historical or legendary, known in England, Scotland, and Wales, a number of whom are not recognized by Butler. A third list which has not been neglected is the Calendar of the Book of Common Prayer. This contains comparatively few names, and omits such universally admired characters as St Francis of Assisi and St Teresa of Avila. The proposed revision of the Prayer Book, known as the "Deposited Book," was rejected by Parliament in 1928, and is therefore not officially recognized; but it has made good many omissions in the Elizabethan book.

In the list given here, as most names, with biographies, appear in Butler's volumes, names and dates taken from this standard work are not specially so indicated. The supplementary names taken from Baring-Gould are noted *BG*; those peculiar to the Prayer Book, when not included in Butler, are marked *BCP*; those which are found only in the Roman Missal (generally feasts of Our Lady) are marked *RM*. There are no female names in the "Deposited Book" that do not appear elsewhere.

The purpose of this Calendar is to indicate, in the limited space available, the Christian names of saints celebrated on any given day of the year. Most of the better-known saints are referred to in some detail in the main body of the book, and further information may be readily obtained from the sources given above.

Some saints are represented more than once because they are commemorated on a different date in different places to avoid a clash; in some cases not only the anniversary of a saint's death, but that of some special event in her life—particularly in the case of Mary—may be kept.

Generally speaking, the form of the name chosen is that most familiar —*e.g.*, Audrey rather than Aethelthryth or Etheldreda. The meaning of every name in the Calendar is given either in the text or in the Supplementary Index.

It is a pity that there is not a name for every day of the year. There are, as a matter of fact, many saints whose names have not been included here; but it is more than improbable that any child would wish to be called, say, Veep or Uncumber!

JANUARY

1. Euphrosyne; Martina *BG*
2. Stephana
3. Genevieve; Bertilia
4. Angela *BG*
5. Emiliana *BG*
6. *Epiphany BCP* (*see* Bertha); Gertrude
7.
8. Pega
9. Marciana; Alix
10. Christiana; Justine
11.
12.
13. Ivette (Jutta); Veronica
14.
15. Ita
16. Priscilla
17. Roseline
18. Beatrice; Christine; Susanna *BG*
19. Martha; Margaret
20.
21. Agnes *BCP*
22. Inez (Josepha)
23. Mary [Betrothal] *BCP*; Margaret
24.
25.
26. Paula; Margaret
27.
28. Agnes (alternative date) *RM*; Mary
29.
30. Martina; Hyacintha; Serena *BG*
31. Marcella

FEBRUARY

1. Bridget
2. Mary [Purification] *BCP*; Joan
3. Margaret
4. Joan; Veronica
5. Agatha; Adelaide
6. Dorothy
7. Juliana *BG*
8. Elfleda
9. Susanna
10. Clare
11. Mary [Appearance at Lourdes]; Victoria; Theodora *BG*
12. Marina; Eulalia
13. Beatrice; Christine; Catherine
14.
15. Jovita; Julia
16. Juliana; Philippa
17. Miriam (Marianne) *BG*
18. Constance (Constantia) *BG*; Augusta *BG*
19.
20. Elizabeth; Paula *BG*; Mildred *BG*
21.
22. Margaret
23. Milburga; Martha; Romana
24.
25. Walburga
26. Isabella
27. Honorine *BG*
28. Angela; Antonia; Louisa

B

MARCH

1. Antonia *BG*
2. Agnes
3. Teresa; Camilla *BG*
4.
5.
6. Colette (Nicolette); Felicity
7. Perpetua *BCP*
8.
9. Frances; Catharine
10. Anastasia; Patricia
11. Aurea; Teresa; Margaret; Alberta *BG*
12. Fina (Seraphina); Justine (Justina)
13. Euphrasia
14. Matilda
15. Lucretia; Louise
16. Eusebia; Columba *BG*
17. Gertrude
18.
19.
20. Claudia *BG*
21.
22. Catherine *BG*
23. Sibyllina
24. Catharine
25. Mary [Annunciation] *BCP*; Lucy; Ida
26. Maxima
27. Lydia *BG*; Augusta *BG*
28. Mary *BG*
29.
30.
31. Jeanne (Joan)

APRIL

1. Catherine; Theodora
2. Mary; Ebba
3. Irene
4.
5. Juliana; Theodora
6. Catharine
7. Ursulina
8. Julie
9. Mary
10.
11. Gemma
12.
13. Ida
14.
15. Bernadette; Grace *BG*; Ita
16.
17. Clare
18. Mary
19.
20. Agnes
21.
22.
23. Helen
24. Marie
25. Franca *BG*
26. Mary [of Good Counsel] *RM*; Alda; Franca
27.
28. Valerie (Valeria); Theodora
29. Mary Magdalen; Antonia *BG*
30. Catherine; Hildegarde

MAY (May is the 'Month of Mary')

1. Isidora *BG*; Bertha *BG*
2. Zoë
3. Maura
4. Monica; Catharine; Helen *BG*
5. Judith (Jutta)
6. Prudence; Elizabeth *BG*
7. Rose; Flavia *BG*
8. Ida *BG*
9.
10. Beatrice; Solange
11.
12. Gemma; Jane
13. Juliana
14. Petronella; Mary
15. Dymphna; Bertha; Madelina (Magdalen); Denise
16.
17. June *BG*
18. Elgiva *BG*
19.
20. Columba; Basilla
21. Helen (alternative date)
22. Rita (Margaret); Julia
23.
24. Joanna *BG*; Aphra *BG*
25. Madeleine Sophie; Mary Salome *BG*
26. Eva; Mariana
27. Melangell (Monacella)
28. Mary
29. Mary Magdalen
30. Jeanne (Joan)
31. Angela; Petronilla

JUNE

1. Candida (Gwen *BG*)
2.
3. Clotilde
4. Vincentia
5.
6. Candida *BG*; Pauline *BG*
7. Anne
8. Calliope *BG*
9. Anna Maria; Pelagia *BG*
10. Margaret; Olive
11. Paula; Alice *BG*
12. Antonina
13. Aquilina
14.
15. Alice; Germaine *BG*
16. Julitta *BG*; Justine *BG*
17. Teresa; Emily
18. Elizabeth
19. Elizabeth; Juliana *BG*
20. Micheline; Florence *BG*
21.
22.
23. Audrey (Etheldreda); Mary
24.
25. Bertha
26.
27. Mary [of Perpetual Succour] *RM*; Madeleine
28.
29. Judith; Salome; Emma
30. Ermentrude

JULY

1. Miriam *BG*; Esther *BG*
2. Mary [Visitation] *BCP*
3.
4. Bertha; Elizabeth *BG*
5. Zoë *BG*; Philomena *BG*
6. Dominica; Modwen; Maria
7. Ethelburga
8. Elizabeth; Priscilla
9. Everilda; Veronica
10. Amelia (Amalburga); Felicity; Rufina
11. Olga; Sara
12. Veronica
13. Mildred; Maura; Sara *BG*
14.
15. Edith; Anne-Marie
16. Mary [Our Lady of Carmel]; Marie-Madeleine
17. Mary [Humility of] *RM*; Marcellina
18. Marina *BG*
19. Justa; Aurea *BG*
20. Margaret *BCP*
21. Julia *BG*
22. Mary Magdalen *BCP*
23. Romula; Anna; Vanna
24. Christina; Felicia
25. Thea; Valentina *BG*
26. Anne *BCP*; Christine *BG*
27. Natalia
28. Irene *BG*
29. Martha; Beatrice; Flora *BG*; Lucilla *BG*
30. Julitta; Maxima
31. Helen

AUGUST

1. Faith, Hope, Charity; Sophia; Eiluned
2. Alfreda
3. Lydia
4.
5. Mary [Our Lady of the Snows]; Aphra
6.
7. Claudia
8. Joan
9. Mary BG
10. Philomena
11. Susanna; Lelia
12. Clare; Hilaria BG
13. Gertrude; Irene BG
14.
15. Mary [Assumption into Heaven]
16. Serena BG
17. Clare; Juliana BG
18. Helen; Beatrice
19. Emily; Thecla
20. Mary
21. Jeanne-Françoise de Chantal
22. Mary [Immaculate Heart of]
23.
24. Aurea BG
25. Patricia; Ebba; Mary Michaela
26. Elizabeth; Rose BG
27. Margaret
28.
29. Sabina
30. Rose
31.

SEPTEMBER

1. Verena; Anna BG
2. Margaret
3. Phoebe
4. Ida; Rosalie; Rose; Hermione BG
5.
6. Bee
7. Regina (Reine) BCP
8. Mary [Birthday of] BCP; Natalia
9. Louise; Seraphina; Wilfreda
10.
11. Theodora
12. Mary [Name of]; Victoria
13.
14. Catharine
15. Mary [Seven Sorrows of: Dolores]; Catharine
16. Euphemia; Edith
17. Columba; Hildegard
18.
19. Mary; Emily
20. Philippa BG; Susanna BG
21. Maura
22.
23. Helen
24. Mary [Our Lady of Ransom: Mercedes]
25.
26. Justina; Lucy
27. Delphina
28.
29. Mariamne
30.

OCTOBER

1. Julia *BG*; Maxima *BG*; Germaine *BG*
2.
3. Therese; Romana
4. Berenice *BG*; Aurea *BG*
5. Flora
6. Faith *BCP*; Mary Frances
7. Justina; Julia *BG*
8. Bridget; Valeria *BG*
9.
10.
11. Mary [Motherhood of]; Julia *BG*
12. Ethelburga
13. Magdalen
14.
15. Teresa
16. Hedwig; Kiara
17. Margaret Mary; Audrey (Etheldreda) *BCP*
18. Gwendoline *BG*
19. Cleopatra; Laura *BG*
20. Mary Teresa; Martha *BG*
21. Ursula
22. Mary Salome *BG*
23. Elfleda *BG*
24.
25. Daria; Margaret
26.
27.
28. Anastasia (Stacey); Cyrilla *BG*
29. Elfleda *BG*
30. Dorothy (Dorothea)
31.

NOVEMBER

1. *All Saints' Day*
2. Maura *BG*
3. Winifred (Gwenfrewi); Sylvia *BG*
4. Frances
5. Elizabeth; Bertilla
6. Joan Mary
7. Helen; Margaret
8.
9.
10. Florentia *BG*
11.
12.
13. Columba *BG*
14. Elizabeth
15. Gertrude *BG*
16. Gertrude; Agnes
17. Hilda; Victoria
18.
19. Elizabeth
20.
21. Mary [Presentation of]
22. Cecilia *BCP*
23. Felicity *BG*
24. Flora
25. Catherine *BCP*
26.
27. Margaret *BG*
28. Catherine
29.
30. Maura, Justina *BG*

DECEMBER

1. Natalia *BG*; Florentia *BG*
2. Viviana; Aurelia *BG*
3. Hilaria
4. Barbara
5. Crispina *BG*
6. Dionysia (Denise); Gertrude *BG*
7. Josepha
8. Mary [Conception of] *BCP*
9. Valeria *BG*
10. Eulalia; Julia *BG*
11.
12. Adelaide *BG*
13. Lucy *BCP*; Odile
14.
15. Mary; Christiana *BG*
16. Adelaide; Mary
17.
18.
19. Thea *BG*
20. Julia *BG*
21.
22. Frances
23. Victoria; Margaret
24. Emiliana; Adela *BG*
25. Eugenia; Anastasia
26. Vincentia
27. Fabiola
28.
29.
30.
31. Melania; Columba

A

ABIGAIL is a Hebrew name meaning 'a father's joy' or 'a source of joy.' In the Bible the story of an early Abigail can be found in chapter xxv of the First Book of Samuel, where she is described as a woman "of good understanding, and of a beautiful countenance." A tactful person and an admirable hostess, she became King David's wife.

Her name began to be used in English-speaking countries soon after the Reformation—the great religious revolution of the sixteenth century, when many Old Testament names came into fashion. In a play called *The Scornful Lady* by Shakespeare's contemporaries Beaumont and Fletcher, Abigail is the heroine's confidential helper. As a result, an abigail came to mean any confidential attendant. Oddly enough, Queen Anne's lady-in-waiting and confidante was named Abigail Masham. Abigails of to-day should, therefore, make perfect private secretaries. One even wonders whether the original bearer took down the Psalms at David's dictation.

Nowadays the short form *Gail* is popular, but the older short forms were *Abbie* and *Abbey*. Readers of Dickens's *Our Mutual Friend* will remember Miss Abbey Potterson, the formidable landlady of the Six Jolly Fellowship Porters, whose dockland customers were convinced that she was related in some mysterious way to the Abbey at Westminster!

Farther up the Thames, in Mortlake cemetery, is a touching epitaph to little Abigail Rockleigh, that runs:

> For years, a child:
> For sparkles of God's grace,
>   A jewel rich:
> Entombed lies in this place.
> Her ashes only here;
> All else is gone to rest.
> God takes them youngest, whom
>   He loveth best.

ADA The origin of this name is not clear, though it prob-ably comes from an old German name or title meaning 'noble,' and may be a shortened form of a longer name of German origin, such as *Adela* or *Adeline*, both of which mean 'noble.' Or it may have had its beginnings in one of those odd-sounding names which the Anglo-Saxons liked so much, such as *Aethelthryth* ('noble strength') or *Aethelgiefu* ('noble gift').

But it has another possible origin: long ago there was a Ger-man Christian name, for both boys and girls, which was spelt *Eda*, sometimes *Etta*. This word meant 'happy' or 'blessed.'

The name reached this country from Germany in the late 1700's, and became immensely popular during the nineteenth century. The poet Byron's daughter, born in 1815, was christened Ada; in his romantic poem *Childe Harold's Pil-grimage* he addresses her as, "Ada! sole daughter of my house and heart."

In fiction Dickens's pathetic ward in Chancery, Ada Clare, is portrayed in *Bleak House*.

The usual pet form of Ada is *Adie*.

Strictly speaking, *Adah* is an entirely different name from Ada, though the two forms have become so mixed up that the difference is no longer generally realized. Adah is a Hebrew word meaning 'ornament.' It is one of the oldest of all names known to us, for, apart from Eve, it is the first female name mentioned in the Book of Genesis (chapter iv).

Later Hebrew tradition makes Adah the wife of Cain, and Byron does likewise in his drama *Cain*. After Cain has killed his brother Abel, Adah goes with her husband and their two children into the wilderness to share his exile.

Adah has been used in this country since the seventeenth century, though it has always been more popular in the U.S.A. One of the most famous actresses in America in the nineteenth century was Adah Menken, whose visit to London in 1864 aroused tremendous enthusiasm. She was also a writer and an admirer of Charles Dickens; in 1868 she dedicated a volume of her poems called *Infelicia* to him.

ADELA This name comes from the Old German word 'adal,' 'noble,' which had its Anglo-Saxon counterpart in 'aethel.' The Normans made it a favourite name, and brought it over with them at the time of the Conquest. William the Conqueror christened one of his daughters Adela; she married Stephen, Count of Blois, and their third son, Stephen, became King of England in 1135.

Its popularity was extended to the Low Countries about the same time on account of the eleventh-century St Adela, Countess of Flanders. Although the name did not spread among the native English at that period, it remained popular on the Continent.

In the nineteenth century, however, by which time the French form had become *Adèle*, it regained favour in this country and became fashionable with the Victorians, as did *Ada*, *Adelaide*, and *Ethel*, its near relatives.

ADELAIDE has the same origin as *Alice* (see p. 31), though it is closer to the words from which it is derived ('adal,' 'noble,' and 'heidis,' equivalent to the modern English suffix '-hood').

On the Continent, particularly in France and Germany, the name has been common for hundreds of years. But in England it was almost unknown until 1830, when Adelaide, daughter of the Duke of Saxe-Coburg Meiningen, became Queen of England on the accession of the Duke of Clarence as William IV.

It was as a compliment to this popular Queen that the capital of South Australia, founded in 1836, was given her name. About the same time in England, especially in London, a great many roads, crescents, etc., were named after her. During the Victorian era the name had a great vogue.

Addy is the usual pet form of Adelaide, though sometimes this name is abbreviated to *Ada*.

ADELINE Like *Adelaide*, Adeline and its other form *Adelina* come from an Old German word meaning 'nobility.' Unlike Adelaide, however, it has been used in this country ever since the Norman Conquest. Twenty years after William the Conqueror landed here the name Adelina Joculatrix, the literal meaning of which is Adeline the Joker, appeared in Domesday Book; but whether this lady was a professional lady jester or a mere humorist we shall never know; all we can be sure of is that she was a landowner in her own right.

Until about 1400 Adeline was common in its various forms, especially in the latinized versions *Alina* and *Alyna*, but afterwards it suffered an eclipse which lasted right up to the nineteenth century, when it came back into fashion. The usual short form is *Aline*.

A famous bearer of this name was Adelina Patti, one of the greatest sopranos of all time. She was born in Madrid in 1843, but became a naturalized British subject and made her home at Craig-y-nos Castle, near Swansea.

The name has been kept alive during this century by the well-known song, composed in 1903, with the sentimental refrain:

> O Adeline, sweet Adeline!
> You're the fairest of them all,
> Sweet Adeline!

AGATHA This name has the simplest of meanings, but is the most difficult to live up to: it is Greek for 'good woman.'

The first known Agatha was certainly all that her name implies: she was St Agatha, a Sicilian girl put to death for being a Christian in the persecution organized by the Roman Emperor Decius in the third century. In the church of the city of Catania, in Sicily, there is the miraculous Veil of St Agatha, believed to be a sure defence against the eruptions of Mount Etna. It is not surprising, therefore, that St Agatha is a patron saint for protection from fire. In England there are four churches dedicated to her.

During the Middle Ages the name was popular throughout Europe in its different forms, the commonest of which were at that time the French form *Agace* and the Latin form *Agacia*. Later it became less common, and was not revived until the nineteenth century.

Fashions in names come and go, so that we never know when any name will gain or lose favour, but at present the only well-known Agatha in England is Agatha Christie, creator of that ingenious crime-solver Hercule Poirot.

Though generally looked on as a pet form of *Agnes*, *Aggie* was originally the pet form of Agatha.

AGNES This name is derived from a Greek word meaning 'pure,' 'sacred,' although, because of its likeness to the Latin word 'agnus,' it is often taken to mean 'a lamb.' On this account, St Agnes, a young Roman Christian put to death during the reign of the Emperor Diocletian, is frequently represented with a lamb in her arms. On her name-day, January 21, lambs are brought from one of the convents in Rome to the Pope at St Peter's, where they are blessed and their fleeces shorn for wool to make pallia. A pallium is a kind of Y-shaped, scarf-like vestment conferred by the Pope on archbishops. There is a world-famous church in Rome dedicated to St Agnes; in England five churches bear her name.

Agnes was already well known in this country by the twelfth century. For over four hundred years it was one of the commonest feminine Christian names. It often used to be written *Annis*, *Annice*, or *Annes*, and because it was similarly pronounced it became confused with *Ann*. As *Anis*, it is still a favourite name among gipsies.

The Spanish version *Ines*, and its anglicized form *Inez*, are occasionally used in this country.

No Agnes is mentioned in the Bible, and probably for this reason, as much as any other, the name went out of fashion after the Reformation. During the nineteenth century, however, it regained some of its popularity, owing in some measure, no doubt, to the success achieved by Keats's *Eve of St Agnes*, written in 1819, and Tennyson's *St Agnes' Eve* (1842).

In Wales, Agnes was turned into *Nest* or *Nesta*, and by the twelfth century it was a common name there, especially in the south. In England the pet forms *Nessie* and *Nessa* are found.

In the fourteenth century that gallant Scotswoman Agnes, Countess of March (called Black Agnes, from the colour of her hair), successfully defended her absent husband's castle at Dunbar against the invading English, in the war which Edward III waged against the Scots. She is referred to in a number of Scottish ballads of that period—for instance:

> She kept a stir in tower and trench,
> That brawling, boist'rous Scottish wench,
> Came I early, came I late,
> I found Black Agnes at the gate.

In fiction there are Agnes Wickfield, the second wife of David Copperfield, and Agnes Grey, a rector's daughter in the novel of that name by Anne Brontë.

AITHNE, or *Aine*, is derived from the Celtic word 'aodh-nait,' which means 'little fire,' and has the masculine equivalent Aidan, the name of a seventh-century saint.

An ancient name, it was in common use in Ireland for hundreds of years. In legend Aine is queen of the fairies of South Munster, and it is said that she lives at Knockany ('the hill of Aine') in County Limerick.

In A. E. W. Mason's novel *The Four Feathers* (1902) there is a young lady from Donegal named *Ethne*, who would never play her violin except with her back to the audience!

Eithne, like Ethne, is another modern version of this name. The portrait of a certain Eithne—a real person—used to appear, as a typical Irish beauty, on Irish Sweepstake tickets.

There are signs that Aithne, in its various forms, is regaining favour in Ireland and even in Scotland, because of its Celtic associations.

ALETHEA, not to be confused with *Althea* (p. 33), is a Greek word meaning 'truth', and thus belongs to the group of abstract virtues—including also *Sophia*, 'wisdom,' and *Irene*, 'peace'—which were so popular in the seventeenth century.

When Charles I was Prince of Wales he travelled to Spain, where he met the Spanish Princess *Maria Aletea*, who nearly, but not quite, became his Queen. It was about this time—in the early 1600's—that the name came into vogue in England. In the records of Durham for the year 1669 there is a reference to an Alethea Brandling; she married a Mr Hitch at the age of nine!

Jane Austen, besides being a novelist, was also a prolific letter-writer, and one of her favourite correspondents was her friend Alethea Bigg.

The name has been popular in Ireland for a very long time, with the pet form *Letty*, which is more usual for *Letitia*.

ALEXANDRA is, of course, the feminine of Alexander, which means 'protector of men.' The first female bearer of the name known to history was Queen Alexandra of Judaea, who died in 69 B.C. There was a Christian martyr St Alexandra, but little is known about her. Few namesakes are known before fairly modern times, though there is an old tradition that the mother of St Thomas of Canterbury (Thomas à Becket) was a Saracen lady named *Alisaundre* whom the saint's father had met on the Crusades. It is said that she found her way from the Nile to the Thames, and that on reaching London she wandered through the streets calling out, "Becket, Becket!"—the only English she knew—until she found him.

The name was in use in England by the thirteenth century, and is found in records of that period both as *Alexandra* and *Alexandria*. But it was not until after 1863, when Prince Albert (afterwards King Edward VII) married Alexandra, eldest daughter of King Christian IX of Denmark, that the name became fashionable. Alexandra Rose Day (June 26) was instituted in 1912 to mark the fiftieth year of her residence in England. Every year on that day artificial roses made by the blind and crippled are sold in the streets, and the proceeds are distributed to hospitals and other institutions which care for the sick. Also named after her are Alexandra Park, in North London, which contains a famous racecourse, and Alexandra Palace, famous for its B.B.C. television studios.

To-day the name, which has a Royal bearer through Princess

Alexandra, daughter of Princess Marina, is sometimes found as *Alexa*, *Alexia*, and *Alexandrine*, with the pet forms *Alex* and *Lexy*.

Queen Victoria's first name was *Alexandrina*; in the form *Aleksandrina*, it has long been a favourite in Russia, like its masculine counterpart, Aleksandr. *Sandra*, originally an Italian short form of the name, has, during the last twenty-five years or so, become an independent name in England.

Alexis may come from the Greek word for 'protection' or from a similar one meaning 'helper.' For a long while it has been a widespread boys' name in Russia, but during the present century, in the early part of which Russian names became quite fashionable in this country, it has been used here occasionally as a girls' name, and seems to be gaining in popularity.

ALICE is a name with a long and obscure history. In its earliest form it appears as *Adalheidis*, an ancient German word, used as a royal title, meaning 'nobility'; *Adelaide*, *Adeline*, *Adela*, and probably *Ada* are derived from the same word. The use of Adalheidis as a title of honour for German princesses is comparable with that of *Augusta*, bestowed on the wives and daughters of Roman emperors.

The next stage through which the name passed was *Adelice* or *Adelicia*, and this, by about the twelfth century, had been shortened to *Alicia*, whence *Alice*.

There are several other forms of the name, among them *Alix* ("la belle Alix" was the wife of Henry I), and *Alison*, which was popular by the fourteenth century. Chaucer, in *The Miller's Tale*, makes Alison the wife of John, a rich old miserly carpenter. She had a roguish eye, small eye-brows, and was "more pleasant to look on than a flowering pear-tree."

Nowadays Alison is the usual Scots form of Alice, the true Gaelic version being *Ailis*, sometimes shortened to *Ailie*. *Allison* is another version. Other pet forms of Alice are *Allie* and *Ally*. The Welsh form of Alice is *Alys*.

Shakespeare introduces an Alice into *Henry V*; she plays the part of an attendant of Princess Katharine.

But the best known of all Alices is, of course, the one created in 1865 by Lewis Carroll. *Alice's Adventures in Wonderland* began as a series of stories told on summer afternoons to some child friends of his, who included Alice Liddell, after whom he named his heroine. Both this book and its sequel, *Through the Looking-Glass and What Alice found There* (1871), enjoyed tremendous popularity and gave the name a great vogue.

Other nineteenth-century Alices in fiction are Alice Beverley, in Frederick Marryat's *Children of the New Forest*, and Alice Brand, "that maiden void of fear," who is the Lady of the Lake in Scott's long poem of that title.

In songs we have Sweet Alice, the charming but over-sensitive heroine of the song beginning, "Don't you remember sweet Alice, Ben Bolt?"

> Who wept with delight when you gave her a smile,
> And trembled with fear at your frown.

A favourite some thirty years ago was *Alice-blue Gown*. Alice-blue is a light shade of blue named after Alice, wife of the American President Theodore Roosevelt.

Famous bearers of recent times include Alice Meynell, the poet, and Alicia Markova, the prima ballerina.

ALMA One of the most famous battles fought during the Crimean War was the Battle of Alma (1854). When news of our victory there reached this country Alma was adopted as a girls' Christian name, and became very popular.

Though rare before that date—in England, at least—Alma already existed as a Christian name. In Latin the word means 'fair' or 'kind,' and the Romans gave the title 'Alma Mater' ('bounteous mother') to several goddesses. To-day the term 'alma mater' is used when referring to one's own university, college, or school.

The name is also connected with a Hebrew word meaning 'maiden' and with a Celtic word meaning 'all good.' In Italian 'alma' means 'soul' or 'spirit,' which may sometimes be the reason for using it.

In Spenser's *Faërie Queene* Alma is the name given to the Lady of the House of Temperance.

For so short and simple-sounding a name, this choice of origins is a wide one. Tastes in names change almost year by year, but just now Alma seems to be enjoying a return to favour.

ALTHEA is a Greek word meaning 'healthy' or 'whole-some,' and should not be confused with the similar-sounding Greek name *Alethea*, meaning 'truth' (see p. 29). The original Althea (more correctly *Althaia*) was the mother of Meleager, a great hunter among the ancient Greeks. She was told by the Fates, when her son was a week old, that his life would end when the log in her hearth was burnt up. Hearing this, Althaia removed it and set it aside for safety; but one day, being in a rage with her son, who had just killed her brothers after an argument, she replaced it, and as soon as it was con-sumed he died.

Both Althea and Alethea came into fashion at the time of the Stuarts. One of the best-known Cavalier poems is Richard Lovelace's *To Althea from Prison*:

c

> When Love with unconfined wings
> Hovers within my gates,
> And my divine Althea brings
> To whisper at the grates. . . .

The "grates" are those of the prison to which he was committed by the Long Parliament for presenting a petition to the House of Commons "for the restoring of the King to his rights."

Althea, being connected with the Greek word 'althos,' 'remedy,' is the name given in botany to the marshmallow and hollyhock genus, in allusion to their supposed medical properties.

AMANDA Of the several names derived from the Latin word 'amare,' 'to love,' Amanda is among the most charming; it means 'lovable.'

The name first appears, as early as 1694, in a Restoration drama entitled *Love's Last Shift*, by Colley Cibber, and in its sequel, *The Relapse*, by Sir John Vanbrugh. In both these plays Amanda is portrayed as the charming young wife of Loveless, a loose-living character who had deserted her; her devotion, however, wins back his love.

The dramatists of the Restoration seem to have taken delight in making up pleasant-sounding names, especially for their heroines. Besides Amanda, there are, for instance, *Clarinda* and *Florinda*, which were fashionable in literary circles in the eighteenth century. The craze for such fanciful names grew until it reached ludicrous proportions, and caused John Gay to cap the lot with *Blowzelinda*! It is not surprising that most were very short-lived; but Amanda has survived.

James Thomson, in his poem *Spring* (1728), introduces the name:

> And thou, Amanda, come, pride of my song!
> Formed by the Graces, loveliness itself.

It occurs again in Tobias Smollett's novel *Peregrine Pickle*, written twenty-three years later. Soon after its appearance in literature Amanda became a baptismal name, and has been in regular, though not common, use ever since.

Amanda has the pet form *Mandy*.

AMELIA The name Amelia is derived from an ancient word, 'amal,' which occurs in many languages with the idea of 'hard work' (compare the English word 'moil').

In ancient Rome there was a noble clan named Aemilius, of which *Aemilia* was the feminine form. It was used by Shakespeare in *The Comedy of Errors* for Aegeon's wife.

The name became widespread in Germany, and there are numerous early records of it in the form *Amalburga*. After the introduction of Christianity into western Europe this Germanic name was equated with Aemilia, to give a more 'cultured' and Christian version. Amalburga became obsolete, and Aemilia became *Amalie* in Germany and *Amelia* or *Emily* (p. 96) in England.

It was not until after Queen Anne's death in 1714, however, when the Elector of Hanover became King George I of Great Britain and Ireland, that the name was used to any great extent in this country. It then became popular very quickly, both as Amelia and Emily, with all classes. William IV's Queen was christened Amelia Adelaide Louisa Theresa Caroline—all favourite names in the early nineteenth century.

The heroine of Henry Fielding's novel *Amelia* (1751), the devoted wife of Captain Booth, is said to be the portrait of Fielding's own wife. Dr Johnson remarked: "The character of Amelia is the most pleasing heroine of all the romances."

Readers of Thackeray's *Vanity Fair* (1848) will recall Amelia Sedley, the wife first of the worthless dandy George Osborne, then of the faithful Captain Dobbin.

Nearer to our own day there is Amelia Earhart, the first woman pilot to fly the Atlantic—an American achievement of the twenties.

Milly, besides being the short form of *Millicent*, is also used as a pet form of Amelia.

An invented form, *Ameliaranne*, names the heroine of a well-known series of children's stories.

AMY Whether in its English form, *Amy*, or its French form, *Aimée*, this name means 'beloved.' There is an older French form, *Esmée*, though nowadays its masculine counterpart, Esmé, is more frequent. The name *Esmé* used to be given to children of both sexes, and in the sixteenth century became a popular name in Scotland.

But the earliest known form of Amy was the Latin form *Amata*; there was a thirteenth-century St Amata, but little is known about her except that she was a native of Bologna, in Italy. The name also often occurred as *Amicia*, which in the course of time was shortened to *Amice*, a common name in its own right about six hundred years ago.

One of the most famous bearers of the name in history was Amy Robsart, who in 1550 married Robert Dudley, Earl of Leicester. It is said that he was so confident that Queen Elizabeth wished to marry him that he had his wife murdered; other accounts say she committed suicide. Her story is imaginatively told in Sir Walter Scott's *Kenilworth*.

Aimée Dubucq de Rivéry, cousin of the Empress Josephine, was captured at sea on her way to a French convent school and became the chief wife and adviser of the Sultan of Turkey.

In Louisa May Alcott's *Little Women* (1868) Amy is one of the four sisters (the others being Jo, Meg, and Beth) of the March family, who lived in New England. Amy, the artistic member of the family, finally marries Laurie, who for a long time had been Jo's companion. In another American classic, Mark Twain's *Tom Sawyer*, which appeared eight years later, the hero counted Amy Lawrence among his several girl friends.

One of the pioneers of British aviation was Amy Johnson, who in 1930 became the first woman to make a solo flight from England to Australia.

ANASTASIA The meaning of Anastasia, which comes from the Greek word for 'resurrection,' places this name in the same class as the masculine name Ambrose, which means 'immortal.' The name, therefore, is most suitable for girls born about Eastertime. The early Christians gave it to newly baptized children to signify that they had arisen to a new life. Perhaps because of its religious connexions—there are two Christian martyrs bearing the name—Anastasia has long been used in Ireland, as well as in America, where it has the pet form *Stacey*.

In England it used to be much more common than it is now. It dates back to the thirteenth century, perhaps even earlier. Then it generally appeared as *Anstey* or *Anstice*, which to-day are not unusual surnames, especially in Devonshire, where it was once popular as a Christian name.

It is in Russia, though, that the name enjoys its greatest popularity, and there it is usually given the forms *Nastasya* or *Nastya*, the pet form being *Nastyenka*. Ever since the Russian Revolution rumours have been circulating that Anastasia, daughter of Nicholas II, the last Tsar of Russia, escaped when the Royal Family was massacred by Red guards in 1918. This mysterious lady has since been the subject of several books, plays, and films.

ANDREA Though common in its masculine form, Andrew, the feminine name Andrea has never been widespread in this country. In France and Italy, on the other hand, it has long been a favourite as *Andrée* and *Andrea*. The French form is occasionally given nowadays to English girls.

Andrea comes from the Greek word 'andros,' meaning 'manly.' The earliest known record of the name in England dates back to 1617.

ANGELA is the feminine form of the old English masculine name Angel, now obsolete as a Christian name. Although the Latin word 'angelus' means 'angel,' the original Greek word 'angelos' signifies 'messenger'—angels being spirits who bring messages to man from God.

The masculine and feminine forms were both probably first used for children born on or near the feast of St Michael and All Angels, celebrated on September 29.

Of the three Italian saints who bear this name, the most famous is St Angela Merici, who founded the Ursuline order of nuns at Brescia in 1537.

Angela, and more so Angel, were used in the seventeenth century, but the Puritans regarded it as presumptuous to christen a child by such a name, and it was barred, together with Michael, Gabriel, and Raphael. As a result, Angela and Angel went almost completely out of use; but whereas Angel was never revived, Angela was restored to favour, though not before the nineteenth century.

A twentieth-century pet form is *Angie*.

Among Angelas of modern times are the two authors Angela Brazil and Angela Thirkell; Angela Brazil was a famous writer of girls' school stories, while Angela Thirkell wrote stately novels.

Other forms of the name are *Angelina* (or *Angeline*) and *Angelica*. The first of these, a popular name in Italy, is not much used in this country now, though it had a vogue here in the middle of the last century, when Edwin and Angelina were used as typical names for sentimental lovers, as may be seen in old copies of *Punch*. Its decline in popularity may have been due to this.

Angelica is a much older name than Angelina; a princess of that name appears as the heroine of the Italian epic poems describing the adventures of Orlando and other famous paladins of Charlemagne's Court. In Boiardo's *Orlando Inamorato* (1495) she is called "the fairest of her sex." Her adventures are continued in Ariosto's *Orlando Furioso* (1516). The name Angelica appears again in 1695 as the witty heroine of Congreve's comedy *Love for Love*.

Among the best-known historical Angelicas was Angelica Kauffmann, a Swiss by birth, who came to London at the age of twenty-five. Her paintings of classical subjects were much sought after, and in 1769 she became the first woman member of the Royal Academy.

ANN(E) After *Jane* this name is currently the most popular girls' name. It appears in a variety of forms—*Ann, Anna, Anne, Anita, Annetta, Annette, Annie, Hannah*, all now Christian names in their own right, and the pet forms *Nan, Nancy* (and its Welsh form, *Nansi*), and *Nanette*. The original from which all these are derived is *Hannah*, a Hebrew word meaning 'grace.' In addition to these there are a good many more versions used on the Continent, where the name enjoys equal popularity.

The story of Hannah, mother of the prophet Samuel, is told in the opening chapters of the First Book of Samuel. She lived about three thousand years ago, which shows how ancient the name is. Hannah is now one of the less common forms of the name in this country, though it was much favoured at the time of the Reformation and continued to be popular throughout the seventeenth century.

It was in the Greek and Latin form, *Anna*, that the name was introduced into Europe. In Virgil's epic poem, the *Æneid*, completed about the time of Christ's birth, there is an Anna, sister of Dido, Queen of Carthage. And, though lacking Scriptural support, tradition has it that St Anna (or St Anne) was the mother of the Virgin Mary. The only Anna actually mentioned by name in the Bible is the one known as the Prophetess, who appears in St Luke ii, 36–38.

The name Anna was particularly popular in the Byzantine Empire, and the earliest female historian, Anna Comnena (1083–1148), wrote a work in fifteen books, called *The Alexiad*, which deals with the history of Byzantium (now Istanbul), where she was born. By the tenth century Anna had spread to Russia, where it has remained a favourite.

In France *Anna* became *Anne*, and it was in this form, and as *Ann*, that it was most widely adopted in England, where the earliest record dates back to 1218, though at that time it was a rare name. By about 1500, however, it had spread to all parts of the country, and since then has retained its popularity in all classes.

It had a great vogue during the eighteenth century, when the pet form *Nancy*, now often given as an independent name, originated. *Nan* and *Nanny* are slightly older pet forms, as are

Han and *Hannie* for Hannah. *Nance*, on the other hand, is distinctly modern. *Annie*, as an independent name, dates from the nineteenth century.

When Anne was chosen as the first of the four names of Queen Elizabeth II's daughter it immediately became even more popular. The Princess was baptized Anne Elizabeth Alice Louise at Buckingham Palace on October 21, 1950.

Historically this was a happy choice, for the name has been borne by six Queens of England—Anne of Bohemia, who married Richard II in 1382; Anne Neville, wife of Richard III; Anne Boleyn, the ill-fated second of Henry VIII's six wives; Anne of Cleves, his fourth wife; Anne of Denmark, wife of James VI of Scotland, who on the death of Elizabeth became James I of England; and Queen Anne, last of the Stuarts.

At the beginning of the eighteenth century it became fashion-able to join the name Anne with Mary, to form *Mary Ann(e)* and *Anna Maria*, as well as *Marian*—but not *Marion*, which is derived solely from Mary (see p. 161). George Eliot, author of *Adam Bede*, was actually called Mary Ann Evans. Benjamin Disraeli's wife was christened Marianne Evans, but was generally known as Mary Anne Evans. In France *Anne-Marie* is still a popular combination.

Both in history and literature Anne, in its various forms, occurs so frequently that mention can here be made of only a few other bearers. Anne of Brittany was the wife of two successive French kings, Charles VIII and Louis XII; Anne of Austria, who, as Regent from 1643, and with the support of Cardinal Mazarin, made France a formidable European power; and Anne, Empress of Russia, who came to power in 1730 on the death of the Tsar Peter II and gave her country a political importance it had never known.

Other famous Annes include Anne Hathaway, who married William Shakespeare in 1582; and Nancy, Lady Astor, who in 1919 became the first woman to sit in the House of Commons.

In literature there are, among countless others, Anne Page in Shakespeare's *The Merry Wives of Windsor*; Anne Elliot in Jane Austen's novel *Persuasion*; *Anne of Green Gables* and *Anne of Avonlea*, well-known girls' stories by L. M. Montgomery; Arnold Bennett's *Anna of the Five Towns*; and *Ann Veronica*, by H. G. Wells; while the most famous Anna of all fiction is undoubtedly the heroine of Count Leo Tolstoy's *Anna Karenina*.

Annie Laurie, one of the most famous of British lyrics, was written by William Douglas at Kircudbright in the seventeenth century:

> Maxwelton braes are bonny
>   Where early fa's the dew,
> And it's there that Annie Laurie
>   Gie'd me her promise true;
> Gie'd me her promise true,
>   Which ne'er forgot shall be,
> And for bonny Annie Laurie
>   I'd lay me doon and dee.

ANNABEL There are few names whose origins are more difficult to unravel than *Annabel*, or *Annabella*, and its near relative, *Arabella*. The likeliest theory is that it is another form of *Amabel*, an old name deriving from the Latin word 'amabilis,' meaning 'lovable,' which is probably also the origin of *Mabel* (see p. 155).

The history of Annabel does not appear to be connected with *Anna* or *Ann*, because, in Scotland at any rate, Annabel was a common name while Ann(e) was hardly known there. In later times, however, it has no doubt become associated with Anna, and its accepted meaning is therefore 'Anna the beautiful.'

Arabella's true origin seems likewise to be forgotten, but may well be a later form of *Orabilis*, Latin for 'yielding to prayer.' It appears in the thirteenth century as *Arbell* and in the odd forms *Arable* and *Orable*; Annabel is most commonly found in early records as *Annaple*.

Arabella is sometimes found in novels of the nineteenth century, but is not now a much used name. Annabel, on the other hand, is still fairly popular, chiefly in Scotland, and during the last half-century has gained in popularity on the Continent. Edgar Allan Poe's lyric *Annabel Lee* (1849) helped to revive the name during the last half of the nineteenth century:

> It was many and many a year ago,
>   In a kingdom by the sea,
> That a maiden there lived whom you may know
>   By the name of Annabel Lee;
> And this maiden she lived with no other thought
>   Than to love and be loved by me.
>
> I was a child and *she* was a child
>   In this kingdom by the sea;
> But we loved with a love that was more than love,
>   I and my Annabel Lee. . . .

Annabella Drummond was an historical character. She lived during the second half of the fourteenth century and became the wife of King Robert III of Scotland. Of the Arabellas in history, perhaps the most famous is Arabella Stuart, first cousin of James VI of Scotland and I of England. Because of her faithfulness to William Seymour, who had Tudor blood, she

was twice exiled from Court. It was doubtless a Stuart sup^
porter who wrote of her after her second exile:

> Where she went and how she fared
> Nobody knew and nobody cared.

Another Arabella to whom a nameless rhymster has been
unkind is recorded in the following epitaph:

> Here lies, returned to clay,
> Miss Arabella Young,
> Who, on the first of May,
> Began to hold her tongue.

ANTHEA This name, of Greek origin, is akin to the Latin
Flora, for both mean 'lady of the flowers.' In ancient Greece
it was given as a title to the goddess Hera, Queen of Olympus,
at her great temple at Argos.

There is no evidence of Anthea being used as a Christian
name in English^speaking countries before the seventeenth
century, when, like many Greek^derived names, it became
popular among the pastoral poets; for instance, there is Robert
Herrick's poem *To Anthea, who may command him Anything*:

> Thou art my life, my love, my heart,
> The very eyes of me:
> And hast command of every part,
> To live and die for thee.

In E. Nesbit's *Five Children and It* and its sequel *The
Phoenix and the Carpet* there is a most likeable Anthea.

ANTONIA is the feminine form of the older name Antony,
or Anthony, said to mean 'inestimable.' Antonia is Latin and
Italian; the Portuguese and Spanish form is seen in the third^

century Portuguese saint *Antonina*, and in those countries this name has long been popular, particularly in its pet form, *Nina*. Many children christened Antonina or Antonia in Catholic countries are named after this saint, but elsewhere the name is given, for the most part, as the feminine form of Ant(h)ony.

In France the masculine form Antoine became *Antoinette* in the feminine; among famous bearers of this name was the Austrian-born Queen Marie-Antoinette, who ended her life on the guillotine during the French Revolution. Antoinette is occasionally given in England, with the pet form *Toinette*.

The usual version in this country is Antonia, the pet forms of which are *Toni*, *Tonie*, and *Tony*. Antonia White and Antonia Ridge are contemporary writers.

AUDREY This is all that time has left of the Anglo-Saxon name *Aethelthryth*, meaning 'noble strength.' Most Anglo-Saxon names ceased to be used after the Norman Conquest, but this particular one survived among the peasantry in the form *Etheldreda*, the short form of which was Audrey.

Among Anglo-Saxon saints few were held in such high regard as St Etheldreda, otherwise known as St Audrey (or *Awdry*). She was born at Ermynge, in Suffolk, in 630, the daughter of a Saxon kinglet named, oddly enough, Anna. She married Egfrid, King of Northumbria, but at the age of forty-three withdrew to the Isle of Ely, where she founded a nunnery, of which she was abbess for six years, until her death in 679. For hundreds of years a fair, called St Audrey's Fair, was held annually on her feast-day, at Ely. Here brightly coloured laces were sold, and those who bought them placed them as a mark of reverence on her tomb. They were known as "St Awdry's laces" or simply "tawdries"; like most goods on sale at fairs, they were cheap both in price and quality, and hence 'tawdry' has come to mean 'showy without taste or worth.'

By Shakespeare's day Audrey, which until the sixteenth century was merely the pet form of Etheldreda, had become an independent name, though it was not regarded at that time as a very fashionable one. In *As You like It* Shakespeare gives it to the country wench who jilts William for Touchstone. In fact it was not until late in the nineteenth century that the name really came into its own. To-day it is probably as popular as it has ever been.

AUGUSTA The Roman emperors, at their accession, assumed the title Augustus. Augusta, 'sacred, venerable,' was the title of honour conferred by them on their wives, sisters, daughters, and mothers. Among the Romans, therefore, it was not so much a Christian name as a mark of majesty.

It was not until the sixteenth century that Augustus and Augusta were given as baptismal names, and then only to babies of royal blood in Germany. When the House of Hanover became the Royal family of Great Britain after Queen Anne's death in 1714 these names were introduced into this country, though they did not become widespread until the nineteenth century. The pet forms adopted were *Gus* and *Gussie* respectively; *Gusta* is also occasionally used.

In Ireland the feminine form became *Augusteen*, while in France it appears as *Augustine*. The Spanish form can be seen in the name of the Maid of Saragossa, *Augustina*, who in 1808, during the Peninsular War, became a heroine overnight. Saragossa was being besieged by the French, and Augustina, then only twenty-two, saw her fiancé shot during a skirmish. She immediately took his place and distinguished herself in the battle which followed. Largely owing to her courage and inspiration, the French were obliged to withdraw after a further siege. This young lady was aptly named, for the town of Sara-gossa derives its name from 'Caesarea Augusta' in honour of the Emperor Caesar Augustus.

Nowadays Augusta is not a common name, but is sometimes chosen for girls born during August.

AVERIL The name Averil comes from two Old English words, 'eofor,' meaning 'boar,' and 'hyld,' meaning 'favour' or 'protection.' In Anglo-Saxon days, when the wild boar roamed the forests of England, it was regarded as a sacred animal, and was hunted not so much for its flesh as for its head, which was offered to the Saxons' pagan deities in sacri-ficial rites. All 'animal-names' were given for religious reasons; see also *Bernadette*, p. 53.

The first known Averil was St *Eberhilda*, or *Everild*, who lived in Yorkshire in the seventh century. A pupil of St Wilfred of York, she founded a nunnery called Everildisham, where she ruled and died. This abbess must have been a very popular person, for even to-day the name, the usual form of which is now Averil, is still found in Yorkshire and the north of England.

Averil should not be confused with *Avril*, taken from the French and meaning April.

AVIS Many people think that Avis is a modern name; in fact it is an exceedingly old Germanic one, though it was not introduced into England until the Normans came over.

Its first-known form was *Haduwig* (whence modern German *Hedwig*), meaning 'refuge in war'; the French softened it to *Edwige*, and the Norman dialect gave it to us as *Havoise*. By degrees this was sweetened to *Havoisia*, *Avicia*, *Avice*, and finally

Avis. In its various forms it is frequently found in medieval records, but nowadays only the forms Avis and, less commonly, Avice are found.

Avis has made a decided change in the generally accepted meaning of the name, for 'avis' is the Latin word for 'bird.' Avis has nothing to do with *Ava*, which is of very recent origin and appears to be a coined name, though it may be an adapted form of the German *Eva*, which is identical in pronunciation.

BARBARA The ancient Greeks applied the term 'barbaros' to all foreigners. The word means 'foreign, strange' (literally, 'stammering'), and the name Barbara is the feminine form.

The story of St Barbara, a third-century Syrian Christian, is one of cruelty and suffering. When her father discovered that she had become a Christian he denounced her to the Governor of Nicomedia, a town some fifty miles west of Istanbul. Barbara refused to renounce her faith, despite being tortured, and finally her father himself beheaded her. As the fatal blow was struck there was a clap of thunder and a streak of lightning, and her father fell dead on the spot. Angels descended and carried the head of the martyred girl to Paradise, while devils took her father down to the bottomless pit. The details of this legend led to St Barbara becoming the protectress against thunder and the patron saint of artillerymen; and the powder-room in old French battleships was known as "la sainte-barbe," this shortened form being the old French pet form of the name.

The true old English version was *Barbary*, which was how Barbara was written and pronounced until comparatively recent times. English pet forms are *Bab* and *Babs*, while in

Scotland most Barbaras are affectionately called *Babbie* or *Baubie*.

Barbara was a fairly common name from the Middle Ages up to the time of the Reformation, when, because it is neither mentioned in the Bible nor an 'abstract-virtue' name, it quickly lost favour. It was only some fifty years ago that it was revived, but since then it has enjoyed much popularity.

In the ballad of Barbara Allen, she goes to see Sir John Grahame, who is dying of love for her. The heartless young lady draws aside the curtain and says, "Young man, I think ye're dyin'." With these words she leaves him and makes her way home, but before she arrives she hears the death-bell toll and, full of repentance, tells her mother:

> O mother dear, O mak my bed,
>   An' mak it saft an' narrow;
> My love has died for me to-day,
>   I'll die for him to-morrow.

Another famous Barbara in literature is Barbara Frietchie, whose story was told in ballad-form in 1863 by John Greenleaf Whittier. When the Confederate general Stonewall Jackson was passing through Fredericktown during the American Civil War Barbara Frietchie, then ninety, hung the Union flag from her window:

> "Shoot, if you must, this old grey head,
>   But spare your country's flag," she said.

The general, moved by her courage, refrained from having the flag hauled down.

In Dickens's novel *The Old Curiosity Shop* there is a little servant-girl called Barbara, "very tidy, modest and demure, but very pretty, too." She becomes Mrs Kit Nubbles.

D

One of the most notable Barbaras of to-day is Baroness Wootton of Abinger; in 1958 she became one of the first four life peeresses. Barbara Sleigh is the creator of Carbonel, the cat, a favourite of children of all ages.

BEATRICE, and its earlier form *Beatrix*, come from Latin and have the meaning 'bestower of blessings.' The usual pet forms are *Bea*, *Bee*, *Beat*, *Beatty*, *Trix*, and *Trixie*. The name occurs as Beatrix in Domesday Book, a mine of information on old names.

Although it was quite common in this country for two or three hundred years after the Norman Conquest, it was little used after about 1250 and by the seventeenth century had gone out of fashion. Its revival about a hundred years ago was partly due, no doubt, to its use in the Royal family (the youngest of Queen Victoria's nine children was christened Beatrice), and partly to its appearance in the literature of that period. In Thackerary's novel *Henry Esmond*, for example, Beatrix is one of the major characters, being the object of James the Pre-tender's love. The same Beatrix reappears in the sequel, *The Virginians*, although there she is no longer a young beauty, but a quarrelsome old woman.

The most famous bearer of the name, however, was un-doubtedly Beatrice Portinari, the "glorious lady of my heart," as Dante called her in his *Vita Nuova* ('New Life'). He first saw her when he was nine years old and she a few months younger! But she was married at an early age to a certain Simone de Bardi, and died before her twenty-fourth birthday in 1290. Dante's passion for her remained unquenched all his life, and in his great poem *The Divine Comedy* she is his guide through Paradise and is idealized as the embodiment of the spirit of love.

One of Shakespeare's most witty and high-spirited female characters is Beatrice, Benedick's sparring-partner in wit and "our dear Lady Disdain" in *Much Ado about Nothing*. Leonato says of her in the play:

> There's little of the melancholy element in her, my lord: she is never sad but when she sleeps, and not ever sad then; for I have heard my daughter say, she hath often dreamed of unhappiness and waked herself with laughing.

Among the most famous ever to have borne the name is Beatrix Potter, author of *Peter Rabbit*.

The Italians, who made up the form Beatrice, pronounce it 'bay-a-tree-chay,' and have a short form *Bice*, pronounced 'bee-chay,' occasionally used in this country.

Nowadays the name is used in almost every country of western Europe, also in Russia. In Wales it was once popular in the form *Bettrys*; the Gaelic equivalent is *Beitiris*.

BELINDA This is an ancient Germanic name made up of two words, the first of which is obscure; the second, 'lindi,' meaning 'serpent,' was used in many old German names. Serpents were once universally regarded as sacred creatures. They were worshipped not only in countries on the mainland of Europe, but also in England by the Anglo-Saxons, in Greece, and as far afield as Mexico. Snake-worship and snake-names are dealt with further under *Linda* (p. 151).

Belinda first appears in the Charlemagne legends, which relate the heroic deeds of this King of the Franks and Christian Emperor of the West, and of his paladins. In these legends Belinda is the wife of one of the paladins, Orlando (Roland).

In England, however, the name was virtually unknown until Queen Anne's reign, when feminine names ending in -inda and -anda became all the rage (see p. 34). In 1714

Alexander Pope's poetic satire *The Rape of the Lock* was published, and in it the heroine's name is Belinda. Of her, Pope
says:

> If to her share some female errors fall,
> Look on her face, and you'll forget them all.

A lock of Belinda's hair is stolen by her suitor; it flies to the
skies, where it becomes a meteor which

> shot through liquid air,
> And drew behind a radiant trail of hair.

Two playwrights who use the name are William Congreve,
in *The Old Bachelor* (1693), and Sir John Vanbrugh in *The
Provok'd Wife* (1697).

As a result of the success of these three works, Belinda began
to be used as a baptismal name early in the eighteenth century,
and has been in use ever since, though it has never achieved
wide popularity.

BELLE It is doubtful whether this was originally a full name,
although it has its own meaning, 'lovely,' 'beautiful,' both in
French, as 'belle,' and in Italian, as 'bella.' Until the last
century it was used merely as a pet form of names ending in
bel or bella, such as *Isabel* and *Arabella*—for instance, *Belle*
is the name given to *Isopel* Berners, in Borrow's *Lavengro*.

Dickens uses *Bella* as an independent name: In *Our Mutual
Friend* Bella Wilfer is a young woman "giddy from the want
of some sustaining purpose, and capricious because she was
always fluttering among little things." Though spoilt and wayward, she has a lively character, such as Dickens loved to
portray in his novels and, probably, in real life, to know.

Nowadays Belle, a commoner form than Bella, seems to be
gaining in popularity as an officially recognized name.

BERNADETTE There are comparatively few names which owe their origin to the bear, but one of them, Bernard, has been popular for hundreds of years, both in this country and on the continent of Europe. The earliest recorded form is Berinhard, which in Old German meant 'resolution of a bear,' though the Anglo-Saxons used it a good deal in the adapted form Beornheard, which means, literally, 'bear-strong.'

The name was particularly favoured in Switzerland (where the St Bernard dogs come from), the Pyrenees, and Scandinavia. In all these regions bears used to be found in abundance, and were considered sacred by the inhabitants, who created many legends about them. It was only natural that in the course of time feminine forms of Bernard should develop—perhaps used originally by parents who had hoped for a son and had had a daughter. Of the feminine forms, *Bernardine* (sometimes also given as a boys' name), *Bernardina*, and *Bernarda* are the best known, though none has ever been popular in this country.

Another feminine form of the name is Bernadette. This was made world-famous in the last century by Bernadette Soubirous (1844–79), who became known as St Bernadette of Lourdes. A French peasant-girl, she claimed that she saw visions of the Virgin Mary, who told her of the healing powers of the waters at Lourdes. The first vision appeared on February 11, 1858, and during the next three weeks she saw the same white-veiled vision sixteen times. Thousands came to see her pray, and word spread of various miracles which happened to people who took the waters there. Great numbers of pilgrims still flock to Lourdes annually in the hope of being cured of their ills by the holy waters.

It was in the Basilica of Our Lady at Lourdes that the novelist Franz Werfel took refuge in 1940 when the German army invaded France. It is said that while in the church he made a vow that he would dedicate his next book to the saint if he succeeded in escaping from France. This he managed to do, arriving eventually in the U.S.A., where in 1942, faithful to his vow, he published *The Song of Bernadette*, which had enormous success both as a book and a film.

BERNICE In the last twenty years or so this has become a much-favoured name, and has almost completely ousted the longer form *Berenice*, which, however, is still not uncommon in France.

Nike (pronounced 'Nikee') was the Greek goddess of victory, and Ber(e)nice means 'bringing victory.' The name, therefore, has a triumphant ring, and it is hardly surprising that it was widespread in the great Greek-speaking empire of Macedonia in the fourth century, when, because of the extensive military conquests of Alexander the Great, Macedonia governed vast areas of Europe and Asia.

Among the conquered territories was Egypt, and during the period 323 to 48 B.C., when Egypt became a Roman province, thirteen Macedonian kings named Ptolemy ruled the country, and the large majority of their wives and daughters were called Berenice.

It is a name frequently met with too in Jewish history. Several princesses of the Herod family were named Berenice, among them the sister of Herod Agrippa II, who in chapter xxv of Acts is referred to as Bernice. The form Bernice, therefore, is by no means a recent introduction, though its pet form, *Berny*, is modern.

BERTHA This ancient name has scarcely altered from its original form: *Berchta*, the Old German word for 'bright.' It was the name of the Emperor Charlemagne's mother, who was known as "Berthe aux grands pieds," 'Bertha with the big feet,' regarded, in spite of her outsize shoes, as a beauty.

From the dim past looms the ancient legendary goddess *Berchta*, or *Perchta*, on whose night, January 6, the Austrian mountain-peasants used to celebrate by dancing and ringing bells. Until recently, at least, she was regarded as a sort of fairy godmother who looked after deserted babies and punished lazy housewives; and the country folk round Salzburg would leave oat-cake and salted herrings for her outside their cottage doors.

Tradition associates the name with the visit of the Three Wise Men to Christ twelve days after His birth, and because of this it often used to be given to girls born on January 6.

Before the Norman Conquest the name was unknown in this country except for Bertha, the Christian wife of King Ethelbert of Kent, to whom we owe the introduction of Christianity into southern England by St Augustine, whom the King and Queen welcomed and befriended. After about 1200 it began to grow in popularity, and contemporary records show that it most often took the form *Berta*. To-day its pet forms are *Bert* and *Bertie*.

The name has been attached to two very different articles: a powerful German gun, which in 1918 shelled Paris at a range of over seventy miles (so called because they were manufactured by the Krupp armament works, which had been inherited by Bertha Krupp); and a wide, frilly lace-collar worn on low-necked dresses, popular in Victorian times, like the name itself.

BERYL comes from the Sanskrit, the ancient literary language of India, and is the name given to certain types of precious stones—*e.g.*, the blue aquamarine, the yellow chrysoberyl, and the greenish chrysoprase. In Persian and Arabic the word means 'crystal' or 'crystal-clear.' The German word 'Brille,' contracted from 'Berille,' also has this origin; it means 'spect-acles,' originally made from crystal, because clear glass was unobtainable in the Middle Ages. Our word 'brilliant' has the same derivation.

As a Christian name it is not very old; no examples of it are found before the nineteenth century. One of the earliest ap-pearances of this jewel-name is in Mrs Riddell's novel *George Geith of Fen Court* (1865), in which Beryl Molozane is the heroine.

Berylla is a modern fanciful variation.

BETH When not a pet form of *Elizabeth* this name is most often a contraction of the Hebrew *Bethia*, meaning 'daughter (*i.e.*, worshipper) of Jehovah.' The name is mentioned in the Bible (First Book of Chronicles, iv, 18) as the wife of Mered and a daughter of Pharaoh.

The English author Mrs Gaskell introduced a Bethia into her last novel *Wives and Daughters* (1865), but it is not a com-mon name to-day, either in fiction or as a given name.

For hundreds of years it was a popular name among the Scots, not because of its Hebrew meaning, but through its connexion with the Celtic word 'beath,' meaning 'life'; the name Macbeth is derived from the same word. Introduced into Scotland from Ireland, its early popularity was in some measure due to the Irish princess who became St *Bee*, or *Begha*. In or about the year 656 she founded the nunnery of St Bees in Cumberland, having been installed by St Aidan, founder of the Northumbrian Church, as the first nun in Northumbria. Her name, though in fact Celtic, was thereafter often anglicized as Beth.

BLANCHE Three forms of this name still used in this country are *Blanch*, *Blanche*, and, less commonly, *Bianca*. The first two are derived from the French; the other comes from the Italian. The meaning of the name is 'white' or 'fair-complexioned.'

There is also a Latin form, *Candida*, hardly used as a Christian name in England, though well-known on account of G. B. Shaw's play *Candida* (1897). There is also a St Candida, at whose tomb, in Whitchurch, Dorset, pennies are still left as offerings. In addition to the meanings given above, the Latin form denotes 'pure,' 'unsullied.'

The first mention of the name in history is in the form *Blanca*. Born in Navarre, she became the Queen of Sancho III of Castile and the mother of Alfonso VIII, King of Castile from 1158 to 1214, who married Leonora of Aquitaine, daughter of Henry II of England. A daughter of this marriage was christened Blanca too, a name which for her was certainly a lucky choice, because the ambassadors of King Louis VIII of France, who wished to strengthen the alliance between his country and Spain, chose her, because of her lovely name, in preference to her sister, who had had the misfortune to be named *Urraca*, Spanish for 'magpie'! In due course this Blanca became the mother of King Louis IX of France, who was canonized in 1297.

About this time the name was adopted in France in the form Blanch or Blanche, and was brought to England by the granddaughter of Louis IX's mother, Blanch of Artois, who married Edmund, Earl of Lancaster. The House of Lancaster adopted the name in England, thereby making it popular here.

Of the Blanches mentioned above, none was more pious or more admired than King Louis IX's mother. Shakespeare introduced her into his play *King John*, whose niece she was:

If zealous love should go in search of virtue,
Where should he find it purer than in Blanch?
If love ambitious sought a match of birth,
Whose veins bound richer blood than Lady Blanch?

Shakespeare used the name Bianca in two other plays—*The Taming of the Shrew* and *Othello*.

The Italian forms *Bianca* and *Biancha*, however, have never been used at all widely in this country, though the name appealed to Robert Herrick, who wrote a charming poem, called *Kissing Usury*, which begins:

Biancha, let
Me pay the debt
I owe thee for a kiss
Thou lent'st to me,
And I to thee
Will render ten for this.

BRANWEN, also found as *Brangwain* and *Brengwain*, is a Welsh name meaning 'beautiful raven,' the raven here being symbolic of a dark-haired beauty. It has long been popular in Wales on account of its historical associations.

The Welsh series of tales known as the *Mabinogion* (= 'juvenile instruction') tells the story of Branwen, daughter of King Llyr, who at one time, long ago, ruled over England, known then as "the Island of the Mighty." She was "one of the three chief ladies of this Island, and she was the fairest damsel in the world." She married a King of Ireland who delighted in the name of Matholwch. How she became connected with Wales is by no means clear, but legend had it that she was buried on the Isle of Anglesea. Her tomb there was opened in 1813, and in it was found an urn which corresponded with the description given in the *Mabinogion*.

Another famous Branwen in legend is the one who figures in the romance of *Sir Tristram*, otherwise known as the Tristan legend, popularized by Wagner's opera *Tristan und Isolde*. Branwen, or Brangwain, was the maid of *Iseult* (in Welsh, *Essyllt*, meaning 'beautiful to behold'), who was betrothed to Mark, King of Cornwall. Tristan was entrusted with the task of bringing Iseult from her home in Ireland, but before they set out her mother gave Brangwain a love potion to hand to her mistress on her wedding-night. Unfortunately during the voyage Tristan and Iseult asked Brangwain for a drink and she handed them the magic cup containing the potion. They fell hopelessly in love, and thus began the tragic romance of which the troubadours of France sang.

A name similar in sound but different in meaning is *Bronwen*, 'white bosom,' which for many generations has been one of the most widespread girls' names of pure Welsh origin. Another Welsh name with the same meaning is *Gwenfron*.

BRENDA is a Shetland name, said to be coined from the Old Norse masculine name Brand, which means 'burning log' or 'sword.' Its popularity outside the northern islands is due to Sir Walter Scott, whose novel *The Pirate* (1821) has for its setting the wild sea country of the Shetlands. The land-holder, Magnus Troil, has three daughters, Ulla, Minna, and Brenda. The sweet-natured Brenda is wooed by Mordaunt Mertoun, son of a former pirate, and, having obtained old Magnus's blessing, he finally marries her.

The early Victorians, who had a great liking for names from the distant past with a pleasant ring to them, seized on Brenda, with the result that it steadily gained ground throughout the 1800's, and its popularity has been maintained during the present century.

In Ireland Brenda is looked on as a feminine form of Brendan, which is a name of Celtic origin thought to mean 'fiery.'

BRIDGET The widespread use of this name is due almost entirely to two saints, one Irish, the other Swedish, who were called Bridget.

Together with St Patrick and St Columba, St Bridget (or St *Bride*, as she is sometimes called) of Kildare is the most popular of Irish saints. Born just over fifteen hundred years ago, as a child she looked after her father's flocks, spending most of the day among the birds and beasts of the field, which grew to trust and love her. When she became a young woman she went to a bishop and told him of her wish to spend her life doing works of Christian charity. The bishop conferred upon her the title 'Sister of Mercy,' whereupon she built for herself a hut or cell, and the place where she built it came to be known as Kildare, 'the cell of the oak.' Her fame spread far and wide through Ireland, and she became the subject of hosts of legends. She lived to be seventy, and died in 523 beloved of all Ireland.

St Bridget of Sweden was born some 850 years after the Irish saint's birth; actually the Swedish name has no real connexion with the Irish, being derived from 'birg hitta,' meaning 'mountain protection.' Her early life was very different from her namesake's; she came of a noble family, married and had eight children, and was a member of the Swedish royal household. But when her husband died she changed her way of life completely, devoting all her time to the founding of a monastery in East Gothland, which became so well known that by the Reformation there were no fewer than seventy-four establishments of the order of St Bridget scattered throughout Europe. On her return from a pilgrimage to the Holy Land, she died in Rome in 1373 and was canonized eighteen years later.

It is interesting to note that the Brigittines of Syon (Isleworth), of the order founded by St Bridget of Sweden, survived Henry VIII's dissolution of the monasteries; they took refuge in Portugal, and returned to England in the early nineteenth century. Now at South Brent, Devon, they still pray daily for their founder, Henry V.

The Irish name Bridget, also found commonly as *Brigid* and *Brigit*, is derived from the Celtic word 'brigh,' meaning 'strength.' Celtic legends refer to a goddess named *Brighid*; daughter of the Sun-god, she was worshipped as the goddess of light and of poetry. Many of the remarkable feats attributed to her became confused afterwards in people's minds with the miracles of the Irish St Bridget.

Together with Mary, Bridget (or *Bríd*, its true Irish form) is nowadays the commonest Irish girls' name; yet, until the 1600's at least, these names were scarcely used in Ireland, as they were considered too sacred to bestow as font names. Once adopted, however, they quickly surpassed all others in popularity—so much so that the pet form of Bridget, *Biddy*, became a nickname for Irish colleens generally. Now *Bridie* is the commoner pet form.

The name was introduced into England about the middle of the fifteenth century, during Edward IV's reign, in the form *Brigitte*, suggesting that its introduction here was from Sweden rather than Ireland, as the then prevalent Swedish form was *Brigitta*. But *Bride*, the usual English form in bygone days, was not far behind in establishing itself here, and it is from this form that our word 'bridewell' is derived. Bridewell, really St Bridget's Well, was built as a hospital in Bridge St, Blackfriars, on the site of a former royal dwelling belonging to

Edward VI. It was later converted into a prison, and the name was used afterwards in this sense for gaols up and down the country.

Bride was also popular in Scotland, where the Irish saint had a large following, and her repute gave rise to at least eighteen places in Scotland called Kilbride, 'cell of St Bridget.'

Many churches, too, have been dedicated to one or other of these saints, the most famous, perhaps, being the St Bride's in Fleet Street, now restored after being severely damaged during an air raid in 1940.

CAMILLA This name originated in ancient Etruria, now Tuscany, the region round Florence. Its meaning is 'an attendant at a sacrifice': the *Camilli* and *Camillae* were the boy and girl attendants respectively.

The Queen of the Volsci, one of the Etruscan tribes, was named Camilla. She was a great leader and, according to Virgil, was so fleet-footed that she could run over a cornfield without bending a blade of corn, and make her way over the sea without wetting her feet! The name of this Queen's mother was *Casmilla*, but her father "drowned one hissing letter in a softer sound" and called his daughter Camilla.

The name was first used in England as early as 1205, though it was rare until after the Reformation, when there was a classical revival in English literature, which was reflected in the sudden popularity of Christian names taken from the Classical authors. Though this vogue did not last long, Camilla became established, and is still occasionally found; but, like *Anthea*, it seems to be used nowadays mostly by families which retain these names in successive generations.

In France, on the other hand, as *Camille* it is still widely used. The French, who have had a liking for Greek and

Roman names since the Revolution, when they looked to ancient Athens and Rome for the model of their new régime, gave the name a great vogue, though it had been in use there, both for boys and girls, since the mid seventeenth century.

Its use in Italy can be traced back even further, for a Camilla appears as the wife of Ansmelo of Florence in an episode of Cervantes' *Don Quixote* entitled *The Fatal Curiosity*, written at the beginning of the seventeenth century.

Probably the most famous use of the name in English literature is in the novel *Camilla*, by Mme D'Arblay, better known as Fanny Burney. This novel, published in 1796, earned her three thousand guineas, which she used to build a cottage near Mickleham, in Surrey, which she called Camilla Cottage.

One of Greta Garbo's finest screen performances was in *Camille* (1937), the plot of which, like that of Verdi's opera *La Traviata*, was taken from the younger Alexandre Dumas' novel *The Lady of the Camellias*.

CAROLINE and its many variations are all feminine forms of Carolus, the Latin rendering of the Old German word 'carl,' 'a man.' In Italy this Latin form became Carlo, and from it are derived the feminine forms *Carla, Carol, Carola, Carolina,* and *Caroline*. In France it became Charles, whence the feminine *Charlotte*, a softer version of the Italian *Carlotta*.

None of these feminine names is anything like as old as the masculine form. Charlotte seems to be the earliest version of the name in this country, the first record of it dating from 1613, when Beaumont and Fletcher's play *The Honest Man's Fortune* was first performed; it included a character named Charlotte. It is recorded again in 1626, but was rare here until the second half of the eighteenth century, when it was made popular by Charlotte Sophia, Queen of George III and mother of his fifteen children.

Charlotte Brontë, perhaps the most famous bearer of the name, was born in 1816. Under the pen-name Currer Bell she wrote her three great novels, *Jane Eyre*, *Shirley*, and *Villette*, all still widely read to-day. Charlotte Yonge was a much more prolific writer of the same period; she was the author of 160 books, including a pioneer work on the history of Christian names.

In Europe the name had a tremendous vogue after the publication, in 1774, of Goethe's *The Sorrows of Young Werther*. In this romance Werther commits suicide in a fit of despondency, leaving his pathetic loved one, Charlotte, in despair. W. M. Thackeray, the English humorist, parodied this morbidly sentimental story, and of the heroine he wrote:

> Charlotte, having seen his body
> Borne before her on a shutter,
> Like a well-conducted person
> Went on cutting bread and butter.

The first known *Carola* was a certain Carola Harsnett, born in 1670. She, no doubt, was named in honour of Charles II, and it is quite likely that there were other Carolas before her, the name being given to daughters born to Royalists during the Civil War, fought between Charles I and Parliament from 1642 to 1649.

Carola has never been widely used in this country, but is still occasionally found, the most celebrated Carola of to-day being Carola Oman, the historian, biographer, and novelist.

Caroline came into fashion when Caroline of Ansbach,

wife of George II, became Queen in 1727. It remained a favourite name for the rest of that century and, although it lost favour to some extent in the 1800's, it has now regained much of its former popularity.

Carol as a name has no connexion, strictly speaking, with Christmas carols. Long popular as a boys' and a girls' name in the U.S.A., it came into vogue in this country, together with *Carole*, during the 1930's, partly on account of Carole Lombard, the film star.

The appearance of *Carolyn* and *Karolyn* is even more recent, but there are signs that these forms are overtaking all others in popularity.

The usual abbreviation of Caroline is *Carrie*, less commonly *Caddy*, while Carolina is shortened to *Lina*, and Charlotte (which a couple of hundred years ago was commonly pronounced 'Shar-lott-ee') has the pet forms *Lottie* and *Chattie*; but the Charlotte in *Bleak House* was called *Charley*.

CATHARINE—See *Katharine*.

CECILY In ancient Rome there was a famous family called the Caecilii, and it is generally supposed that its founder must have been blind, for this is the meaning of the Latin word 'caecus,' from which the name originated.

Easily the most celebrated member of this family was the martyred St Cecilia. She is the patron saint of music, particularly church music, and is generally represented seated at an organ, whence the belief that she invented this instrument. Her playing and singing are said to have been so beautiful that, in the words of Alexander Pope, in his *Ode for Music on Saint Cecilia's Day* (1713):

E

Of Orpheus now no more let poets tell,
  To bright Cecilia greater power is given;
His numbers raised a shade from hell,
  Hers lift the soul to heaven.

St Cecilia's Day is often chosen for choir festivals. Wherever music is loved her name has remained popular, even though it has assumed other forms in the course of time.

The commonest forms met with nowadays in this country are *Cecily* and *Cicely*. In former times *Sisley* was widespread; other forms occasionally found are *Cecil* (now almost exclusively a boys' name, though still used for girls in some families and borne by the distinguished historian Cecil Woodham-Smith), *Cécile* (the usual French form), and *Cecilie* (either an early English rendering of the Latin form *Cecilia* or in imitation of the German *Cäcilie*).

The name was introduced into England at the time of the Norman Conquest, for William the Conqueror had a daughter named Cecilia. More famous in history, though, is Cecily, the twelfth daughter of Ralph Neville, Earl of Westmorland. She was the mother of Richard III. Her good looks gained her the title 'the Rose of Raby,' while her behaviour won her the less flattering nickname 'Proud Cis.' She lived in the fifteenth century, by which time the name must already have been well established, for Chaucer gives the name Cecily to the heroine (St Cecilia) of his *Second Nun's Tale*.

During the Middle Ages the normal spelling was Cecilia, which is as one might expect, because in those days records were kept in Latin. The written and spoken forms of names were, however, often quite distinct, and it is probable that already in medieval times this name was pronounced *Sisley*, which is remarkably close to its modern pronunciation, as well as resembling the modern Irish form, *Sisile*.

The name continued in favour right up to the Reformation, when, like the majority of non-scriptural saints' names, it suffered an eclipse. It had a revival in the early eighteenth century, and its renewed popularity was enhanced when Fanny Burney's novel *Cecilia* appeared in 1782.

Nowadays the usual pet form is *Cis*, sometimes *Cec* (pronounced 'sess').

CELIA There is a hill in Rome known as the Caelian Hill, said to be named after an ancestor of the ancient Roman Caelian clan, which, it is supposed, took the name from 'caelum,' Latin for 'the heavens.' Celia, therefore, means 'heavenly.'

In England the name often used to be spelt *Caelia*, but since about 1700 its normal spelling has been as we know it to-day. In the literature of the Elizabethan period and the seventeenth century it was very popular, being used especially in poetry, like *Phyllis* and *Amaryllis*, for any lady-love. Shakespeare had a Celia, Rosalind's cousin in *As You like It*, and Edmund Spenser's Dame Celia is the heavenly mother of the three theological virtues Faith, Hope, and Charity in *The Faerie Queene*. Ben Jonson's immortal lyric, "Drink to me only with thine eyes" is addressed *To Celia*; Jonathan Swift speaks for many husbands when he satirically remarks:

> Five hours (and who could do it less in?)
> By haughty Celia spent in dressing.

When the name *Cecilia* returned to favour in the eighteenth century (see above) it often assumed the shorter form Celia, and both these forms were used to render the Irish version, *Sile*, pronounced like *Sheila*.

On the Continent the French form, *Célie*, was in vogue in

the eighteenth century both as a font name and in pastoral poetry. Related names are *Celeste* and *Celestine*, both occasionally given in this country.

CHARITY "Faith, Hope, and Charity, but the greatest of these is Charity." The ancient Latin version of the Scriptures known as the Vulgate uses the word 'caritas' for Christian Love, which is what Charity means in the Bible.

In seventeenth-century England the austere Puritans, wishing to do away with church ritual and accept as their sole authority the "pure Word of God," frowned on the use of non-scriptural saints' names and chose for their children names from the Old Testament, many of them obscure and almost unpronounceable, or 'abstract-virtue' names, among which Charity was highly favoured. Other girls' names of this kind were *Grace*, *Truth* or *Troth*, *Patience*, *Verity*, and *Prudence*. John Bunyan, who expressed the Puritans' attitude to life, introduced Charity into his allegorical *Pilgrim's Progress*, placing her in the "Palace Beautiful."

At one time it was customary when triplets were born to baptize them *Faith*, *Hope*, and *Charity*, the names of the daughters of the third-century martyr St *Sophia* (Greek 'sophia'='wisdom'), who is usually represented holding her three daughters in her arms. The Joshua Reynolds window at New College, Oxford, shows the virtue of Charity protecting children nestling under her robe.

Dickens, in *Martin Chuzzlewit*, gives the names *Charity* and *Mercy* (another 'abstract-virtue' name) to the daughters of Mr Pecksniff; to every one, though, they were known as *Cherry* and *Merry*, and still to-day Cherry is the usual pet form of Charity, a less common contraction being *Chattie*, shared with *Charlotte*.

CHARMIAN This name, the original form of which was *Charmion*, is derived from a Greek word meaning 'joy.' In history she is remembered as the kind-hearted attendant of Cleopatra, and is introduced into Shakespeare's *Antony and Cleopatra* (1608) and Dryden's *All for Love* (1678).

CHLOE, pronounced 'clo-ee,' is a Greek word meaning 'a green shoot,' and should therefore be especially appropriate for girls who have 'green fingers.'

It was a title given to Demeter, goddess of fruits and crops, and thus came to be regarded as a name particularly suitable for country girls, though it was in a city, Corinth, that St Paul converted a Chloe to Christianity. Chloe was popular in poetry as a name for country girls ever since she was portrayed as the shepherdess beloved by Daphnis in the Greek pastoral romance *Daphnis and Chloe* some fifteen hundred years ago. It was popularized in this country by the poets of the Elizabethan and Stuart periods. Sir Philip Sidney has a Chloe in his famous idyll *Arcadia* (1590), while Thomas D'Urfey (1653–1723) writes thus of his *Chloe Divine*:

> Chloe's a Nymph in flowery groves,
> A Nereid in the streams;
> Saint-like in the temple she moves,
> A woman in my dreams.

At the beginning of the nineteenth century the name became a favourite one among the coloured people of America, and it is therefore no mere coincidence that Harriet Beecher Stowe chose it for her character Aunt Chloe in *Uncle Tom's Cabin* (1851). In this novel, which did much to arouse anti-slavery sentiment before the American Civil War, Chloe is the wife of the faithful old slave, Uncle Tom.

CHRISTINE Of the several names derived from 'Christ,' Christine and Christina are nowadays the most commonly used in this country. These names derive from the Greek word 'chrio,' meaning 'I anoint'; the Greek term 'Christos,' 'the Anointed One,' was used by the Greeks to translate the old Hebrew word 'Messiah.'

The first record of the name dates from the third century, when St Christina lived; a Roman noblewoman, she was martyred about 295. It is after her that most Italian Christinas were named. Among them was Christina Rossetti (1830–94), the poet who wrote Goblin Market; though born in England, she was of Italian parentage.

It was from Italy, late in the eleventh century, that the name reached England, Ireland, and Scotland, becoming specially popular in Scotland, mainly in the forms Kirsty and Kirsteen. The true Gaelic forms are Cairistine and Ciorsdan. In England the most usual form was Christian, a name used by both sexes, which only in recent times has yielded its popularity to the forms Christine and Christina. The Scandinavian form is seen in Kirsten Flagstad, the great Norwegian concert singer.

Christabel, 'fair follower of Christ,' is a more fanciful form of these 'Christian' names. It first appeared in the old ballad Sir Cauline, as Christabelle, the daughter of "a bonnie king of Ireland," and was already a widely used name in the north of England when Coleridge published his mysterious fragmentary poem Christabel in 1816. This poem, however, made the name popular in other parts of the country, one famous bearer of it being Christabel Pankhurst, of that celebrated family who fought for votes for women at the beginning of this century.

Another form of the name, but one hardly used nowadays in England, is Christiana. Bunyan, in Pilgrim's Progress, devotes the second part (1684) of his great allegory to the journey of Christiana, wife of Christian, to the Celestial City.

Pet forms of the name are taken from both halves of it—*Chris* and *Chrissie*, and *Teenie* and *Tina*; Tina is also used as a pet form of *Clementina*. In Scotland the pet form *Christie* is sometimes used, as by Charles Reade in his novel *Christie Johnstone* (1855), the story of a Scots fishergirl.

CLARE In Latin this name has a double meaning: 'bright' and 'illustrious.' In old songs it is said that the Emperor Charlemagne (742–814) had a daughter called Princess *Clara*, but the first famous historical character to bear the name was St Clare of Assisi, friend of St Francis and foundress, in 1212, of the order of nuns known variously as Poor Clares or Clarisses. The first convent of Poor Clares in England was founded about 1293. St Clare was proclaimed patron saint of television in 1958 by Pope Pius XII, because of her reputed power of seeing events at a distance ('television' means literally 'seeing at a distance').

The name began to be used in this country about seven hundred years ago, being found both in the Latin form, Clara, and in its English version, Clare. Since then it has been adopted, in a variety of fanciful forms, by poets, playwrights, and novelists, especially in the seventeenth and eighteenth centuries. *Clarinda* and *Claribel* are both characters in Spenser's *Faërie Queene*, while one of the first English novels, published in 1748, was Samuel Richardson's *Clarissa Harlowe*. Much older is the noble-sounding *Esclairmonde*, found, together with *Clarimond*, in French medieval romance. All these variations have enjoyed a literary vogue at one time or another, but have rarely been used as font names.

In the nineteenth century Clara came into fashion, and is often found in Victorian literature. Dickens, for example, uses it for David Copperfield's devoted old nurse and friend, Clara Peggotty. During the present century Clare has been more favoured than Clara, though both forms have lost ground to the French version *Claire* in very recent years.

CLAUDIA derives from the name of an ancient Roman patrician family, and is said to be connected with 'claudus,' the Latin word for 'lame.' The poet Martial celebrates a beautiful Claudia of Britain about A.D. 60, which seems to indicate that hers is one of the oldest surviving names in this country.

It was about the same time as Martial was composing his famous epigrams that the Emperor Claudius conquered part of south-east England and the British prince Caractacus was captured, together with his family, and taken in chains to Rome. When he saw them there Claudius was so impressed with their noble bearing that he set them free. One of the Prince's daughters soon afterwards became a Christian, and at baptism took the name Claudia. Tradition has it that this is the Claudia mentioned in St Paul's Second Epistle to Timothy (iv, 21).

Other forms of the name are *Claudine* and *Claudette*, French versions which have been used from time to time in this country.

In Wales Claudia is regarded as a name closely akin to *Gladys* (see p. 116).

CLEMENCY It is difficult to say whether Clemency is the most common form of this name nowadays; *Clemence* is perhaps as often found. *Clementina*, once popular, is no longer much used, nor *Clementine*, which remains familiar, however, on account of the "forty-niner's" daughter in the old song.

All these variations derive from the masculine form Clement, which in turn comes from the Latin word 'clemens,' meaning 'mild,' 'merciful.' The earliest recorded English form, *Clementia*, was in use here as far back as 1200. The Romans had a goddess Clementia, worshipped as the goddess of Pity. Statues show her holding a lance in one hand and a goblet in the other—the lance to defend the oppressed, and the goblet to refresh the weary.

From the German-invented form *Klementine* came the English version *Clementina*, which was popular here following the appearance, in 1753, of *Sir Charles Grandison* by Samuel Richardson. In this novel the hero is loved by the amiable Italian lady Clementina, but he chooses to marry instead the affected orphan Harriet Byron.

Clem is the pet form of all these versions, as well as of the boys' name Clement.

One of the foremost writers of to-day is Clemence Dane—the pen-name of Winifred Ashton.

CONSTANCE This name, taken from the Latin word 'constantia,' means 'constancy' or 'perseverance.' In Roman times the masculine form was famous far and wide through Constantine the Great, who in 313 ordered the toleration of Christianity throughout the Roman Empire. The feminine form, *Constantia*, was used in the Imperial families of Rome, and even spread to Greece—a rare occurrence, as the Romans usually borrowed Greek names.

In England the name was introduced at the time of the Norman invasion, and was soon in general use. Its commonest form during the Middle Ages was *Custance*, used by Chaucer in *The Man of Law's Tale*.

Constance of Brittany, mother of the unfortunate young Prince Arthur, is one of the characters in Shakespeare's *King*

John; but it was probably John of Gaunt's second wife, Constance of Castile, whom he married in 1371, who kept the name popular in England right up to the Reformation, when it went out of fashion.

Its use between then and the nineteenth century was mainly in royal and aristocratic circles, but during the Victorian age it leaped back into popularity in its original form, Constantia.

Very few babies these days are christened Constantia, but Constance, with its pet form *Connie*, is by no means uncommon.

CORA, together with its charming but rather unusual diminutive, *Corinna*, is derived from the Greek word 'kore,' meaning 'girl, maiden.' *Kore* or *Cora* was a title given to Persephone (Proserpina), who, while innocently gathering flowers one day, was seized by Pluto, king of the Underworld, and carried off in his chariot to the infernal regions to be his bride. When her mother Demeter at last tracked her down Kore was allowed to spend half the year above in the sunlight of the upper world, but was obliged to spend the other half with her gloomy husband among the Shades.

The name Cora does not appear to have been used in this country until the middle of the last century, although it was by then already known in America. James Fenimore Cooper used it in his novel *The Last of the Mohicans* (1826), in which the ill-fated heroine was Cora Munro.

Corinna, a variation of Cora, dates back to at least the fifth century B.C. A Greek poetess by this name once vanquished the great Pindar in a public poetry competition. It became a favourite name among the lyric poets of the seventeenth century, including Robert Herrick, of whose many lady-loves Corinna was but one.

The French author Madame de Staël gave the French form

of the name to her novel *Corinne* (1807). Another French version is *Coralie*, which came into existence just after the Revolution. The comparatively recent name *Coral* may be an adaptation of this, but is more probably a 'jewel-name,' like *Beryl*, *Esmeralda*, etc.

CYNTHIA Mount Cynthus in Greece was regarded as sacred to the goddess Artemis, who was given the title "the Cynthian," much as Catholics to-day talk of "Our Lady of Lourdes." But Cynthus contains that curious combination of letters, -nth-, which constantly occurs in words (*e.g.*, Labyrinth, Rhadamanthus, Corinth) taken by the Greeks from the early Minoan people from whom they conquered their country. So the goddess of Mount Cynthus must have been the ancient Mother Goddess of the Earth whom the Minoans worshipped, taken over by the Greek invaders and given the name of their own goddess who appeared to them most to resemble her.

Two thousand years ago, the Latin poet Propertius addressed poems to a girl friend called Cynthia. The name was again extensively used by the Elizabethan poets, and was one of the several names applied to Queen Elizabeth (the commonest was *Gloriana*). Since then it has been in and out of favour, but has probably never enjoyed such popularity as it does now.

DAISY The daisy, with its golden sun-like centre and pink-edged white petals that close with the approach of night, derives its names from the Anglo-Saxon 'dæges éage,' 'day's eye.' Chaucer says:

> That wel by reson met hit callë may
> The dayësye, or elles the ye of daye,
> The emperice and flour of flourës alle.
> (Prologue to *Legend of Good Women*)

Like most flower-names, it seems not to have been used as an independent name until the last century. It was at first a translation of *Marguerite*, a French girls' name identical with the French word for a daisy. The English name *Margaret* has nothing to do with daisies, strictly speaking, being from the Persian for 'child of light' (see p. 157). In Old French 'marguerite' only meant 'pearl,' a meaning it has now lost except for biblical references, but it added the meaning 'daisy,' presumably because this flower came to be looked on as 'the pearl of flowers.' Marguerite de Navarre (1492–1549) was called "marguerite des marguerites" ('pearl of pearls') by her brother François I. Another famous Marguerite of Royal French blood was Marguerite de Valois (1553–1615), among whose jewels was a necklace of pearls mounted in the shape of daisies.

The name Daisy was in use in America, too, in the nineteenth century; the American novelist Henry James used it in the title of a short story, *Daisy Miller*, published in 1879, which tells of the experiences of a young American girl on her first visit to Europe.

Daisy Ashford was only nine when she wrote *The Young Visiters*, an extremely funny and imaginative story, published in 1919.

Perhaps the most famous Daisy of all is the one who was asked in Henry Dacre's famous song of the 1890's to "give me an answer, do!"

DAPHNE The Greek word 'daphne' means 'bay-tree,' 'laurel,' and the name Daphne may therefore be compared with *Laura*, from the Latin word 'laurus,' 'laurel.' But whereas Laura has long been in use as a Christian name, Daphne was unknown until the turn of this century. It is now fairly widespread, the most famous bearer being the novelist Daphne du Maurier.

The first Daphne appears in Greek mythology as a nymph. The Sun-god Apollo fell in love with her, but she was terrified of him and fled, calling on the gods to protect her. This they did by changing her into a bay-tree!

Using this myth, Giulio Caccini composed *Dafne* (1596), the first Italian opera, as distinct from a musical drama.

The pet forms are *Daph* (or *Daff*) and *Daffy*.

DAWN This name, a coinage of the late nineteenth century, is becoming increasingly popular. It is a literal rendering of the Latin word 'aurora.' *Aurora* was the Roman goddess of dawn, and as a Christian name it has been popular in France, in the form *Aurore*, for over four hundred years. In England Aurora had a certain vogue in the nineteenth century, owing partly to Byron and partly to Elizabeth Barrett Browning. In *Don Juan*, written in 1818, Byron introduces

> Aurora Raby, a young star who shone
> O'er life, too sweet an image for such glass,
> A lovely being, scarcely form'd or moulded,
> A rose with all its sweetest leaves yet folded.

In Elizabeth Barrett Browning's romance *Aurora Leigh* (1857) the heroine is a talented girl who, being left without financial resources, learns to support herself by her pen.

Aurora has the pet forms *Orrie* and *Rora*.

Dawn Powell, born in 1897, was an American satirical novelist and dramatist; she was one of the first bearers of the name. The first novel of the celebrated American writer Edna Ferber was *Dawn O'Hara*, published in 1911.

Other names connected with the dawn are *Lucy* (see p. 153); *Zora*, the Arabic word for 'dawn'—quite a common girls' name in Australia; *Gwawr*, the Welsh for 'dawn'; and *Roxana*, from the Persian for 'dawn' and the title of a novel (1724) by Daniel Defoe. *Roxana* and *Roxane*, popular in the U.S.A., have the pet form *Roxy*.

DEBORAH is the Hebrew word for 'bee' and later, possibly because of the bee's musical humming, it came also to mean 'eloquence.' Deborah may be compared with another pretty name, *Melissa*, the Greek word for 'bee.'

The first mention of this ancient name is in the Book of Genesis, xxxv, 8. Deborah was Rebecca's faithful nurse, so greatly mourned after her death that the tree under which she was buried became known as the "oak of weeping."

The second scriptural bearer of the name lived about three thousand years ago, when the Israelites were under the yoke of the Canaanites. There were at that time ten tribes, without central government, and six of these answered the summons of the prophetess and judge Deborah to rise up against the tyrannical Canaanites. The Israelites were victorious, and Deborah sang a famous Song of Triumph after the victory. The story of this Deborah is told in Judges iv, and in the following chapter is the Song of Deborah, considered one of the oldest poems in the Old Testament, and so expressive that it may explain the later meaning of the name—'eloquence.'

The Puritans, who loved Old Testament names, made this one very popular in the seventeenth century. John Milton named his youngest daughter Deborah, a fitting name for such an eloquent poet's child.

Readers of Mrs Gaskell will remember Deborah Jenkyns in *Cranford* (1853): "Then came Miss Jenkyns—Debōrah, as she liked Miss Matty to call her, her father having once said that the Hebrew name ought to be so pronounced."

Nowadays, of course, the stress is always on the first syllable;

in fact, the modern variant, *Debra*, dispenses with the o completely. The usual pet forms are *Deb*, *Debs*, and *Debby* or *Debbie*, though formerly the commonest abbreviation was *Debir*.

DEIRDRE is an ancient Irish name which may mean 'the raging one,' from the old Celtic word 'derdriu,' or possibly 'the broken-hearted one,' from the Gaelic word 'deoirid.' The original bearer was the heroine of one of the *Three Sorrowful Tales of Erinn*, a legend adapted as a tragedy, *Deirdre* (1907) by W. B. Yeats, and also by J. M. Synge in a verse drama, *Deirdre of the Sorrows* (1910).

The name does not appear to have been used baptismally until these two modern Irish playwrights popularized it in poetical and artistic circles. Both Yeats and Synge, however, may have been inspired by William Sharp, whose *Deirdre* (1903) was one of the several tales and romances written by him, under the pen-name Fiona Macleod, to promote the Celtic Renaissance, which aimed at reviving interest in Scotland's and Ireland's heroic past.

DENISE, the feminine form of Denis, was recently imported from France to fill the gap left for centuries by the neglect of the older form *Dionysia*. This makes clear its derivation: for Dionysus, otherwise known as Bacchus, was the god of wine and of drama. There may seem to be little connexion between wine and the stage, but among the ancient Greeks a yearly festival was held to celebrate the wine-harvest, with dances, songs, and recitations, which developed into the Greek drama. The name of Dionysus means simply 'the God of Nysa'; Mount Nysa, his holy mountain, is in modern Afghanistan.

Denise used to be a common name in this country, particularly during the Middle Ages. The most usual pet forms then were *Dennet* and *Diot*, and in records it was generally written in its Latin form, Dionysia. Since its revival in the present century it has become quite popular both in this country and the U.S.A., where the versions *Dion*, *Dione*, and *Dionetta* are found. *Denyse* is a fanciful variation.

A remarkable Denise of to-day is Denise Robins, author of over a hundred novels.

DIANA In the ancient Aryan languages 'Dy-' meant 'god'; this survives in our word 'divine.' But a d frequently became pronounced like a z or a j, as in the Greek Zeus and the Latin Jupiter, which merely mean 'god' and 'god the father.' The Roman god Janus was probably originally the same divinity as Jupiter, but when he had a separate temple he became regarded as a separate god. Oddly enough, the god Janus (also Dianus) had a wife, *Jana*, but she became known as *Diana*. As he was the great sky god, she was looked upon as the lesser sky goddess, and so became the goddess of the night, symbolized by the moon.

When the Romans began to absorb the civilization of the Greeks they started to adopt Greek gods and goddesses, claiming that any Greek divinity was the same person as the Roman god or goddess whose character and functions were most like. Hence the Roman Diana was claimed to be the Greek Artemis, actually a far more picturesque personality; she was not only the moon goddess, but protectress of wild animals (sometimes their huntress too). She would have nothing to do with men; when the sportsman Actaeon discovered her bathing she was so furious that she changed him into a stag which his own hounds tore to pieces.

The most notable temple of Artemis was at Ephesus; it was one of the Seven Wonders of the ancient world. When St

Paul preached Christianity there the image-makers, who did a roaring trade, started a riot. Holding an indignation meeting in the stadium, they roused the people, who shouted, "Great is Diana of the Ephesians" continually for two hours, till they were pacified by the town clerk. The goddess's name in the English version of this passage (Acts, xix) is given as Diana, but in the original Greek it is Artemis.

Diana's reputed birthplace is Delos, in the Aegean Sea; hence she came also to be known as the Delian goddess, and the name *Delia* is derived from this small island.

Diana was not used as a Christian name in this country until well into the sixteenth century, a little after its adoption in France in the form *Diane*. It was made popular there by the beautiful Diane de Poitiers (1499–1566), whose black-and-white favours her Royal lover, Henri II, always wore at tournaments.

Shakespeare introduced a Diana into *All's Well That Ends Well*, written about 1600, and it appears quite often in the poetry of the seventeenth century. It was not until about 1750, however, that the name came into general use in England, and it was at this time too that it became shortened familiarly to *Di*, just as it is to-day.

Diana Vernon, one of Sir Walter Scott's most popular female characters, appears in *Rob Roy* (1817) as the niece of Sir Hildebrand Osbaldistone; she is portrayed as a high-spirited woman of great beauty and sparkling talents.

Just now the name seems to be very much in vogue among actresses, including Diana Churchill and Diana Wynyard in England, and Diane Cilento from Australia.

DINAH The names *Dinah* and *Diana* are often confused with each other, though in fact they are quite distinct. Dinah

F

means, in Hebrew, 'judged,' and was the name of the daughter of Jacob and Leah.

Like many Old Testament names, this one began to be used during the seventeenth century when the Puritans held sway in this country. The early Puritan settlers in New England made it popular in the New World, and it is still widespread in the U.S.A., though nowadays there it is more commonly found among coloured people. It was the name given in *Uncle Tom's Cabin* (1851) to the negro cook in the St Clare household.

Elsewhere in literature a Dinah appears in Laurence Sterne's *Tristram Shandy*, while in George Eliot's *Adam Bede* Dinah Morris is the main female character—a factory girl and Wesleyan preacher sensitive to others' needs.

A popular ballad of Victorian times was *Vilkins and his Dinah*, which begins:

> It is of a rich merchant I am going to tell,
> Who had for a daughter an uncommon nice young gal,
> Her name it was Dinah, just sixteen years old,
> With a very large fortune in silver and gold—
> *Singing too-ra-li, too-ra-li, too-ra-li-ay.*

Her father finds her a husband, but she wants to live single a year or two more, at which her father calls her bold and threatens to disinherit her.

DOLORES comes to us from Spain, where it was used in conjunction with *Maria*. Until recently Maria, always identified in the minds of Spaniards with the Virgin Mary, was not given as an independent name but was combined with such attributes of the Virgin Mary as *Dolores* (=Maria de los Dolores, 'Mary of the Sorrows') and *Mercedes* (Maria de las

Mercedes, 'Mary of the Mercies'). As Our Lady of Sorrows, the Virgin Mary is represented with her heart pierced with seven swords, emblematic of her seven Sorrows—the prophecy of Simeon, the flight into Egypt, Jesus lost in Jerusalem, Jesus' meeting with his mother on the way to Calvary, Mary at the Cross, Jesus' dead body laid in his mother's arms, and Jesus laid in the tomb.

In America and this country, however, Dolores stands as a name on its own. The pet forms are *Lola* and *Lolita*. Lola is nowadays often given as an independent name in the U.S.A., with the pet form *Lo*.

Until it became a popular name in Hollywood in the 1930's Dolores was used almost exclusively by Roman Catholics.

DORA Now a name in its own right, Dora was at one time used as a short form of *Dorothy* or *Theodora* (see p. 85), or as an English adaptation of the German name *Dore*. It does not figure as an independent Christian name before the nineteenth century, and one of the earliest uses of it in literature is in some verses, by the Scottish poet Thomas Campbell, written in 1836:

> Dora's eyes of heavenly blue
> Pass all painting's reach;
> Ringdoves' notes are discord to
> The music of her speech.

A Dora also appears in a poem by Tennyson written in 1842. Thirty-eight years previously the name had been given to a daughter of the poet William Wordsworth who had a sister called Dorothy.

Dora Spenlow, in *David Copperfield*, is the pretty but unpractical 'child-wife' of the hero, who loves to sit by him and hold his pens for him as he writes, while the housework is neglected.

In E. Nesbit's famous 'Bastable' books for children there is Dora Bastable, the eldest girl of that enterprising family of Would-Be-Goods and Treasure Seekers.

Doretta and *Dorette* are diminutive forms occasionally given. The pet form *Dorrie* is shared with Doreen, Dorothy, and Doris.

DOREEN Of all the Irish girls' names which have found favour in this country, Doreen or, in its native form, *Doirean*, is to-day probably the most popular. It is said to be derived from a Celtic word meaning 'sullen,' but it seems unlikely that Irish-speaking parents, knowing the word, would wish to inflict such an unprepossessing attribute on their children. It is more likely that, like many Irish girls' names ending in -een, including *Kathleen, Maureen, Eveleen*, which are diminutives of *Katharine, Mary*, and *Eve*, Doreen is a diminutive of *Dora* or *Dorothy*.

The name was first used in England about sixty years ago. *Doreen* was the title of a novel, which appeared in 1894, by Edna Lyall, the hero of which is the Irish revolutionary leader Michael Davitt.

DORIS In Greek mythology Doris was the daughter of Oceanus and Tethys and mother of fifty daughters, known as Nereids, who were the sea-nymphs of the Mediterranean.

But Doris was also the name of a mountainous region in Greece which was the home of the Dorians, one of the great Hellenic races. The name, therefore, means 'a Dorian girl.' Some authorities claim that it means 'bountiful,' or 'she of good gifts.'

Although Greek in origin, Doris was also a popular name with the Romans, and in both languages is often found in poetry. In England too it was a favoured name in drama and poetry. William Congreve, the Restoration dramatist, introduced it in his translation of a satire by the first-century Roman poet Juvenal; and a Doris appears in a play, *The Confederacy* (1705), by Congreve's friend Sir John Vanbrugh.

As an English Christian name, though, Doris goes back only to the latter part of the last century. It very quickly became a favourite name, but its popularity has declined during the last fifty years or so.

DOROTHY The name Dorothy is a compound of two Greek words, 'doron,' 'gift,' and 'Theou,' 'of God.' *Theodora* is another form of the same name, the order of the two Greek words having been reversed. Dorothy may be compared with its Anglo-Saxon counterpart *Godgiefu*, which was later given the Latin form *Godiva*.

The third-century martyr St *Dorothea* was one of the many Christians put to death during the reign of the Roman Emperor Diocletian. On her way to execution a young man taunted her with the words, "Send me some fruit and roses, Dorothea, when you get to Paradise." Later that evening, while he was at dinner, an angel appeared with a basket of apples and roses and said, "From Dorothea in Paradise," then vanished. The playwrights Philip Massinger and Thomas Dekker dramatized this legend in *The Virgin Martyr* (1622).

In England Dorothy has always been a more popular form than Dorothea, though the latter was in vogue in early-Victorian times. The name came into use in Shakespeare's time, and though there is no Dorothy in his plays, there is a *Doll*—Doll Tearsheet in *The Second Part of King Henry IV*—

which shows that this popular abbreviation was being used as early as the name itself. Another short form is found in Ben Jonson's play *The Alchemist* (1610), where one of the characters is *Dol* Common.

Dorothy became such a popular name that after 1700 its pet form *Doll*, or *Dolly*, became the name of the best loved of all young girls' playthings. In Scotland a doll is known as a *Doroty* or *Dorrity*, early Scottish forms of the name. The true Gaelic version is *Diorbhail*.

Other pet forms are *Dot*, *Dottie*, and *Dodo*, while of the many fanciful variations of the name the most charming are perhaps *Doralicia* and *Dorinda*, the latter at one time much favoured in Ireland. *Dodie*, another variant, is famous through Dodie Smith, the playwright who wrote *Dear Octopus*. *Dora*, sometimes used as a pet form of Dorothy, is treated separately on p. 83.

In fiction there are: Dorothea Brooke, the heroine of George Eliot's novel *Middlemarch* (1872); Dorothy, in *The Wonderful Wizard of Oz* (1900) by Lyman Frank Baum, the American children's classic which was made into a successful film in 1939; Dot, the cheery, chubby young wife of John Peerybingle in Dickens's *The Cricket on the Hearth*, very fond of her husband and very proud of her baby; and another delightful Dickens character, Dolly Varden, the locksmith's daughter in *Barnaby Rudge*, who marries Joe Willet and lives with him at the Maypole Inn. She gave her name to a special kind of hat with one side bent downwards and abundantly trimmed with flowers.

DULCIE With the exception of *Douce*—an uncommon name on this side of the Channel—Dulcie is to-day the only form used of the names deriving from the Latin *Dulcibella*, 'sweet-beautiful,' which at one time or another have been popular in this country. Among the commonest were *Dulce*, *Dulcena*, *Dowsabel*, *Dowse*, and *Ducia*.

In the Middle Ages Dowse and Dowsabel were very common names—so common, in fact, that by the sixteenth century they had passed into the language with the meaning 'sweetheart.'

A Spanish form was *Dulcinea*, and Cervantes chose this as the name of Don Quixote's lady-love; or rather, the chival-rous knight chose it himself, for when his faithful squire Sancho Panza first pointed her out she was nothing more than a "stoutly-built sturdy wench" named Aldonza, riding an ass. Don Quixote, however, convinced that she was the victim of enchantment, gave her the romantic name Dulcinea, and described the lady of his dreams thus: "Her flowing hair is of gold, her forehead the Elysian fields, her eyebrows two celestial arches, her eyes a pair of glorious suns, her cheeks two beds of roses, her lips two coral portals that guard her teeth of oriental pearl, her neck is alabaster, her hands are polished ivory, and her bosom whiter than the new-fallen snow."

EDITH As spelt and pronounced to-day, Edith is a com-paratively modern name, for it was not until the nineteenth century that its extensive popularity was revived for the first time since the Norman Conquest. Its widespread use in Anglo-Saxon times, mainly in the form *Eadgyth*, meaning 'prosperous war,' ensured its survival, for a while at least, in England after the coming of the Normans. Their arrival marked the rapid disappearance of the majority of Anglo-Saxon names, because they found it difficult to pronounce them and therefore dis-couraged their use. Already in Domesday Book, undertaken by William the Conqueror in 1086, the hard-sounding *Eadgyth* had been softened to *Edeva*, from which comes the modern pet form *Edie*.

Two English saints of the name, St Edith of Wilton and St Edith of Polesworth, had helped to popularize it in Anglo-Saxon times. Both lived in the tenth century and both were Saxon abbesses.

In 1042 Edward the Confessor succeeded Hardicanute as King of England, and three years later he married Edith, only daughter of Earl Godwin, who at that time was the power behind the throne. On Edward's death in January 1066 Harold II became King, and his wife, whom he had married in the previous year, was also an Edith. Why he chose this lady as his wife and not Edith Swan-neck, who had borne him five children, is conjectural, but after Harold was killed at the battle of Hastings on October 14, 1066, it was Edith Swan-neck who identified him on the battlefield.

Henry I, the youngest and only English-born son of William the Conqueror, married the Saxon princess Edith, a direct descendant of King Alfred the Great. However, in deference to the Normans' difficulties with Saxon names, her name was changed to *Matilda*. She became Queen in 1100, after which date the name became progressively scarcer until its revival, referred to above, in the last century.

To-day Edith is still a popular name, and there are quite a number of well-known people who bear it, including Dame Edith Sitwell, whose poetry and prose have a wealth of imagery expressed in a highly individual style, and Dame Edith Evans, one of the outstanding actresses of this century, who made her début in 1912 as Cressida in Shakespeare's *Troilus and Cressida*.

Still remembered is Edith Cavell, the heroic English nurse who during the First World War helped many British soldiers to escape before she was taken by the Germans and executed on October 12, 1915.

E. (*i.e.*, Edith) Nesbit was famous for children's books in which delightfully natural children meet magical creatures. Her blend of real and unreal was completely novel, and her stories are as well loved to-day as in the early 1900's.

EDNA The origin of this name is obscure, though its most likely derivation is as a contracted form of *Edwina*, which comes from two Anglo-Saxon words meaning 'rich friend.' It may, on the other hand, be a contraction of another Anglo-Saxon name, *Edana*, which became obsolete about the time of the Norman Conquest. Or it may, in some cases, be taken from the Hebrew word 'ednah,' which means 'rejuvenation.' This name occurs in the apocryphal Book of Tobit as the wife of Raguel and mother of Sarah, who married Tobias.

At all events, Edna suddenly sprang into popularity as a Christian name in the second half of the last century, since when it has been in widespread use.

Two famous novelists bear the name. Edna Lyall (1857–1903) is the pen-name of Ada Ellen Bayly; her novels, the best-known of which are *Won by waiting* and *Donovan*, were widely read in late-Victorian times. The American novelist, short-story writer, and playwright Edna Ferber is best remembered for her novel *Show Boat* (1926), later made into an operetta.

EILEEN Eileen and *Aileen* have their origin in a Gaelic word meaning perhaps 'pleasant,' perhaps 'overjoyed.' Both forms of this name are used in Ireland as substitutes for *Helen* or *Evelyn*. Its use in England dates only from the last decade or so of the nineteenth century, a period when many Irish names became popular in this country.

EILUNED This charming Welsh name, which is just as commonly found with the spellings *Eluned* and *Elined* (which is how it is pronounced), is derived from 'eilun,' meaning 'idol.' In Wales it continues to be a very popular name, and in this century has occasionally been given by English parents. *Lyn*, *Lynn*, and *Lynne* are the pet forms, and these have recently been bestowed a good deal as independent names. Lyn is also a common boys' name in Wales.

The medieval French form was *Linet*, the name of a heroine of Arthurian romance; her story is told by Sir Thomas Malory in *Morte d'Arthur*, completed in 1470. Tennyson, too, has related the story of Gareth and *Lynette* (his own spelling of the name) in his *Idylls of the King*. The poet describes her thus:

> A damsel of high lineage; and a brow
> May-blossom; and a cheek of apple-blossom;
> Hawk-eyes; and lightly was her tender nose
> Tip-tilted like the petal of a flower.

Since the appearance of Tennyson's poem in 1872 Lynette has from time to time been used as a font name, as also has *Linnet*.

ELAINE Like *Linet* and *Lynette* (see *Eiluned*, above), Elaine figures both in Malory's *Morte d'Arthur* and in Tennyson's *Idylls of the King*. Elaine, an old French version of the Greek name *Helen*, was known as "the lily maid of Astolat." In Arthurian legend she is a princess, daughter of King Pelles and mother of Sir Galahad, the son born to her by Sir Lancelot, whom she loved "with that love which was her doom."

Elaine came to be used as a Christian name after the publication of Tennyson's poem.

The Welsh name *Elain*, meaning 'fawn, young hind,' is really an entirely different name.

ELEANOR This name, like *Elaine*, is a variation of *Helen*. It reached England by way of France in the twelfth century, when its usual forms were *Alienor* (which is how Eleanor of Aquitaine, Henry II's wife, was known) and *Alianore*, the name of King John's daughter. In the Middle Ages Eleanor, in its various forms, was a much more popular name than Helen, perhaps mainly on account of Eleanor of Castile, "Good Queen Eleanor," wife of Edward I, whom he married in 1254, when he was fifteen and she ten. She died in 1290 at Harby, in Nottinghamshire, and Edward, broken-hearted, had her body brought to Westminster Abbey, erecting memorial crosses, known as Eleanor Crosses, at each place where the funeral procession rested on the way—Grantham, Lincoln, Stamford, Geddington, Northampton, Stony Stratford, Woburn, Dunstable, St Albans, Waltham, West Cheap, and "the little village of Charing."

From 1154 until 1399, the period during which the House of Plantagenet ruled England, the name was a favoured one in this country, particularly among the aristocracy. After 1400 its popularity waned for several generations, reappearing in the early part of the seventeenth century, as often as not in the three-syllable form *Elinor*. It is interesting to note that "pretty, witty" *Nell* Gwynn's real name was Elinor; she died in 1687 at the age of thirty-seven. Another form found about this time was *Ellenore*: the name of the first foundling entered in the register of the Temple Church, London, in 1700 was Ellenore Temple.

Nowadays, however, the commonest form is undoubtedly Eleanor, though variations are not uncommon. The Italian and German forms, *Eleonora* and *Eleonore* respectively, are sometimes given in this country, as also are their contractions, *Leonora* and *Lenore*. The usual pet form is *Ellie*, the name of "the little white lady" in Charles Kingsley's *Water Babies*.

In literature there are Elinor Trent, much better known as Little Nell, in *The Old Curiosity Shop* by Dickens; and Elinor Dashwood, who in Jane Austen's novel *Sense and Sensibility* represents 'sense,' as opposed to her sister Marianne's 'sensibility.'

Among the greatest actresses of all time was Eleonora Duse, born near Venice in 1859. Distinguished Eleonors of modern times include Eleanor Roosevelt, wife of Franklin Delano Roosevelt, thirty-second President of the U.S.A., and Eleanor Farjeon, the poet and writer of children's stories.

ELIZABETH Like many names of Hebrew origin, Elizabeth contains a reference to the Deity, for 'El' is Hebrew for 'God'; the full meaning of this name is 'God has sworn' or 'oath of God'—said to be an allusion to the covenant made with Abraham. The original form, recorded as *Elisheba*, was borne by Aaron's wife, who lived about 1200 B.C.

For over four hundred years Elizabeth has been an immensely popular name in this country, as well as on the Continent of Europe and in many other parts of the world. There are few, if any, names which have a longer list of variants and pet forms than this one. Apart from the alternative spelling, *Elisabeth* (which in England has never been as common as the spelling with a z), there are the forms *Eliza, Elsie,* and *Elspeth*—all now independent names—and the pet forms *Bess, Bessie, Bessy, Bet, Beth, Betsey, Betsie, Betsy, Betta, Bette, Betty; Libby, Lilibet, Lilla, Lillah, Lisa, Lisbet, Lisbeth, Lise, Liselotte, Liz, Liza, Lizzie, Lizzy*; and *Tetsy* and *Tetty*. Some of these have also been given as font names. In addition there are several continental forms occasionally used in this country, of which the most familiar are the French *Babette* and *Elise*, the German *Ilse*, and the Italian *Bettina*. One important omission in this list is *Isabel*, which is treated separately on p. 130.

This remarkable variety of forms is reflected in the old nursery rhyme:

> Elizabeth, Betsy, Betty and Bess
> Went out one day to find a bird's nest,
> They found a nest with five eggs in it,
> They each took one and left four in it.

Elizabeth is indeed a royal name. In 1464 Edward IV, of the House of York, married Elizabeth Woodville. When their eldest daughter, Elizabeth, married Henry VII in 1486, the struggle between the Houses of York and Lancaster came to an end. One of the children of this marriage was the future Henry VIII, father of Elizabeth, the Virgin Queen (her mother being Anne Boleyn), who ruled from 1558 to 1603. She gave her name to the greatest era in English history—"the spacious times of great Elizabeth," as Tennyson expressed it— an era in which England became a world power politically and which was the blossom-time of English literature. The spirit of that glorious age of adventure and discovery also marks the second Elizabethan age, which began in 1952 on the accession of our present Queen, named after her mother, whose maiden name was Elizabeth Angela Marguerite Bowes-Lyon.

In all walks of life for many generations there have been famous Elizabeths. Saint Elisabeth of Hungary was fourteen when she was betrothed to Ludwig, landgrave of Thuringia. She was renowned for her generosity to the poor. One day she filled the skirts of her dress with food and set out to distribute it among the poor in the town. On the way she happened to meet her husband, who asked her what she was carrying. "Only roses," she replied, for she was afraid of him; and when the landgrave looked he found that her lap was indeed filled with red and white roses, though it was not the season for them. Then, looking up at his wife, he noticed a luminous cross above her head. When her husband died of the plague in 1227 St Elisabeth devoted the rest of her short life to tending the sick and sheltering the poor.

Another bearer of the name who devoted her life to helping the needy was Elizabeth Fry (1780–1845). She was a Quaker, and did much to promote prison reform, as well as finding shelter for the homeless, setting up various charitable institutions—and bringing up a family of eleven!

Among the numerous other Elizabeths who are famous may be mentioned Elizabeth Montagu (1720–1800), who founded the celebrated 'Blue-stocking Club' and was also a fabulous entertainer: at her London home in Portman Square she threw parties for nobility and chimney-sweeps alike; Elizabeth Barrett Browning, the English poet whose *Sonnets from the Portuguese* were inspired by her love for the poet Robert Browning, whom she married in 1846; Elizabeth Hastings, the lady whom "to love," said Laurence Sterne, was "a liberal education"; Betsy Ross (1752–1836), said to have made the first American flag at the special request of George Washington; and Elizabeth Talbot, Countess of Shrewsbury, better known as Bess of Hardwick, who in the sixteenth century married four husbands and inherited a fortune from each, with which she spent the rest of her life building enormous houses.

In literature the examples are equally numerous. Elizabeth Bennet, in Jane Austen's best-known novel, *Pride and Prejudice*, overcomes her prejudice against her suitor, Darcy, when he conquers his pride; in *Little Women* (1868), by the American author Louisa May Alcott, "Elizabeth—or Beth, as everyone called her—was a rosy, smooth-haired, bright-eyed girl of thirteen, with a shy manner, a timid voice, and a peaceful expression. . . . Her father called her 'Little Tranquillity' "; in Shaw's *Pygmalion* (1913) Liza Doolittle, the Cockney flower-girl, is transformed into a 'fair lady' of society; another Liza is the titular heroine of W. Somerset Maugham's first novel, *Liza of Lambeth* (1897), which presents a social study of life in the slums of London in the late nineteenth century and which caused a furore on its appearance; Betsy Prig, the friend of the immortal Mrs Gamp in Dickens's *Martin Chuzzle-wit*; Elspeth, in three of Sir Walter Scott's novels, *Guy Manner-ing, The Antiquary*, and *The Monastery*—an indication of the popularity of this form north of the Border; and countless others.

ELLA Once a widely used name, Ella has of late become less common. It is one of the many Christian names introduced into England at the time of the Conquest, being derived from a Norman name, itself from an ancient Germanic word mean-ing 'all.'

As a masculine name, however, it had already been in use for several hundred years among the Anglo-Saxons in the form Ælla, the name of a sixth-century ruler of the Anglian kingdom of Deira.

Ella, as a girls' name, almost died out between about 1350 and 1850, when, like many old English names which had become obsolete, it was revived by the Victorians. Since then it has been in constant, though not frequent, use.

Its revival in this country more or less coincided with its adoption in America, one of the earliest bearers there being the lush, sentimental verse-writer Ella Wheeler Wilcox (1850–1919), who enjoyed great popularity in her day.

Ella Shields was a favourite music-hall star and male

impersonator at the turn of the century, while to-day one of
the outstanding jazz singers is Ella Fitzgerald.

ELLEN Although now regarded as an independent name,
Ellen is actually one of the many forms of *Helen* (see
p. 122). It is also sometimes used for *Eleanor*. In Scotland
Ellen has long been the most popular form of both these
names, and Scott chose it for the heroine of his narrative poem
The Lady of the Lake (1810), daughter of the outlawed James
Douglas.

Probably the most famous English Ellen was Dame Ellen
Terry, the distinguished actress who from 1878 to 1898 was Sir
Henry Irving's leading lady.

ELSA Strictly speaking, this name has nothing to do with
Elsie, though the two are often confused. Whereas Elsie is a
pet form of the Hebrew-derived name Elizabeth, Elsa comes
from two Old German words and means 'noble maiden.'
The Scots have a charming version, *Ailsa*, which seems to be
more popular now than ever before, and which has lately been
adopted in England.

In these days of fashion-consciousness most people will
have heard of Elsa Schiaparelli, the Italian-born dress-designer
who became a French citizen and established her first salon
in Paris in the late 'twenties.

EMILY *Emily* and *Amelia* are Latin forms of the original
Roman clan name Aemilius.

It was the fourteenth-century Italian poet Boccaccio, author
of the famous *Decameron*, who made Emily widely popular in
Europe in the early days of the Renaissance. She figures in his
Il Teseide, written about 1341, the plot of which was taken

over by Chaucer for his *Knight's Tale*, in which the name is variously spelt *Emelie*, *Emelye*, *Emily*, etc. Chaucer describes her thus:

> . . . *Emilie*, that fayrer was to sene
> Than is the lilie upon his stalke grene,
> And fresher than the May with flourës newe.

In Shakespeare's day the commonest version was the Latinized one, *Emilia*, the name of the villain Iago's wife in *Othello*. This form was still in common use in the eighteenth century, and in the literature of that period Emilia is often found—as, for instance, in Tobias Smollett's novel *The Adventures of Peregrine Pickle* (1751), in which an Emilia is the lady-love of the spendthrift Peregrine.

It was not, however, until the House of Hanover became the ruling dynasty in England, following the death of Queen Anne in 1714, that the name achieved any real measure of popularity here, although its history can be traced back to the time when Christianity was introduced into western Europe (see *Amelia*, p. 35). Generally found as *Amalie* and *Amalia* in Germany, the name was adopted here as Emily; even the German-born princesses living at the English Court found themselves being called Emily.

Since that time, and until this century, Emily remained a popular name, but now, like its counterpart, Amelia, it is tending to go out of fashion. Emily is occasionally found as *Emilie*—the modern French version—*Emmelina*, and *Emmeline*, the last-named reminding one of that self-assured young lady of A. A. Milne's who, after disappearing for several days, came back, calmly announcing:

> Sillies, I went and saw the Queen,
> And she says my hands are *purfickly* clean!

G

Readers of Dickens's *David Copperfield* will recall Emily
Peggotty, better known as Little Em'ly, the pretty and attrac⁄
tive niece and adopted daughter of Daniel Peggotty; she runs
off with Steerforth, who later abandons her.

Emily Brontë, the younger sister of Charlotte and the elder
sister of Anne, is most famous for her great novel *Wuthering
Heights*, which appeared under the pen⁄name Ellis Bell in
1848. Another celebrated Emily of the last century was Emily
Davies, the first Mistress of Girton College, Cambridge, and a
pioneer of higher education for women.

In the *Bab Ballads* by W. S. Gilbert, published in 1869, the
story is told of Emily Jane:

> Emily Jane was a nursery maid,
> James was a bold lifeguard,
> John was a constable, poorly paid
> (And I am a doggerel bard).

> Rivals for Emma were John and James,
> And Emily liked them both:
> Though she couldn't tell which had the strongest
> claims—
> (And I couldn't take my oath).

—which shows, incidentally, that *Emma* has been used as a pet
form of Emily.

EMMA is a very old name, derived, like *Ermintrude* (see p. 101),
from the name of some obscure Teutonic hero. Originally
confined to the Franks, by about A.D. 900 it had become
common in France, too, whence it reached England.

Queen Emma, a Norman by birth, married King Ethelred
"the Unready" in 1002, and by doing so established the first
royal link by marriage between this country and Normandy.

Their elder son was Edward the Confessor. Having become a widow in 1016, Queen Emma married Ethelred's successor to the throne, Canute, the following year. Both Saxon and Norman chroniclers speak highly of the Queen, who was known as "the Fair Maid of Normandy." On her arrival in England she became so popular with the English that they bestowed on her the 'lucky' name of *Elfgiva* ('elf-gift'), and in the Saxon Chronicle she is called Emma Elfgiva.

In those days Emma occurred in a variety of forms, such as *Ymma*, *Imma*, and *Eme*, but by the early twelfth century it had settled down into the simplest possible version, *Em*. With its pet form *Emmot*, Em continued to be the commonest form right up to the eighteenth century, when Emma came back into fashion. To-day the usual pet forms are *Em* and *Emmie*.

The famous Lady Hamilton, whom Nelson loved, was a late eighteenth-century Emma; in 1816 Jane Austen gave the name to a novel portraying a conceited but talented heroine, Emma Woodhouse.

ENA, and the similarly pronounced *Ina*, are both now font names, though originally they were pet forms of names ending in -ena and -ina. Ena is also a short form of *Eugenia* (Greek, 'well-born'), besides being sometimes used in Ireland to represent the Celtic name *Aithne* (see p. 29), and in Wales as an alternative form of *Enid*.

It does not seem to have been used as an independent name before about 1880. Queen Victoria's granddaughter *Victoria Eugénie* was known as Princess Ena; in 1906 she married Alfonso XIII, the last King of Spain.

ENID This is an unsuspected Welsh name, from the word 'enaid,' meaning 'life' or 'soul.'

To call a woman "a second Enid" was the greatest compliment in the age of chivalry. Chrétien de Troyes, who lived in the second half of the twelfth century, wrote many romances based on popular legends, and one of his early works was *Erec et Enide*.

In the *Red Book of Hergest*, a Welsh manuscript of the fourteenth century, the story is retold, with many interesting variations, though the scene—the Court of King Arthur—is the same. After it had been translated by Lady Charlotte Guest (the translation was completed in 1849) the name became very popular in Wales, being pronounced there with a short e, unlike the English pronunciation, 'Eenid.'

In England, however, the name did not come into use until after 1859, when Tennyson published his version of the story, in *Geraint and Enid*. Tennyson says of his heroine:

> . . . Enid, whom her ladies loved to call
> Enid the Fair, a grateful people named
> Enid the Good . . .

Among the famous Enids of to-day are Enid Blyton, the writer of numerous best-selling children's books, and Enid Bagnold, author of *National Velvet* and *The Chalk Garden*.

ERICA This name is the feminine form of Eric, which means 'ever-ruling.' In both the masculine and feminine forms it is an old-established name in Scandinavia, where the modern equivalents are Erik and *Erika*.

In this country Erica has been known as a Christian name for rather less than a hundred years, but has never been in widespread use. During the late-Victorian period, when plant-names such as *Daisy*, *Violet*, and *Rose* were in favour, Erica became accepted in some parents' minds as a plant-name too, seeing that it is the botanical name for *Heather*—which also became a popular name about the same time and for the same reason. Its continued use, in this country at any rate, is due more to this association than to its original Scandinavian one.

ERMINTRUDE, sometimes spelt *Ermentrude* or *Irmintrude,* is derived from two words—Ermin, the name of an ancient Germanic hero, and 'drudi' or its Anglo-Saxon equivalent 'thryth,' meaning 'strength.' The first element is also seen in the name *Emma* and in the long-popular German girls' name *Irma,* sometimes given in this country.

Ermintrude has been used about equally in romantic fiction and in real life. It has the pet form *Trudie,* which it shares with *Gertrude.*

ESTHER

And he [Mordecai] brought up Hadassah, that is, Esther, his uncle's daughter: for she had neither father nor mother, and the maiden was fair and beautiful.

This text, taken from the Book of Esther, xx, 7, shows that the real name of this Esther, the first known bearer of the name, was *Hadassah,* which is the Hebrew word for 'myrtle.' She was a captive Jewish girl who was exiled to Persia during the reign of Ahasuerus. This king had just deposed his consort, Vashti, and chose Esther in her place, dispensing with her Hebrew name and giving her a Persian one meaning 'star.' Esther is, in fact, another form of *Ishtar,* the Babylonian goddess of love.

The Book of Esther describes how she, a young woman of outstanding courage, risked death to save her exiled people from the plots of Haman, arch-enemy of the Jews.

Esther came to be used as a Christian name in England about the time of the Puritans—that is, during the seventeenth century, when Old Testament names came into fashion at the expense of non-scriptural saints' names (regarded as idolatrous) and names of pagan dieties. Soon after its introduction, the pet forms *Essa*, *Essie*, *Ettie*, and *Etty* were also in common use.

In France the name became popular for a time following the production in 1689 of Racine's sacred drama *Esther*, which was performed by the girls of Saint-Cyr, a school founded for daughters of impoverished noblemen. But neither in France nor in England has Esther ever been a much-used name, and *Hester*, a Latin version with the pet forms *Hetty* and, less commonly, *Harty*, has fared no better in the three hundred years or so it has been in use.

Jonathan Swift, author of *Gulliver's Travels*, fell in love with two Esthers—Esther Johnson, whom he addressed as *Stella*, and Esther Vanhomrigh, whom he called *Vanessa*. These two names are treated on p. 197.

There are several well-known Esthers and Hesters in fact and fiction. The real name of Dr Johnson's great friend Mrs Thrale was Hester Lynch Salusbury, though he used to call her *Queeny*. She was born in 1741, thirty-five years before Lady Hester Stanhope, niece of William Pitt, whose household she managed during the last three years of his life. In 1810 she left England and travelled widely in the East, finally settling down on Mount Lebanon, where the local tribesmen came to regard her as a prophetess. A famous Esther of the present century is Esther McCracken, the playwright, best known for *Quiet Wedding* and *Quiet Week-End*, its successor.

ETHEL In Anglo-Saxon times the word 'æthele' meant 'noble,' as did the Old-German word 'adal' (modern German 'edel'): hence the origin of such names as *Ethel*, *Adela*, *Alice*, etc. (see p. 31).

There are a large number of names in old English records which begin with 'æthel,' but it was never used as a name without some accompanying word, usually a noun, as in *Aethelgiefu*, meaning 'noble gift,' and *Ethelburga*, 'noble protection.' There are nineteen saints dating from Anglo-Saxon times whose names begin with Aethel-, among them *Aethelthryth*, who became known as St *Audrey* (see p. 45).

In fact Ethel did not come into use as an independent name in England until well into the nineteenth century. One of the earliest uses of it was by Thackeray, who introduced a character named Ethel Newcome into his novel *The Newcomes* (1855). By the end of the century, however, it was enjoying great popularity.

The name is borne by two famous twentieth-century novelists: Ethel Mannin, prolific author of novels about working-class people, and Ethel M. Dell, who specialized in brutal, overpowering heroes.

EUNICE means, in Greek, 'happy victory,' and was at one time pronounced 'you-nice-ee,' with the stress on the middle syllable, though nowadays its usual pronunciation is 'you-niss,' with the stress on the first syllable, as in its pet form, *Euny*.

The mother of St Paul's friend and disciple Timothy was the first Christian bearer of the name, and in the Second Epistle of St Paul he refers to "the unfeigned faith that is in thee; which dwelt . . . in . . . thy mother Eunice."

In this country it began to be used as a Christian name about three hundred years ago, but it has never been common, while on the Continent it seems to be completely unknown.

EUPHEMIA Derived from the Greek for 'pleasant speech,' Euphemia is an uncommon name nowadays in its full form, although, in Scotland at least, it is still often met with as *Effie* and *Euphame*. The name also has the implied meaning of 'silence,' for when the ancient Greeks prepared for a sacrifice the priest would call out, "Speak pleasantly, citizens!" meaning that nobody present should utter an unlucky word that might anger the gods; so for safety's sake, nobody spoke at all.

St Euphemia was a fourth-century martyr of Bithynia whom, according to legend, the lions in the arena refused to devour. Her courage became known far and wide, and thus her name spread over most of Europe, reaching England about 1100.

In England the name has never been at all popular in any form, and examples in English literature are few, though a famous one is *Eppie*, the waif in George Eliot's novel *Silas Marner* (1861). In Scotland, on the other hand, it has long been a favoured name, and figures a good deal in Scottish literature. For instance, in Scott's novel *The Heart of Midlothian* (1817), Effie Deans is the daughter of the Scottish cow-feeder affectionately known to his friends as Douce (=kindly) Davie. Robert Burns uses another form of the name in his poem *Eppie Adair*:

> An' O! my Eppie,
> My jewel, my Eppie!
> Wha wadna be happy
> Wi' Eppie Adair?

King Robert II of Scotland, the first member of the royal Stuart dynasty, married Euphemia, Countess of Moray, in 1355.

Other forms of Euphemia, most of them mainly Scottish, are *Ephie, Euphan, Euphie, Phemie* (pronounced 'fay-me'), and *Phamie*.

EVE At first sight it is far from easy to recognize this name in its first shape, but it is hardly surprising that it should have changed considerably since it was first bestowed, in the form *Hawwah*, on Adam's wife—"And the man called his wife's name Eve; because she was the mother of all living" (Genesis, iii, 20). According to Milton's poetic vision of her in *Paradise Lost*,

> Grace was in all her steps, heaven in her eye,
> In every gesture dignity and love.

There is an old superstition that children christened Eve are always long-lived, and this may account for the popularity of the name even before the Reformation, when the use of Old-Testament names was uncommon. In olden times it was not unusual to give the name to the female of twins, the brother, of course, being christened Adam.

In Ireland the name *Aoiffe*, which is Gaelic for 'pleasant,' was replaced by the similar-sounding Eve, which has been a favourite name among the Irish for hundreds of years, together with its diminutive *Eveleen*. As early as the twelfth century Eve and Aoiffe were being freely interchanged, as, for example, in the case of the wife of "Strongbow"—Richard de Clare, Earl of Pembroke. From Ireland the name reached Scotland, where it is found in some of the oldest Scottish family-trees; the modern Gaelic version is *Eubha*. The pure Welsh form is *Efa*.

In medieval English records the name first appears in the mid twelfth century, its usual form being the Latin one, *Eva*. This was the less common form during the nineteenth century until the appearance of Harriet Beecher Stowe's novel *Uncle Tom's Cabin* in 1852, in which the pathetic character Little Eva made a tremendous impact on the Victorian reading public. To-day both Eva and Eve are still used as font names, though neither is as popular as it was at the turn of the century. The usual pet form is *Evie*.

Eva Turner is one of the greatest sopranos of this century.

EVELYN Until the nineteenth century, Evelyn as a Christian name was almost entirely confined to persons descended from the celebrated Evelyn family, which includes the diarist John Evelyn, a contemporary of Samuel Pepys.

In the form *Aveline*, the French for 'hazel-nut,' the name was brought over to this country in the eleventh century by the Normans. Aveline was the name of William the Conqueror's great-grandmother, and it was often given to members of the old Norman nobility. From it developed the form *Eveline*, always used only as a girls' name, and later Evelyn.

Evelina, the Latin form of Eveline, became fashionable after the appearance, in 1778, of Fanny Burney's novel *Evelina, or The History of a Young Lady's Entrance into the World*; but in the present century neither of these forms is as popular as Evelyn, which is used both as a boys' and a girls' name.

The similar-sounding Irish name *Eveleen*, besides being a diminutive of Eve, is also used to represent the Gaelic name *Eiblin*, which means 'pleasant.'

FAITH This 'abstract-quality' name, always associated with Hope and Charity, came into use as a Christian name in England after the Reformation, since when it has never become obsolete, though it is no longer nearly as common as it was three hundred years ago.

In ancient Rome Fides, Latin for 'faith,' was worshipped as the personification of faithfulness and honour.

In early Christian times there was a St Faith, the sister of Sts Hope and Charity; she is said to have been martyred at the age of nine. Another St Faith was martyred in A.D. 303 in France, where she came to be called Sainte *Foy*—from which word is derived the old English expression 'by my fay,' meaning 'by my faith.' St Faith's Chapel in Westminster Abbey still shows an interesting wall-painting of its patron, one of the oldest paintings in the country.

The variant *Fay*, in use only since the last decade of the nine-teenth century, has lately been more popular than Faith; though properly meaning 'faith,' Fay is often taken to mean 'fairy.' This meaning may have been in Herman Melville's mind when he gave the name *Fayaway* to a character in *Typee* (1846), a romance of the South Seas.

Probably the best-known Fay is that fine actress Fay Comp-ton, who made her stage début in 1911, with Pelissier's *Follies*.

FELICITY Felicitas was a Roman goddess of good luck; statues and medals show her holding in one hand a rod twined with serpents, like the staff of Mercury, and in the other hand a cornucopia, or horn of plenty. After this goddess were named two saints, one of whom was the personal attendant of St Perpetua during the reign of the Emperor Septimius Severus (193–211). Together they were thrown to the lions in the amphitheatre at Carthage, near modern Tunis. The other was thrown into a vat of boiling oil after being forced to watch her seven sons put to death. The courage and faith of both these martyrs made their name known, and it was adopted in many parts of Europe.

The name took on a variety of forms, including *Felice* (which was often confused with *Phyllis*), and *Felicity*, which was intro-duced as an abstract-virtue name by the Puritans and has remained the most popular form of the name in this country ever since. In an English register of 1641 the odd spelling *Phelisstie* is found.

Felicia, first noted in England in the twelfth century, is a feminine version of Felix, Latin for 'lucky'; still occasionally

found, it was the first name of the once popular poet Mrs
Hemans, author of *Casabianca* ("The boy stood on the burning
deck . . .").

The usual pet form is *Fee*.

FIONA Oddly enough, the name Fiona originated as the
pen-name of a nineteenth-century Scottish author, William
Sharp, who wrote a series of tales and romances based on
ancient Celtic folklore (see p. 79, under *Deirdre*). His choice
was a happy one, because there is a whole host of old Irish
names beginning with 'finn-' or 'fionn-,' which in Gaelic
means 'fair' or 'white,' and which corresponds exactly with
the Welsh name-element 'gwyn-' or 'gwen-.' According to
legend, Ireland was inhabited in remote times by giants, among
them the great, semi-mythological hero Finn, also called Fionn
or Fingal.

Further evidence of the antiquity of 'fionn-' names is seen
in another old Irish legend, that of *Fionnguala* (='white
shoulders'), the daughter of Lir; she was changed into a swan
and made to swim on the rivers and lakes of Ireland for hundreds
of years, until the introduction of Christianity into that island.

In Ireland Fionnguala is often shortened to *Finola* or *Nuala*,
or disguised under the name *Penelope* (p. 180); in Scotland it
becomes most commonly *Finella* or *Fenella*, as in Sir Walter
Scott's novel *Peveril of the Peak*, where Fenella, daughter of
Edward Christian, falls in love with Julian Peveril, and
assumes the name *Zarah*, a "Moorish sorceress."

In the last decade or so Fiona has become a very popular
name in England.

FLORA was the Roman goddess of flowers and of spring-
time, and during her festival, which took place annually from

April 28 till May 3 and was known as Floralia, revels were held similar to, but wilder than, our former May Day celebrations. She was also the goddess of fruits and vines.

A St Flora was put to death in Spain in 850. Spaniels, so-called because this breed of dog was introduced from Spain, were often named after her in the seventeenth century.

In the Scottish Highlands Flora was commonly used as a refined version of the Gaelic name *Finghin*, meaning 'beautiful offspring,' and was especially popular in the clan Macdonald. Flora Macdonald, its most famous historical representative, actually called herself *Florie*. When the Young Pretender, Prince Charles Edward, was defeated at the Battle of Culloden in 1746 she disguised him as her maidservant and brought him safely across the sea to the Isle of Skye, from where he later escaped to France.

Other names akin to Flora are *Florence*, *Flower*, and *Fleur*. Flower has been a rare name ever since it was first used in the eighteenth century, but Fleur, its French equivalent, has been fairly popular since Galsworthy gave it to one of the Forsytes in his famous saga. The Americans have taken a liking to it in the present century. Fleur Cowles was the personal representative of ex-President Eisenhower at the Coronation. The old French version of Fleur was *Flore*. The equivalent Welsh name, *Fflur*, has been in use since at least the twelfth century.

Among the well-known Floras of to-day are Flora Klinckmann—appropriately named, for she is a flower painter—and Dame Flora Robson, who made her first appearance as an actress in 1921 in Clemence Dane's *Will Shakespeare*.

FLORENCE In medieval times, when the Christian name Florence was first used, it appeared commonly both as a boys' and a girls' name, the longer forms being Florentius and

Florentia respectively. It derives from the Latin word 'florens' which means 'flowering,' 'flourishing.' As a boys' name had largely died out by the sixteenth century, except in Ireland where it is still occasionally given to boys; but as a girls' name it survived, though it became somewhat rare.

By the turn of the nineteenth century it was hardly known, but on July 4, 1820, a baby was christened Florence who was to become so famous that within the space of fifty years thousands of girls, not only in England, but all over the world would be named in her honour. She was Florence Nightingale, the "Lady with the Lamp." She was named Florence because that was the city of her birth—in the same way that her elder sister had been christened *Parthenope*, the Greek name of her birthplace, Naples. The original Parthenope was a Siren who threw herself into the sea because she was unable to beguile Odysseus by her singing; she was cast ashore at Naples, which thereafter bore her name.

In her long life—she lived to be ninety-two—Florence Nightingale did an enormous amount to relieve the suffering of the sick and wounded, and she is particularly remembered for her nursing of the casualties of the Crimean War. Robert Holden, a Crimean veteran, said of her: "She was a grand lady to us soldiers, a regular mother, so kind, so gentle, and we often wondered if she ever went to sleep, because she was always at work among the sick, day and night."

So, in the second half of the nineteenth century, the name became tremendously popular, its pet forms being *Florrie*, *Flo*, *Floss*, and *Flossie* ('flos' is the Latin word for 'flower') as well as the now less common *Floy*, the pet name of Florence Dombey, who marries Walter Gay in Dickens's *Dombey and Son*

The Irish equivalent of Florence is *Blatnaid*, the diminutive form of 'blat,' meaning 'blossom,' 'flower-bud.'

FRANCES The name Frances, meaning 'free woman,' is the feminine form of Francis. The Franks (*i.e.*, the 'free men') were a confederacy of German tribes who for a long time fought with the Romans, before settling permanently in Gaul in the fifth century. They regarded themselves as the only truly free people, and their name came to be given to modern France.

The earliest recorded form of the name, *Francesca* ('little French lady'), dates from the thirteenth century, when it was borne by St Francesca of Rome; a model mother and wife, she was said to be attended by her guardian angel in visible form. She was named after St Francis of Assisi.

The story of the tragic lovers Paolo and Francesca da Rimini, who lived in the same period as St Francesca, is told by Dante in the fifth canto of his *Inferno*.

In England the name did not appear in any form until it was given to Henry VII's granddaughter. His daughter Mary, who had been Queen of France and then married the Duke of Suffolk, had her first daughter christened Frances in memory of her first husband; the English, however, called the girl simply *Frank*. She was the mother of Lady Jane Grey. Nowadays the French form is *Françoise*.

Fanny, one of the pet forms of Frances, first appeared in the late seventeenth century, since when it has often been used as an independent name. Frances Burney, born in 1752, lady-in-waiting to Queen Charlotte, and author of the famous novels *Evelina*, *Cecilia*, and *Camilla*, was generally known as Fanny, as also was Frances Kemble, the actress, born in 1809. Other pet forms are *Fan*, *Fran*, *Francie*, and *Frankie*. *Frankie and Johnny* is a popular old American ballad which tells how the girl Frankie shot unfaithful Johnny "with a forty-four gun" because "he was her man, but he done her wrong."

The name is rendered in Gaelic by *Frangag*.

St Frances Xavier Cabrini, born in 1850 in Italy, is the only American citizen to be canonized. She became an American citizen in 1909 and died eight years later.

Other well-known bearers of the name are: Frances Hodgson Burnett, who was born in Manchester but emigrated to Tennessee, where she wrote *Little Lord Fauntleroy* in 1886 and *The Secret Garden* in 1911; Frances Pitt, J.P. and author of numerous books and articles on nature subjects; and Fanny Blankers-Koen, the Dutch athletics champion. In the last century Frances Trollope supported her invalid husband and children by writing novels and travel books; somehow or other she found time to produce 115 books! She was the mother of the more celebrated author Anthony Trollope.

In Frome churchyard is the touching epitaph of little Frances Soame, who died aged ten days:

> The cup of life just to her lips she pressed;
> Found its taste bitter, and denied the rest,
> Averse. Then, turning from the light of day,
> She softly sighed her little life away.

GENEVIEVE The name Genevieve comes, via French, from two Germanic words: 'geno,' 'race,' and 'wefa,' 'woman.' Its oldest known forms are *Genovefa* and *Genoveva*; Genevieve of Brabant, heroine of medieval legend, is referred to in records in all these forms, though nowadays she is known as St Genevieve, like her French namesake, the patroness of Paris.

In the year 451, when the Huns were sweeping across Gaul under their leader Attila, the "Scourge of God," the citizens of Paris panicked and prepared to flee; but St Genevieve, then thirty, told them to put their trust in God and they would be saved. As if by a miracle, Attila and his hordes bypassed the capital, leaving it unscathed. Episodes from St Genevieve's life are depicted in a series of mural paintings in the Panthéon in Paris. It is due to her that the name is such a popular one in France, where it is found as *Geneviève*.

One of the earliest uses of the name in this country occurs in the poetry of Coleridge—for instance, in his sonnet *Genevieve*:

> Maid of my Love! sweet Genevieve!
> In Beauty's light you glide along;
> Your eye is like the star of eve,
> And sweet your voice as seraph's song.

A sentimental ditty of Victorian times was called *Genevieve*. A few years ago a hilarious film appeared about a veteran car of the same name.

GEORGINA There are several feminine forms of George, which comes from a Greek word meaning 'tiller of the soil.' In England no feminine form existed, except for an isolated *Georgia* in the sixteenth century, until after 1714, when *Georgiana* and *Georgina* came in as a sign of loyalty to the Hanoverian kings. Lady Georgiana Spencer, born in 1757, the wife of the fifth Duke of Devonshire, was a celebrated beauty whom both Reynolds and Gainsborough painted. The most usual form in England nowadays is Georgina.

Georgette is the French form, sometimes used in this country; it was after the modiste Georgette de la Plante that the material was named. Georgette Heyer, the popular novelist, is the best-known bearer of this form in England to-day.

In America the commonest form is *Georgia*, but bearers of this version are usually named after the State of Georgia, as in the case of the painter Georgia O'Keefe.

Georgie and *Gina* are the usual pet forms.

H

GERALDINE Hundreds of years ago an adventurous member of the Gerhardini family of Florence left Italy for England, where he settled. One of his descendants, Maurice Fitzgerald, led several of his relatives to Ireland in the invasion organized by Henry II. There they became Earls of Kildare, a line of noblemen so powerful that the so-called Cross of St Patrick on the Union Jack is, in fact, the device from their shield.

But it was not until their power was waning, in the time of Henry VIII, that the poet Henry Howard, Earl of Surrey, fell in love with Lady Elizabeth Fitzgerald, whom he called "the Fair Geraldine" in his poems. This name was his invention, and it continued to be regarded as a romantic appellation rather than a Christian name until after 1800. After the publication in 1816 of Coleridge's poem *Christabel*, in which a mysterious stranger named Geraldine seeks hospitality at the heroine's castle, the name sprang into popularity.

The masculine form, Gerald, means literally 'spear-resolution,' and is derived from two Old-German words.

In the nineteenth century the name became widespread in Ireland, the country of its origin, and by 1900 was quite commonly found both in England and in America; the famous American soprano Geraldine Farrar was born in 1882.

Nowadays the name is in constant, though not widespread, use in this country, where the Italian form *Giralda* is also sometimes used.

GERTRUDE Meaning 'spear-strength' (or possibly 'spear-friend' or 'spear-wizard'), Gertrude is an ancient Germanic name, first borne, it would seem, by one of the Valkyries—the Norse goddesses who conducted the slain heroes from the battlefield to Valhalla, the palace of bliss.

In the seventh century a Flemish nun, St Gertrude of Nivelles, was made patron saint of travellers, and people setting out on a journey in those days would invoke her protection by drinking a cup of blessed wine.

But a better-known bearer of the name is the German mystic St Gertrude the Great, so gentle that mice would run up her staff; she is generally so represented. It was chiefly through her that the name became widely used on the Continent, from where it reached this country. Here in England it was well established by the time Shakespeare used it for the Queen of Denmark, Hamlet's mother, who in earlier records is referred to as *Gerutha*.

The once common pet forms *Gatty* and *Gattie*, peculiar to England, show how common the name became here, giving rise to several surnames, including Gatt and Gatty. Nowadays the usual pet forms are *Trudie*, *Gert* (as used by one of that inimitable music-hall pair, Gert and Daisy), and *Gertie*. These forms date from the nineteenth century, when the name was revived after falling into disuse for a couple of hundred years.

Gertrude Lawrence, who played opposite Noël Coward in several of his sophisticated comedies, was of Anglo-Danish parentage and was christened *Gertrud*, the normal spelling in Scandinavia.

Gertrude Stein, the American poet and novelist, was a subject of wide literary controversy during the 1920's for her peculiar style of writing, of which "A rose is a rose is a rose" is a sample.

On August 6, 1926, Gertrude Ederle, an American swimmer, became the first woman ever to swim the English Channel, her time being 14 hours 31 minutes from France to England.

GILLIAN and *Juliana* (see p. 142), are really the same name, but as they have come to be regarded as entirely distinct from each other, they are treated here separately.

In medieval times Gillian was a common girls' name, and the pet form most usual then was *Gill*, often spelt *Jill*; so common was it, in fact, that it became synonymous with a sweet-heart or a girl generally, as in the expression, "Every Jack has his Jill."

The old nursery rhyme about Jack and Jill is thought by some to be a relic of an old Norse myth, in which the two children are supposed to have been kidnapped, while drawing water, by the moon, on which they can still be seen with the bucket hanging from a pole resting on their shoulders.

Another old pet form was *Gillet* or *Jillet*, but when this acquired the meaning of 'a jilt' towards the end of the seventeenth century, it quickly lost favour. The name went out of use and was not revived until the present century, when it has added the new form *Jillian*. Nowadays, too, Jill is often used as an independent name. Some Gills prefer to pronounce their name with a hard g, as in Gilbert.

GLADYS is often said to be the Welsh equivalent of *Claudia* (see p. 72), but its true Welsh form, *Gwladys*, suggests that it should properly be derived from 'gwledig,' meaning 'ruler over a territory.' There is no doubt, however, that Gladys and Claudia have been linked for many hundreds of years.

Except for Cornwall, where the forms *Gladuse* and *Gladusa* were occasionally met with, the name remained exclusively Welsh until well into the nineteenth century. By the early 1900's it was being quite freely used outside Wales, and is now one of the most widespread of all Welsh names, having the pet form *Glad*.

Famous bearers of to-day include G. B. (Gladys Bronwen) Stern, the novelist; Gladys Mitchell, the writer of thrillers; Gladys Young, the radio actress, who began broadcasting in 1926, and Gladys Ripley, the contralto. Then, too, there is the heroic Gladys Aylward, the little servant-girl who set out with a single suitcase for China, where, as a missionary, she saved the lives of hundreds of children.

GRACE Derived from the Latin 'gratia,' this name means 'grace' in the sense of the undeserved favour of God. It was adopted as such by the Puritans after the Reformation, though it had existed previously, chiefly in the form *Gracia*.

In classical mythology the three Graces—*Aglaia* ('the glorious'), *Euphrosyne* ('joy'), and *Thaleia* ('plenty')—were worshipped as goddesses. The Greek word for 'grace' is 'charis' (pronounced 'karriss'), and connected with it is 'chairein', 'to rejoice.' *Charis* and *Charissa* are still sometimes used as Christian names in this country.

Grace is particularly popular in Ireland, where it usually represents the Irish girls' name *Grainne*, meaning 'love.' The first recorded bearer was a daughter of King Cormac Mac Art; she was wooed by Finn the Mighty, but eloped with his nephew Diarmuid. She is one of the great heroines of Irish legend.

The name is rendered in Gaelic by *Giorsal*.

In favour throughout the seventeenth century, Grace more or less went out of use, like most Puritan names, in the 1700's. Its revival was partly due to the much publicized heroism of Grace Darling, who, with her father, the lighthouse-keeper of the Farne Islands, off the Northumberland coast, rescued nine survivors from the *Forfarshire* when it was wrecked there in 1838.

Among notable modern bearers of the name may be mentioned Gracie Fields, the actress and variety artiste who was born in Rochdale. *Gracie*, though properly a pet form of Grace, is nowadays sometimes given as an independent name.

The Italian form, *Grazia*, is also occasionally given in this country. The Italian novelist Grazia Deledda won the Nobel prize in literature in 1926.

The following ingenious epitaph was composed for a certain Grace Stephens, who died in 1652:

> What though, enclosed in silent cell,
> Grace for a space in dust may dwell;
> This truth we find in Sacred Story—
> Death cannot long keep Grace from Glory.

GRISELDA Though the name Griselda or *Griseldis*, which is of Germanic origin, may mean 'stone of heroism,' or 'grey battle(maid),' it is always thought of as typical of the virtue of patience, from the famous old tale of Patient Griselda. Her unpleasant husband subjected her to a series of humiliations and cruelties, all of which she bore submissively. Originally Italian, the story was used by Chaucer in his *Clerke's Tale*, and was presented in dramatic form by Shakespeare's contemporary, Thomas Dekker, under the title *Patient Grissil*—which shows another form of the name, common in Shakespeare's day, but hardly ever used now.

Other Griseldas in fiction are the heroine of Mrs Molesworth's *The Cuckoo Clock*, and Griselda Grantly, the archdeacon's daughter in Anthony Trollope's *Barchester Towers*.

The name has long been a great favourite in Scotland, especially in the forms *Grizelda* and *Grizzel*, with their pet forms *Griz*, *Grizzie*, *Girzie*, and *Grittie*. It was used a good deal by Scottish writers of the early nineteenth century, such as

Susan Ferrier. A much earlier bearer of the name was Lady *Grizel* Baillie, born in 1665, who is best remembered for her songs, of which the most famous is probably, "And werena my heart licht, I wad dee."

GWENDOLEN In the last hundred years or so several Welsh girls' names have achieved popularity in England, and of these few have established themselves so firmly as Gwendolen, sometimes spelt *Gwendoline, Gwendolyn, Gwendaline,* or *Guendolen.* The name means 'white circle,' probably in allusion to an ancient moon-goddess, who may have borne this name as a title, in much the same way as *Cynthia* and *Phoebe* were titles of the Greek moon-goddess, Artemis. It appears many times, in various guises, in Welsh history and legend.

Queen *Guendoloena,* the legendary wife of King Locrine, who in mythical history was the son of Brute, the first King of Britain, was divorced by her husband, who then married *Estrildis.* Gathering together an army, Guendoloena defeated her husband and threw Estrildis and her daughter *Sabre* into the Severn—hence *Sabrina,* the other name for the river.

In Arthurian legend Guendolen was a fairy with whom King Arthur fell in love. Soon after their child *Gyneth* was born, however, the King decided to abandon his wife; but she persuaded him not to leave before drinking a parting-cup. As he put it to his lips a drop of the liquor fell on his horse, which "leapt twenty feet high" and then dropped dead. Arthur dashed the cup to the ground, thereby destroying the fairy palace. As for Guendolen, she was never seen again.

Another Guendolen was the wife of the wizard Merlin. There are three saints of the name, one of whom was the aunt of St David, patron saint of Wales.

To-day the most popular forms are *Gwen,* very often found

as a font name, besides being the pet form of the longer versions, *Gwenda* ('fair and good'), and Gwendolen. 'Gwen' is the feminine form of 'gwyn' in Welsh, and, besides meaning 'white,' may also signify 'fair,' 'beautiful,' or 'blessed.' Other related names—all feminine and all quite popular in Welsh-speaking areas—are *Gweneira* ('white snow'), *Gwenllian* ('fair flaxen'), and *Gwenonwy* ('lily of the valley').

GWYNETH This is an old Welsh name which also appears as *Gwynedd*, signifying 'blessed' or 'happy,' and *Gwynaeth*, meaning 'a state of bliss.' *Gyneth*, the daughter of King Arthur, mentioned under Gwendolen above, is yet another form of the name, which is sometimes found Latinized as *Venetia*. In 1625 Sir Kenelm Digby married a celebrated beauty of the day, Venetia Stanley. In 1837 Benjamin Disraeli made *Venetia* the title of a novel.

The name Gwyneth or *Gwynneth*, with its pet forms *Gwyn* and *Gwinny*, is popular in Wales, but is only occasionally bestowed in England.

HARRIET Both *Harriet* and *Henrietta* are feminine forms of Henry. In the Middle Ages by far the most usual masculine form of the name was Harry, which explains why Harrison is a much commoner surname than Henryson.

The meaning of the original German name (Haimirich) from which all the other forms, masculine and feminine, were derived is 'home rule.' The oldest known feminine version is *Harriot*, still sometimes used, and the usual pet form of this used to be *Harry*, though nowadays this is reserved for boys and *Hatty* is used for girls. Henrietta has the modern pet forms *Etty* and *Hetty* (also pet forms of *Hester*, p. 102) and *Etta*. In America the forms *Harriette* and *Henriet* are quite common.

Henrietta was a rare name in this country until it was brought over in 1625 by Charles I's wife, the French princess *Henriette Marie* (or *Henrietta Maria*), named in compliment to her father Henry IV. The tongue-tied English Court, however, found it difficult to pronounce the French form, and called her *Hawyot*. It is interesting to note that Oliver Cromwell named one of his daughters after this Queen—a choice he must have regretted when the troubles between his adherents and the Royalists developed later! The Queen's daughter, who married the Duke of Orleans, had the same name as her mother, but was known to her friends as *Minette*.

In his poem *Squire Thomas*, George Crabbe says of the heroine:

> Harriot was in truth
> A tall, fair beauty in the bloom of youth;
> And from the pleasure and surprise, a grace
> Adorn'd the blooming damsel's form and face.

The most famous writer to have borne the name is Harriet Beecher Stowe, born in Connecticut in 1811, whose novel *Uncle Tom's Cabin* (1851) did much to arouse anti-slavery feeling before the Civil War. Among the famous Harriets of to-day is Harriet Cohen, the pianist.

HAZEL In England, this name first came to be used towards the end of the last century, when several flower- and plant-names, such as *Heather*, *Myrtle*, *Lavender*, and *Ivy* were introduced.

One of the earliest uses of Hazel as a Christian name is in an American drama called *Hazel Kirke*, which appeared in 1879. The name Hazel is connected in meaning with *Evelyn*, which comes from an Old French word meaning 'hazel-nut' (see p. 106).

HELEN This most famous of all Greek names means 'the bright one,' coming from a root-word 'ele,' signifying 'light.' There is a host of variations, of which *Elaine, Eleanor,* and *Ellen* are treated separately on pp. 90, 91, and 96, respectively. In addition the names *Eileen* and *Aileen* (p. 89) are used in Ireland for Helen.

The first recorded mention of the name in this country occurs, about 1100, as *Elena*—which is the modern Italian and Spanish form. *Helen* and *Helena* first appear in England in the early years of the sixteenth century with the classical revival of the Renaissance.

Helen of Troy, who symbolizes female beauty in its most perfect form, was the husband of Menelaus, King of Sparta. Her elopement with Paris brought about the ten-year siege of Troy.

In the course of time she became associated with the Faust legend, and Marlowe, in his play *Doctor Faustus,* written towards the end of the sixteenth century, refers to her in the tremendous speech beginning:

> Is this the face that launched a thousand ships
> And burnt the topless towers of Ilium?
> Sweet Helen, make me immortal with a kiss;
> Her lips suck forth my soul; see where it flies!

The mother of Constantine the Great was named Helena. According to an old tradition, she was a daughter of Old King Cole, the Prince of Colchester, who, the nursery rhyme tells us, was a "merry old soul." There is a statue of her at Colchester Town Hall. About 326, when she was over eighty, she made a pilgrimage to the Holy Land, where she is said to have discovered the site of Calvary and dug up the true Cross of Christ. So popular was her memory that 135 churches in Britain bear her name.

In Shakespeare the name Helena appears twice, as a young Athenian lady in love with Demetrius in *A Midsummer-Night's Dream*, and as one of the main characters in *All's Well That ends Well*.

Helen is an extremely popular name in Scotland, where the form Helena, on the other hand, is almost unknown. The Gaelic form is *Eilidh*, and the Welsh, *Elen*. In America *Helene* is widespread, in imitation of the French form, *Hélène*. The pet forms *Nell* and *Nellie* are common to Helen and Eleanor. *Lena*, a contraction of Helena, has become a name in its own right.

Well-known modern bearers include Helena Rubinstein, the American cosmetics expert; Helen Hayes, the American actress; and Helen Keller, one of the most remarkable women of our times, who, though deaf and blind since the age of nineteen months, writes, and lectures all over the world.

HERMIONE Though *Hermia* seems to have died out after *A Midsummer-Night's Dream*, Hermione, the other feminine form of Hermes—again used by Shakespeare, in his *Winter's Tale*—has survived. The Greek god Hermes, whose Roman counterpart was Mercury, was the messenger of the gods and protector of travellers.

In Greek legend Hermione was the daughter of Helen of Troy and Menelaus.

Though Hermione has never been a common name, it is by no means unknown to-day. The leading bearers of the name in this country are the two actresses and wits, Hermione Baddeley and Hermione Gingold.

The names *Hermine, Herminia,* and *Herminie* are different in origin; they are derived from the German boys' name Hermann, which means 'army man.'

HILARY Like *Carol* and *Evelyn*, Hilary (or *Hillary*, as it is sometimes spelt) is one of the few names still used in modern times both as a boys' and a girls' name. It comes from the Latin word for 'cheerful,' and is connected with the word 'hilarious.'

In medieval days the forms *Hilaria* and *Hilaire* were found, the first being the Latin and the second the French form. As a girls' name, it became rare about Chaucer's time, but was reintroduced at the turn of the present century, since when it has grown considerably in popularity.

> I always felt sorry for Hilary:
> She longed to be lissom and willery—
> But alack and alas,
> When she looked in the glass
> She was cushiony, bolstery, pillery!
>
> But now she's grown up, as Hilaria
> (The Latin name, rhyming with 'area'),
> If she looks she will find
> That the fates have been kind,
> And she's slenderer, gracefuller, fairier.
>
> (B.L.S.)

HILDA, from an Old German word meaning 'battle(maid),' was the name of the chief of the Valkyries in Scandinavian mythology. In Scandinavia and England *Hild* was found as an independent name, but in Germany it was only used as part of a compound name (compare the Anglo-Saxon element 'Æthel-', referred to under Ethel, p. 102). Thus, among the many ancient German names using this element are the obsolete *Hildiridur*, 'battle-hastener,' *Hildemar*, 'the glory of Hilda,' and the modern *Hildegard*, 'battle-spear'—a popular name to-day in America, found also as *Hildegarde*—and *Hildegund*, 'battle-maid of war.' The same element was also used as a suffix, as in *Gunhilda*, an inverted form of *Hildegund*, and *Clotilda*, or *Clotilde*, 'loud battle(maid),' which have survived.

The most famous bearer in England was St Hilda, or *Hild*, as she was known before being given a Latin ending to her name, who in 657 founded Whitby Abbey, over which she ruled for twenty-two years. It is said that even now, in certain lights, looking through the arch of an empty window, can be seen

> The very form of Hilda fair
> Hovering upon the sunny air.

Hilda has always been a popular name around Whitby, but elsewhere in England it fell into disuse about 1300. Helena Swan, in her *Girls' Christian Names*, written in 1900, remarked: "After a long hiatus, it has again become a very popular name in England, there being just now a tendency to revive old names, from a growing feeling for and interest in the poetry of the past, and the sense too of the need for a change, a need for something distinctive."

Hylda is a modern variant.

HOPE was first used as a Christian name in the seventeenth century by the Puritans, who delighted in coining 'abstract-virtue' names, such as *Faith*, *Charity*, *Prudence*, and *Honour*.

The ancient Romans worshipped the goddess Spes, who personified Hope; concerning her Greek counterpart there is a beautiful allegory that, when Epimetheus opened the vessel brought to him by Pandora, from which all kinds of evils were scattered over the earth, Hope alone remained behind. She is represented as a youthful figure.

An anchor is the symbol of Hope, just as Faith has a Cross or Bible, and Charity a burning heart.

The Russian word for 'hope' is 'nadezhda,' which, in its Frenchified form, *Nadine*, has been used as a Christian name in both France and England for about a hundred years. *Nada* and *Nadia* are the less common Serbo-Croat forms.

IDA This name is of Teutonic origin, and is derived either from the verb 'idja,' 'to work hard,' or from 'itis,' 'a woman.' It was introduced into England by the Normans, and in Domesday Book there is mention of a certain Ida, Countess of Boulogne, a wealthy heiress. There are several names in German and Scandinavian mythology containing the root-element of Ida, among them the Norse goddess *Iduna*, goddess of spring and guardian of the golden apples which the gods tasted whenever they wished to renew their youth.

After being in disuse for some five hundred years Ida was revived in the nineteenth century. Its popularity then was no doubt partly due to Tennyson's poem *The Princess*, which appeared in 1847. The heroine is portrayed as the "new woman," foundress of a university to which only women are admitted. The Gilbert and Sullivan comic opera *Princess Ida,* which appeared thirty-seven years later, is a "respectful operatic perversion of Tennyson's *Princess*."

The name has no connexion with the Mount Ida in Crete or Phrygia, but in Ireland it has taken the place of the ancient Celtic name *Ita*, which meant 'thirsty.' There is an Irish St Ita, whose name-day is April 15.

Among famous modern bearers are Ida Haendel, the violinist; Ida Bailey Allen, the American cookery expert; and Princess Ida Labia, who lives in South Africa and is the owner of one of the largest private collections of Old Masters in the world.

IMOGEN This is probably a unique example of a name coming into being through a printer's error! It seems that when Shakespeare sent the manuscript of his play *Cymbeline* to the printers they misread his *Innogen,* which was intended to suggest 'Innocence,' for Imogen, thinking perhaps that it was meant to signify 'last born,' the only possible interpretation of the name as it stands.

Thanks to this mistake, we have gained a very pretty name with a most romantic namesake. It is certainly more attractive than the ancient British *Ignoge,* a mythical princess, and than the real *Imagina,* who was the Duchess of Luxemburg in 1400. Besides, it is the only one of these to survive, as with the poet Imogen Guiney and the musician Imogen Holst. Other modern forms are *Imogine* and *Imogene*; the name is sometimes shortened to *Immy.*

There is also the poem by Walter de la Mare *To Imogen* that sings of the night which

> shall see
> Unwearying as her stars, still Imogen
> Pausing 'twixt death and life in one hushed word.

INGRID has always been a widespread name in Scandinavian countries, but never elsewhere until recently, when the Swedish film star Ingrid Bergman made it popular in parts of Europe and in America.

The name means 'Ing's ride.' Ing, in Norse mythology, was the god of fertility and crops, and of peace and prosperity. His cult, which extended over the whole north, had its greatest influence in Sweden—in fact he is looked on as the ancestor of the Swedish kings. Ing's 'ride' refers to his steed Gallin-bursti, 'the golden-bristled boar,' which, from its tearing up the earth with its tusks, represented the seed-sowing time.

Ing gave his name to several long-established boys' and girls' names—for instance, Ingvar the Viking, the terror of Anglo-Saxon England, and, among the feminine forms, *Ingeborg*, 'Ing's protection,' and its short forms *Inga* and *Inge*, all used frequently on the Continent and occasionally in this country.

IRENE comes from the Greek word 'eirene,' which means 'peace.' In ancient Greece *Eirene* was worshipped as the god-dess of peace, and because of its happy associations was later adopted in many parts of Europe as a Christian name; but in this country it does not occur until about 1880, though it had been previously used in English classical dramas and in poetry.

Till recently the name was always pronounced 'eye-ree-nee' in England, with the stress on the middle syllable, but the American fashion of pronouncing it 'eye-reen' has lately spread to this country.

In the third century, when the Roman Emperor Diocletian ordered St Sebastian to be shot to death with arrows for being a Christian, it was a pious woman named Irene who tended him after the archers had failed to inflict a death-blow. The Christian calendar contains three other saints of the name, all of whom were martyred.

The seventeenth-century poet Robert Herrick seems to have known a somewhat formidable lady of the name, judging by his poem *Upon Irene*:

Angry if Irene be
But a minute's life with me:
Such a fire I espie
Walking in and out her eye,
As at once I freeze, and frie.

In 1749 a classical tragedy called *Irene* was staged by David Garrick; its author was Dr Johnson, the lexicographer, who had taken years to write it—in spite of which it was a complete failure.

Famous modern bearers include Madame *Irène* Juliot-Curie, the French physicist whose mother, Marie Curie, discovered radium; Irene Dunn, the celebrated actress; Irene Scharrer, the pianist; and Irene Curzon, Baroness Ravensdale of Kedleston, one of the first four life peeresses created by the Queen. It is also borne by one of the daughters of Queen Juliana of the Netherlands.

Renie, the pet form of Irene, has nothing to do with *Renée*, the feminine form of the French name René, meaning 're-born.'

IRIS Though generally associated with the flower, this name is the Greek word for 'rainbow,' and in classical mythology Iris was the personification of the rainbow who carried messages across her many-coloured bridge from the gods to men. Shakespeare, in the masque in *The Tempest*, introduces Iris in this way. The flower was given its name by the ancients on account of its beautiful and varied colours; hence also the name given to the coloured part of the eye.

The use of Iris as a Christian name dates from the nineteenth century, though it did not become at all common until after 1900. Perhaps the earliest use of it was by Shelley (1792–1822) in his poem *On A Painted Woman*:

I

To youths who hurry thus away,
How silly your desire is
At such an early hour to pay
Your compliments to Iris.

Stop, prithee, stop, ye hasty beaux,
No longer urge this race on;
Though Iris has put on her clothes,
She has not put her face on.

ISABEL *Isabel, Isabella,* and *Isobel* are all variants of *Eliza-beth* (see p. 92). In the Middle Ages Elizabeth, the older form of the name, became *Ilsabeth,* which in turn was changed to *Isabey* or *Isabeau*; the latter remained the usual form for many generations in the south of France, but elsewhere the second part was changed to 'belle' ('beau' being the masculine form of 'belle,' French for 'beautiful,' 'handsome'), and thus the present-day form *Isabelle,* shortened to *Isabel,* was reached.

When, in the early thirteenth century, the French King Philippe-Auguste married Elisabeth of Hainault he asked her to adopt the name Isabella, which she did, thus making it a popular name in Court circles. Soon it spread beyond the French Court, and became particularly favoured in Scotland (which in those days had very close ties with France) and in Spain. Isabella I, also known as "the Catholic," was Queen of Castile; when she married Ferdinand II of Aragon their dominions were merged, thus creating a unified Spain. It was this Queen who equipped the expedition of Columbus in 1492.

Isa is probably a short form of the name, though it has some-times been used as if independently derived from the Old-German word for 'iron.' This version is found chiefly in Scot-land and America, but there have been so many forms of

Isabel—such as *Bel, Bell, Bella, Belle, Ib, Ibbot, Ibby,* and even *Nib*—that Isa is, in most cases, just yet another variation. Certain it is, at any rate, that Robert Browning, in the letters he wrote to his friend Isabella Blagden, always addressed her as "Dearest Isa." Even *Tibbie* was used, but this name, as used for a cat, comes from Old Flemish 'Tybalt,' the cat in the stories of *Reynard the Fox.* In Scotland the forms *Isbel* and *Ishbel* are found.

Most surnames with Christian-name elements in them are derived from masculine forms; Ibbotson is an uncommon example of a surname originating from a girls' name—*Ibbot.*

Famous bearers include Isabella Beaton, author of the famous encyclopaedia of cookery, the *Book of Household Management,* and inventor of paper patterns; Isobel Baillie, the soprano who has achieved a leading position in oratorio; and Lady Barnett, the television personality.

IVY, the clinging vine, signifies faithfulness in the language of flowers. Like *Hazel, Myrtle,* etc., it has only been used as a personal name within the last century, or less.

Ivy Joslin, the domestic science expert, and Ivy Compton-Burnett, the novelist, are among the well-known present-day bearers of the name.

JACQUELINE Jacqueline and *Jacquetta* are French diminutive forms of Jacques, the French version of our James or Jacob. Jacob, in Hebrew, means 'supplanter,' and it was chosen by Rebekah, wife of the Patriarch Isaac, for her second son, because she had a presentiment that he would supplant his elder brother, Esau.

It was from the Belgian province of Hainault that the feminine form first reached England. Jacqueline of Hainault,

Henry V's sister-in-law, was generally known in England as Dame *Jack*. The same King had a second sister-in-law, Jacquetta of Luxemburg, showing that both forms were early in use. Another of our kings, Edward IV, had a devoted old nurse who compiled a collection of recipes and folk-stories known as *Mother Jack's Book*. Jacqueline Pascal, sister and helper of the great French thinker and mathematician Blaise Pascal, is another historical example of the favourite French form. A noted modern French bearer of the name is Jacqueline Auriol, the world's only woman test pilot and the first woman ever to break through the sound barrier. Jacquetta Hawkes, the archaeologist and wife of J. B. Priestley, is the best-known modern bearer of the more English version.

In Shakespeare's play *Love's Labour's Lost*, *Jacquenetta* is found as the name of a young country girl. Although Jacqueline and its variants began to fall out of favour about Shakespeare's time, the name now enjoys renewed popularity, having recently acquired a new variant, *Jacquelyn* (compare *Carolyn*, a modern form of *Caroline*). The usual pet form is *Jackie* or *Jacky*.

Another feminine version of the name is *Jacoba*, more often found as *Jacobina*. This became widespread in Scotland during the eighteenth century when it was commonly bestowed by Jacobites, as was *Jamesina* for the same reason. These names are still by no means uncommon there to-day, though little used elsewhere.

Jemima(h) has often been used as a feminine form of James; it is, however, really an entirely different name, meaning 'dove' in Arabic and 'day' in Hebrew, though its pet form, *Jem*, was once a common shortening of James. The original bearer was a daughter of the much-plagued Job. Much more recent, and fictional, is Jemima Puddleduck, Beatrix Potter's gullible duck.

JANE Of all the many feminine forms of John, none has been as popular during the present century as Jane. *Jane, Jean, Joan, Joanna, Jeannette, Janet, Jessie, Jenny, Sheena*—these are some of the commoner names, all nowadays given independently, derived from the original form, *Johanna*, which in Hebrew means 'grace of God.'

Until the sixteenth century Jane was a very rare name, the usual version during the Middle Ages being Joan. The first Jane of note in English history was Jane Seymour, the third wife of Henry VIII; she died a few days after giving birth to Henry VIII's only son, the future Edward VI. Lady Jane Grey, born in the same year that Jane Seymour died, was a great-granddaughter of Henry VII. By the time she married, at the age of sixteen, she was fluent in Greek, Latin, Italian, French, and German—reminding one of another Jane, in Hilaire Belloc's *Cautionary Tales*, who

> though barely nine,
> Could spout the Catechism through,
> And parts of Matthew Arnold too.

Queen for only nine days, following the death of Edward VI, Lady Jane Grey was seized and imprisoned, and soon afterwards was executed with her husband, Lord Dudley, on Tower Hill. She was then just seventeen.

Since Tudor times Jane has been in and out of fashion, but was never more popular than it is to-day. It was also widespread from about 1750 until 1850, when it was often used in conjunction with other names—for example, Mary Jane. It had become so common by the middle of the last century that the Victorians discarded it in favour of one or other of the alternative forms of the name. In the past fifty years, though, it has returned with a vengeance, and is now a great favourite:

on more than half a dozen occasions since 1950 it has headed the list in the annual summaries of the Births Columns of various national newspapers. A recently introduced form of the name is *Jayne*.

Being a simple, one-syllable name, Jane does not lend itself to shortening; but variation is possible through its pet forms, the commonest of which are *Janey* or *Janie* and *Jen* or *Jenny* (sometimes spelt and pronounced *Jinny*). *Jenny*, of course, is also a pet form of *Jennifer*, as well as being a name in its own right. But in the old nursery rhyme in which Jenny Wren is the sweetheart of Robin Redbreast it stands for Jane:

> I'll dress you like a goldfinch,
> Or any peacock gay;
> So, dearest Jen, if you'll be mine,
> Let us appoint the day.

Janet was originally a diminutive form of Jane, though nowadays it is looked on rather as an independent name. Particularly popular in Scotland, it was adopted there from the French *Jeannette*. *Jan*, *Netta*, and *Nettie* are pet forms of Janet. Earlier forms, still occasionally found to-day, were *Jannet* and *Jennet*, and it was from the latter that Jenny evolved. In recent times such elaborations as *Janice*, *Janette*, *Janetta*, *Jenetta*, *Jeannine*, *Janina*, *Janine*, and *Jeneen* have added to the host of varieties descended from Johanna. *Jessie*, sometimes used as a form of Janet, is treated separately on p. 137.

The Scots Gaelic form is *Sine*, which in English becomes *Shena*, *Sheena*, or *Sheenagh*. In Ireland Jane is rendered by *Sinéad*, and the diminutives Janet and Jenny by *Sinéidín*. The Welsh equivalents are *Sian* or *Siwan*.

In fiction there are well-known examples of all forms of the name. Jane Eyre, the penniless orphan in the novel of that name (1847), is Charlotte Brontë's most famous heroine; a Jane features in E. Nesbit's *Five Children and It* and its sequels; *Janice Meredith* is the name of an historical novel (1899) by the American author Paul Leicester Ford; *Janet's Repentance* is one of George Eliot's *Scenes of Clerical Life*; Jinny, in Virginia Woolf's *The Waves*, is a pretty child who grows up to be a great beauty; and, in verse, there is that charming little poem *Jenny Kissed Me* by Leigh Hunt, and, in lighthearted vein, A. A. Milne's Jane, who asked:

> Why should I want to be bad at the Zoo?
> And should I be likely to say if I had?
> So that's why it's funny of Mummy and Dad,
> This asking and asking, in case I was bad,
> "Well—
> Have you been a good girl, Jane?"

Among the best-known bearers of the name in real life are: Jane Austen, one of the most accomplished of English novelists, whose greatest works were published between 1811 and 1818, the year after her death at the age of forty-two; Jenny Lind (christened Johanna), known to her Victorian admirers as the "Swedish Nightingale" on account of her fine coloratura soprano voice; and Scottish-born *Jennie* Lee, Member of Parliament and widow of Aneurin Bevan.

JEAN, and its modern French equivalent *Jeanne*, derive from the medieval French form *Jehane*, a name which is connected with *Jane* and *Joan*. Jean has long been popular in Scotland, from where, in early-Victorian times, it spread to England. It is now used quite independently of its associations with other forms of the name, all of which originate from *Johanna* (see p. 133).

The name is also quite popular in America, where Stephen Foster's *Jeannie With the Light Brown Hair* was written over a hundred years ago. Long before that, however, Jeannie, or *Jeanie*, was the favourite pet form of the name in Scotland, where the commonest diminutive is *Jeannette*.

Among the famous Jeans of the past may be mentioned Jean Ingelow, the poet from Boston in Lincolnshire, whose bonneted figure shines unexpectedly from a window in the magnificent church there; and Jean Armour, whom Robert Burns married in 1788, the year in which he wrote the follow-ing lines to her:

> There's not a bonnie flower that springs
>   By fountain, shaw, or green,
> There's not a bonnie bird that sings,
>   But minds me o' my Jean.

JENNIFER is a Cornish form of *Guenevere*, the name of King Arthur's wife. Except in Cornwall, Jennifer was virtu-ally obsolete until about thirty years ago, when it began to be used in other parts of the country. To-day it is a popular name throughout England.

Guenevere or *Guinevere* (in Welsh *Gwenhwyfar*), which means 'fair and yielding,' is still occasionally used as a Christian name, though sometimes disguised under such forms as *Ganor*, *Gaynor*, *Ginevra*, and in Scotland the stately sounding *Vanora*. *Gwinny* is a pet form of *Guenevere*, as well as of *Gwyneth*.

America seems to have adopted the name Jennifer quite early in this century. *Jennifer Lorn*, the title of an imaginative novel by the American Elinor Wylie, was published in 1923.

Jennifer, also spelt sometimes, *Jenifer*, *Jenefer*, or *Jennefer*, has the pet forms *Jen* and *Jenny*.

JESSIE was first used as a pet form of *Janet* in the eighteenth century in Scotland, where it quickly became an independent name. The following lines were written by Robert Burns to eighteen-year-old Jessie Staig in 1793:

> O fresh is the rose in the gay dewy morning,
> And sweet is the lily at evening close;
> But in the fair presence o' lovely young Jessie,
> Unseen in the lily, unheeded the rose.

Jessie, or *Jessy*, is also, of course, a pet form of *Jessica*, a name which in medieval times was almost exclusively Jewish; it was used as such by Shakespeare in *The Merchant of Venice*, but has hardly been used since as a Christian name until very recently. Jessica, in Hebrew, means 'God is looking,' and appears in the form *Iscah* in the Authorized Version (Genesis, xi, 29).

The third use of Jessie is as a pet form of the rather uncommon names *Jessamine* and *Jessamy*, which are versions of the flower-name *Jasmine*. This is derived from the Arabic and Persian *Yasmin*, a common girls' name in Arab countries and famous in England through James Elroy Flecker's *Hassan*. *Jess* is an alternative pet form of all these names.

JOAN Like *Jane* and *Jean*, this name is a feminine form of John, a contraction of the Latin Johannes, which derives from the Hebrew Iohanan, meaning 'grace of God'; Joan is a contraction of *Johanna*, which, in the form *Joanna*, occurs twice in St Luke's Gospel.

In England the first record of the name appears in the second half of the twelfth century, having been introduced from the south of France, as *Jhone* and *Johan*. The first English bearer seems to have been Jhone, daughter of Henry II, but by the reign of Edward II, crowned in 1307, the familiar Joan was the usual spelling. Thus it is an earlier name than *Jane*, which was scarcely known until the sixteenth century, or *Jean*, a later Scottish variant. It is for this reason that Jeanne d'Arc, the Maid of Orleans, burned at the stake in 1431, became known in this country as Joan of Arc, and not as Jane or Jean of Arc.

By Shakespeare's time Joan had become so common in England that it lost favour to the newly introduced Jane. Joan went right out of fashion, and in 1890 was considered an obsolete name. It was revived early in the present century and is now once again very popular.

In Puritan England *Joanna* became widespread, vying for a time with *Jane* in popularity. A remarkable bearer of the name was Joanna Southcott, the religious fanatic who in 1802 prophesied that she would give birth to the second Messiah.

Johanna came into use as a Christian name about 1750; this was the usual way in which the name was recorded in registers during the Middle Ages, being the Latin version, and it became fashionable among the aristocracy of the late eighteenth century. Neither name has been much used during this century, though Joanna is showing marked signs of recovery. *Joanne* is a recent version which is becoming increasingly popular.

The Spanish form of John is Juan, which becomes *Juana* in the feminine; *Juanita*, its diminutive, is shortened to *Nita*, which has been adopted in England as an independent name.

The Irish form is *Siobhán*, pronounced 'Shoo-vawn,' with the stress on the second syllable; this is a favourite among Irish girls' names.

Famous modern Joans include Joan Hammond, who, besides being an operatic and concert singer, is a champion golfer, and Joan Grant, the novelist.

Perhaps the most famous of all, though, is the Joan of Darby and Joan, the model of loving old couples; the original couple are said to have been a certain John Darby, who died in 1730, and his wife.

> What lovely names for girls there are!
> There's Stella like the Evening Star,
> And Sylvia like a rustling tree,
> And Lola like a melody,
> And Flora like a flowery morn,
> And Sheila like a field of corn,
> And Melusina like the moan
> Of water. And there's Joan, like Joan.
>
> (Eleanor Farjeon)

JOSEPHINE The original feminine form of this name was *Josepha*, corresponding to the latinized boys' name Josephus, whence our modern version Joseph. This Hebrew name means 'addition' or 'increase'; the Patriarch Joseph was the child of Jacob's old age.

In every Catholic country the name, both in its masculine and feminine forms, became tremendously popular after 1621, the year in which the Pope fixed a festival-day in honour of St Joseph, husband of Mary the mother of Jesus.

The widespread use of Josephine in Napoleon's time was due to his first wife, the Empress *Joséphine*, whom he married in 1796. Her real Christian names were *Marie Josèphe Rose*; Joséphine is a French diminutive of Josèphe. The commonest French pet forms are *Josée*, *Fifi* and *Fifine*, while in England they are *Jo*, *Joe*, *Josie*, and *Pheeny*.

Josephine is the heroine of Gilbert and Sullivan's comic opera *H.M.S. Pinafore, or The Lass that loved a Sailor* (1878). She is the captain's daughter, who spurns the advances of wealthy Sir Joseph Porter because she is in love with a "common sailor" named Ralph Rackstraw.

In American literature there is Jo March, who figures in *Little Women* and its sequels *Little Men* and *Jo's Boys*, by Louisa May Alcott.

JOYCE During the Middle Ages, when this name was fairly widespread, the most common form was *Josse*—the popular form of *Judocus*, name of a seventh-century Breton prince who became a hermit and was canonized. His cult had a large following in the north and west of France, as well as in the Low Countries, where the usual Flemish form was *Jooss*. One of the French variants was *Joisse*, and it was partly from this and partly from the Latin rendering *Jocea* that our Christian name Joyce originated.

In medieval times it was both a boys' and a girls' name, though by Chaucer's time it was disappearing as a boys' name. In old registers the name was entered as *Jocea* or *Jocosa*, the latter giving the false impression that the name is connected with the Latin word for 'merry' or 'joyful.'

It is very probable that *Jocelyn* or *Joscelyn*, till recently only a boys' name, has the same origin as Joyce, being a diminutive form of it.

Joyce, in its various versions, did not entirely die out after the fourteenth century, though it was rare until the late nineteenth century when it suddenly returned to favour; to-day it is a much-liked name.

The name *Joy* really has no connexion with Joyce, but is an 'abstract-virtue' name, like *Faith*, *Mercy*, etc., which were popular with the Puritans. It was revived at much the same time as Joyce.

Modern bearers of these names include Joyce Grenfell, a

delightful character entertainer; Joyce Lankester Brisley, creator of *Milly-Molly-Mandy*; and Professor Jocelyn Toynbee, scholar and archaeologist.

JUDITH This ancient Hebrew name is sometimes looked on as the feminine form of Judah, meaning 'the praise of the Lord,' though its literal meaning is 'woman of Judaea,'— *i.e.*, a Jewess. The first recorded bearer was *Jehudith*, wife of Esau; but more famous was Judith of Bethulia, who, in the Book of Judith—which forms part of the Apocrypha—saved her countrymen by killing the invading general, Holofernes, with her own hands.

The name found its way to England in the ninth century, when it was confused with an Old-German name, *Jutta*, meaning 'war,' already in use among the Anglo-Saxons. This was the name of Alfred the Great's mother, who set her sons a reading competition that started Alfred's interest in education.

In Norman times Judith had the peculiar pet form *Jugge*; nowadays, though, the usual one is *Judy*, which is so prevalent, particularly in Ireland, that it is often given as an independent name. It is the name of Punch's wife, and has been since about 1700, when the first show of this kind was performed in England; at that time, Judy was very much in vogue.

Judith Shakespeare was the Bard's elder daughter, his younger being Susanna. It is curious that, though he called his son Hamlet, he gave his daughters none of the delightfully unusual girls' names used in his plays.

To-day Judith Anderson, the Australian actress, is a notable bearer; and Judy Garland will be remembered far outside her native United States as the child star of *The Wizard of Oz*, and to-day as a much-travelled singer.

JULIA The Roman family of the Julii were originally noted for their long hair, which gave them this name meaning 'hairy' or 'downy'; though poor Julius Caesar grew bald early in life and was only too delighted to be awarded the privilege of wearing a laurel wreath to disguise the fact.

So imperial a name as Julia naturally spread throughout the Roman Empire and led to several variations, among them *Juliana*. An early victim of the Roman persecutions of Christians, St Juliana was honoured in the Low Countries, her remains having been brought to Brussels. It was also the name of the mother of William the Silent, creator of the Netherlands, and is borne to-day by the Queen of that country. Juliana Horatia Ewing was the author of *Jackanapes* and other delightful children's books written a hundred years ago, but still widely read.

Another famous bearer was the fourteenth-century prioress of Sopwell nunnery, at St Albans, who was "the Diana of her Age for Hunting and Hawking; skilful also in Fishing, and wrote Three Books of these Exercises, commending the practice thereof to the Gentry of England" (Thomas Fuller). Contemporary with her was the hermit Juliana (or *Julyan*) of Norwich, who died, a centenarian, in 1443, having written her *XVI Revelations of Divine Love*, a book which had a profound influence on religious thought in later-medieval times.

The common medieval form was *Julian* or *Julyan*—whence Juliana—and from these the pet forms *Gill*, *Jill*, *Gillian*, etc., were derived. These are treated separately on p. 116.

Julia itself dates from the sixteenth century, having been taken by Shakespeare from the Italian version, *Giulia*, for a character in *Two Gentlemen of Verona*. But the most belauded Julia is to be found in the poems of Robert Herrick, in which she appears to have every possible feminine perfection; the most celebrated of his poems to Julia is the one beginning:

Cherrie-Ripe, Ripe, Ripe, I cry,
Full and faire ones; come and buy.
If so be, you ask me where
They doe grow, I answer; There,
Where my Julia's lips doe smile . . .

Julia became an extremely popular name about 1700, since
when it has never fallen from favour.

The diminutive form of the Italian Giulia is *Giulietta*, from
which Shakespeare contrived the English version *Juliet* in
Romeo and Juliet. A pet form of this name, used in the play by
Juliet's nurse, is *Jule*. *Juliette* is another form, used both in
England and France, as is *Julie*. An older form than either is
Julienne, much in vogue with the Normans.

JUNE This popular name, derived from the name of the
month, has only been in use for just over fifty years, except for
a few rare instances in the late-nineteenth century.

Other names from months are *April* and *May*. April, sometimes elaborated to *Aprille*, and sometimes bestowed in its
French form, *Avril*, is even more recent than June as a Christian
name. May, on the other hand, has been in use for more than a
century (Queen Mary, wife of George V, was called May
before her accession), but its use in Victorian times was more
as a pet form of Mary or Margaret than as a 'month-name.'

Some *Julias* and *Augustas* are so christened because their
birthdays fall in July and August. None of the other months
of the year seem ever to have been used as girls' Christian
names, except *January*, the heroine of Muriel Spark's *Robinson*.

KATHARINE This name of many shapes comes from the
Greek word 'katharos,' meaning 'pure,' 'clean.' The first
known bearer was the fourth-century St Katharine of Alexan-

dria, according to legend an Egyptian princess so learned that she confounded the arguments of all the wise men of Egypt with her defence of Christianity. She was put to death after torture with a spiked wheel—hence the rotating firework called a Catherine wheel. Her tomb can still be seen in a monastery on Mount Sinaï, where her reputation has eclipsed even that of Moses.

It was from the Crusaders to the Holy Land that the name reached Europe, becoming widespread in England in the twelfth century, when, through mystery-plays and ballads, the legends surrounding the Egyptian saint became increasingly numerous. Among these legends was one that the saint helped young women to find husbands. In Dorsetshire until comparatively recent times village girls would visit her chapels at Milton Abbas and Abbotsbury reciting:

> Sweet Saint Katharine, send me a husband,
>   A good one, I pray;
> But arn [*any*] a one better than narn [*none*] a one.
> O Saint Katharine, lend me thine aid,
> And grant that I may never die an old maid.

One of the most outstanding figures of the Middle Ages was the Italian St Catharine of Siena. It was she who induced the Pope to return to Rome from his exile at Avignon in the fourteenth century, and afterwards her advice was sought by leaders of Church and State throughout Europe. She is patroness of the Order of Dominicans, and of Italy.

The usual forms of the name are *Katherine* or *Katharine*, and *Catharine* or *Catherine*. It was once a favourite Royal name, borne, among others, by the wife of Henry V, three of Henry VIII's wives, the Queen of Charles II, the wife of the French King Henri II—Catherine de Medici, mother of three kings —and two Russian empresses.

Katharine has never lost its popularity since it became an English Christian name over eight hundred years ago. In that long period it has developed a large variety of forms which have been in and out of vogue. Of the many variants, those most frequently used to-day are *Kate*, *Kitty*, *Kathleen*, *Kay*, and *Karen*, all of which, besides being diminutive or pet forms of Katharine, are nowadays commonly used as independent names.

Kate was the commonest pet form in Tudor times, but lost favour about 1700 and remained in disuse until the last century, when Kate Greenaway's drawings of children started a fashion in children's clothes. Other forms of Kate are *Katie* (for example, Katie Glover, the heroine of Scott's *Fair Maid of Perth*), and *Katy*, made famous both in the U.S.A. and in this country by the author Susan Coolidge, best remembered for the series that began with *What Katy Did* in 1872. In Goldsmith's comedy *She Stoops to Conquer* (1773), Kate Hardcastle is the pretty, spirited daughter of Squire Hardcastle; she "stoops" to the condition of a barmaid in order to "conquer" the bashfulness of young Marlow, whom she loves.

Kitty is probably an even older pet form than Kate, being often found in medieval times. It too lost favour for a while, but was revived in the late seventeenth century. Kitty Fisher, who found Lucy Locket's purse in the nursery rhyme, was a real lady of the Court of Charles II; and Kitty Clive was a celebrated comic actress of the eighteenth century, whose performances at Drury Lane were much admired by Garrick, Dr Johnson, and Horace Walpole, and who was a friend of the musician Handel. In Sussex a wren is known as a Kitty Wren instead of a Jenny Wren. Other forms of Kitty are *Kittie* and *Kit*.

Kathleen, or *Cathleen*, is the Irish equivalent of Katharine,

K

though it is commonly used in England too as a baptismal name nowadays. It seems to have been modelled on the medieval form *Catlin*, the modern Gaelic version being *Caitlin*. *Kathleen Mavourneen* is a lovely old Irish ballad of the last century; modern bearers include Kathleen Hale, creator of Orlando, the Marmalade Cat, and the singer Kathleen Ferrier. *Katty* is occasionally found as a pet form of Kathleen.

Kay, sometimes used as a pet form of Katharine, but more often independently, probably originated as a diminutive of Katharine or any of its variants, though it may also have been suggested simply by the initial K. Two famous actresses who have enhanced the popularity of this name are Kay Hammond and the late Kay Kendall.

Karen, the Danish form of Katharine, is very popular in the U.S.A., and has also become widespread in recent times in this country. Karen, by the way, has no connexion with *Keren*, which is a Hebrew name, in full *Kerenhappuch*, originally borne by one of the daughters of Job, and meaning 'horn of antimony,' used by the Jews as eyelash paint—successfully, it would seem, in the case of Keren and her sisters Jemimah and Keziah, for "in all the land were no women found so fair as the daughters of Job" (Job, xlii, 15).

Katharine itself occurs so often both in real life and in fiction that it is impossible to mention more than a few examples. Perhaps the most famous bearer in literature is *Katharina* (a form still occasionally used today) in Shakespeare's *The Taming of the Shrew*; she owed her nickname "the shrew" to her fierce temper. Catherine Earnshaw is the heroine of Emily Brontë's *Wuthering Heights*. In real life there was Catherine McAuley, of Dublin, who in the early nineteenth century founded the Irish Order of Mercy; and Katherine Mansfield, the New Zealand writer. Today, there are Katharine Hep⁄burn, the American actress, and Katharine Elliot, D.B.E., Baroness Elliot of Harwood, one of the first four life peeresses, created in 1958.

Other versions of the name not previously mentioned are *Kathryn* (mainly American); *Catriona* (almost exclusively Scottish, and the title of a novel by Robert Louis Stevenson); *Katrine* and *Katrina*, mainly Scottish forms which may have come from the Italian version *Caterina*; *Catrin*, the Welsh form, which has the diminutive *Cadi*; and the pet forms *Casey*, *Cathy* or *Cathie*, and *Kathy* or *Kathie*.

LAURA, like the masculine equivalent Laurence, comes from the Latin word for 'laurel' or 'bay⁄tree,' emblem of victory and poetic inspiration—hence the title 'poet laureate.' The name was already established in England by 1200, to⁄gether with the diminutive form *Lauretta*.

Undoubtedly the most celebrated bearer was the lady to whom Petrarch addressed his sonnets. He first met her in 1327, and from her gained the inspiration for some of the finest love⁄poetry ever written, making the name Laura as widely known as his contemporary Dante made Beatrice.

After the Renaissance it continued to be used throughout Europe, though less frequently, and a variety of forms de⁄veloped, of which the French ones *Laure*, *Laurette*, and *Lorette* have survived, and are sometimes given as font names in this country. The French pet form *Loulou* is not unlike its old English counterpart, *Lolly*.

Other forms of Laura still used from former times or of recent invention are *Laurencia* and *Laurentia*—both as old as, if not older than, Laura itself; *Laurinda* and *Lorinda*—eighteenth⁄century elaborations on the same model as *Clarinda*, *Dorinda*, etc., which were then all the rage; *Loretta*, a variant of the Old French form *Lorette*, both of which were diminutives of Provençal *Lora*; and *Laurel*, especially popular in America. The pet form of Laura and its many variants is *Laurie*.

A famous Laura of modern times is Dame Laura Knight, the artist, whose speciality is circus and stage subjects.

LAVINIA The origin of this name seems to be connected with the town of Lavinium, a few miles south of Rome. Legend has it that when Aeneas, the Trojan hero, went to Italy he formed an alliance with King Latinus, whose daughter Lavinia was offered to him in marriage. But as she had already been promised to Turnus, a neighbouring monarch, war broke out between the two kingdoms. It was agreed to settle the issue by single combat between the two suitors; Aeneas won and made Lavinia his bride. Lavinium, previously called Latium, was renamed after her, and by her Aeneas became the ancestor of Romulus, the legendary founder of Rome.

Lavinia was a widely popular name during the Renaissance, when it was sometimes found as *Lavina*, still occasionally used. Lavinia also occurs once in Shakespeare—as the daughter of Titus Andronicus in the play of that name; of her Demetrius says:

> She is a woman, therefore may be woo'd;
> She is a woman, therefore may be won;
> She is Lavinia, therefore must be lov'd.

It went out of fashion until the eighteenth century, when it enjoyed renewed popularity. In 1730 the poet Thomson retold the biblical story of Boaz and Ruth, but substituted the names Palemon and Lavinia. More modern is Lavinia the heroine of G. B. Shaw's *Androcles and the Lion*.

The pet form of Lavinia is *Vinny*, while Lavina is shortened to *Vina*.

LEILA Like *Esther* and *Beryl*, this is a Persian name, meaning 'dark-haired.' In Persian romance the story of *Leilah* and Mejnoun holds much the same place as that of Cupid and Psyche among the ancient Greeks. Byron used the name in one of his long poems with an Oriental setting—*The Giaour*, thus launching a fashion with it in the early nineteenth century.

Whether spelt in the above way or as *Lila* or *Lela*, this name has no connexion with *Lily* (see p. 150), nor with *Lilla(h)* (p. 92), nor with the Latin-derived *Lelia*.

LESLEY *Lesley* and *Leslie*, the usual feminine and masculine forms respectively (though they are interchangeable), are derived from the place-name or surname, both of which are Scottish. There is a Leslie in Aberdeenshire and another in Fife, each called after a family of that name.

Though hardly used as a Christian name before this century, there was at least one exception, whom Burns immortalized in his lyric *Bonnie Lesley*, in real life Miss Lesley Baillie:

> Thou art a queen, fair Lesley,
> Thy subjects we, before thee;
> Thou art divine, fair Lesley,
> The hearts o' men adore thee.

LETITIA This name, with its pet forms *Letty* or *Lettie* and, less commonly, *Tisha* and *Titia*, is from the Latin word 'laetitia,' meaning 'joy.' In the eighteenth century *Laetitia* was the commonest version of the name. The earliest recorded English form was borne by *Lettice* Knollys, wife of Queen

Elizabeth I's ill-fated favourite, the Earl of Essex. His expedition to Ireland seems to have made the name popular among the colleens, no doubt taking the place of some ancient native name. Lettice is a contraction of Letitia and of the Italian form *Letizia*, the name of Napoleon's mother.

A poem by Charles Tennyson Turner, *Letty's Globe*, describes Letty's delight with this new toy, telling how

> . . . while she hid all England with a kiss,
> Bright over Europe fell her golden hair.

LILIAN No one can be quite sure how or where this name originated. Some authorities claim that it is derived from an old Venetian name *Ziliola*, itself a diminutive of *Zilia*; if this is so, then the name *Lily* would be connected with *Celia*, for *Zilia* was Latinized into Celia. A rather more likely origin is that it came from a pet form of *Elizabeth*—such as the English (mainly Cornish) *Lilibet*, as our present Queen was called in childhood, or the German *Lili*, as in the song *Lili Marleen*.

Whatever its true origin may have been, the name is nowadays connected in people's minds generally with the lily flower, and Lily has, in common with several other flower-names, been in use as a given name since the nineteenth century.

As *Lillian*, it can be traced back as far as Shakespeare's time; even then it was probably associated with the flower, which, according to tradition, sprang from the repentant tears of Eve as she made her way into the wilderness after being driven from Paradise. In Christian art the lily represents purity.

The simple form Lily, occasionally *Lilly*, is no longer usual. Lily Pons, the French operatic coloratura soprano, is a well-known example; another was the Edwardian beauty and actress Lily Langtry, known as the "Jersey Lily" from the place o her birth; and *Lily of Laguna* was a popular song of the First World War. *Lilian* is the more usual version to-day: Lilian Bayliss founded the Old Vic theatre; and Lilian Wyles was, until recently, the holder of a post probably unique for a woman—Chief Inspector of the C.I.D.

The variant *Lillian* was borne by the famous American actress Lillian Gish, whose first great rôle was in the film *The Birth of a Nation*. Lillian Hellmann is a celebrated American playwright. Another form of the name, chiefly Scottish, is *Lilias*; it was given to a daughter of Rider Haggard, author of *King Solomon's Mines*, *Nada the Lily*, etc.

The usual pet form is *Lil*.

LINDA This name comes from the Old German word 'lindi,' meaning 'serpent'—a creature which, from remote times, has been held in awe and worshipped by people of many races. The wingless dragon of German legend is called the *Lindwurm* ('snake-worm') and its blood was supposed to make him who bathed in it invulnerable.

Although often regarded as a frightening creature, the serpent was also looked on as a symbol of wisdom; in St Matthew is found the text, "Be ye therefore wise as serpents, and harmless as doves." Another attribute, their suppleness, was not ignored by the Norsemen of old, who would complement their womenfolk by comparing them with the slender, graceful serpent: indeed, the word 'lind' is connected in origin with our word 'lithe.' Thus, the old German name *Ethelind* meant literally 'noble serpent' and, by inference, 'noble and supple'; there are many such names containing the 'lind' element.

In Spanish 'linda' means 'pretty', and is used as a diminutive ending of several names current in that country.

Linda was not used in England until quite late in the nineteenth century. To-day the usual pet forms of it and its fanciful variant *Lynda* are *Lindy* and *Lin*.

LORNA Like *Myra*, *Pamela*, *Thelma*, *Vanessa*, and *Wendy*, Lorna is an invented name. It was created by R. D. Blackmore in his novel *Lorna Doone* (1869), perhaps with reference to the title of the Marquis of Lorne (*Lorne* is an alternative, but less common, form of the name), or, more probably, by association with the old English word 'lorn,' meaning 'forsaken' or 'lost,' as in 'forlorn.' Readers of Dickens will recall Mrs Gummidge, in *David Copperfield*, who is always talking of herself as "a lone, lorn creetur."

The plot of *Lorna Doone*, which bears the subtitle *A Romance of Exmoor*, hinges on the feud between the Doones—a band of high-born Devonshire outlaws—and the young hero John Ridd, whose father they had killed. When he grows up John protects Lorna against her own family and finally marries her.

Since the appearance of this very popular book Lorna has often been used as a baptismal name.

LOUISE Louise is the French and *Louisa* the Latin form of Louis, which means 'famous in war.' Although very popular in France from early times, Louise was not adopted as a Christian name in England until the seventeenth century, when Louise de Keroualle, a Breton by birth, became Charles II's favourite and was created Duchess of Portsmouth.

Louise remained the usual form until the eighteenth century, when it was superseded by Louisa. To-day, the popularity of these two forms is about equally shared. Other versions sometimes met with in this country are the Italian, *Luisa*, and the German, *Luise*. The usual pet forms are *Lou* and *Louie*. The diminutive *Lulu* is shared with *Lucy*.

Two famous novelists of the last century bore the name. The American Louisa May Alcott produced her most famous work, *Little Women*, in 1868—the same year as the English novelist Louise de la Ramée (better known as *Ouida*, which was a baby mispronunciation of Louise) wrote *Under Two Flags*.

Loïs, if pronounced as two syllables, is another form of the name, taken from a Latinized feminine variation, *Aloysia*, which is clearly connected with the French name *Héloïse* or *Éloïse*, sometimes found in England as *Helewise*.

If, on the other hand, *Lois* is pronounced as one syllable, it is a Greek name, of unknown meaning. It was used by the Puritans, who presumably took it from the Second Epistle to Timothy, in the first chapter of which we learn that Timothy's grandmother was a Lois. Through the Puritan emigrants, this form became popular in America, particularly in New England.

LUCY From the Latin word 'lux,' meaning 'light,' came the Roman names *Lucius* and *Lucia*, which usually denoted that the bearers were born at daybreak. There was in Roman mythology a goddess named *Lucina*, who was patroness of childbirth, making children see the light of day. Though rather uncommon, Lucina is still given occasionally as a font name in this country.

St Lucy, or Lucia, a Sicilian martyr put to death in 303, was a much venerated saint of the Middle Ages. It was chiefly because of her that the name became widespread in medieval Europe. It reached England about the time of the Norman invasion, establishing itself here mainly in the forms *Lucy* and *Luce*.

Shakespeare used the name Luce for a character in *The Comedy of Errors*, written about 1591. In the same play there is also a *Luciana*, while elsewhere he uses the name *Lucetta*—a diminutive of Lucy still found in France (occasionally in England too) as *Lucette*.

This diversity of forms was further increased by the eighteenth century, when *Lucinda* and *Lucasta* came into vogue. Both began as poetic variations of Lucy; Lucasta was invented by the poet Richard Lovelace, who, in *To Lucasta, on Going to the Wars*, wrote:

> I could not love thee, deare, so much,
> Lov'd I not Honour more.

The lady to whom he addressed these lines is usually supposed to have been Lucy Sacheverell, and he coined the name from 'lux casta,' *i.e.*, 'chaste light,' 'chaste Lucy.'

Other forms include *Lucilia*, *Lucilla*, *Lucille*, and *Lucile*, all diminutive variations of Lucia. Lucilla was a name borne by many Roman empresses, and its modern French equivalent, Lucille, has become known in this country of late, partly on account of the actress Lucille Ball, and is sometimes given as a font name. *Lucky* is a pet form of all these names, though it is commoner in America than in this country.

Lucy Locket, who lost the purse which Kitty Fisher found, was a real person; she belonged to the Court of Charles II. The original of her near-namesake, Lucy Lockit, in *The Beggar's Opera* (1727) by John Gay, was Lucy Fenton, Duchess of Bolton. Another opera—Donizetti's *Lucia di Lammermoor*, first produced in London in 1838—was based on Sir Walter Scott's novel *The Bride of Lammermoor*, whose ill-fated heroine was Lucy Ashton.

LYDIA The name Lydia means, quite simply, 'a Lydian girl.' Lydia, a district of Asia Minor, reached the height of its power under its last king, the fabulously wealthy Croesus, who was all-powerful until he was misled by a juggling oracle, which resulted in his kingdom being destroyed in 546 B.C. The Lydians, who are credited with the invention of coinage, were great merchants, and were noted for their exquisite playing on "flutes and soft recorders."

Lydia, the widow of Philippi mentioned in Acts xvi, took her name from this district, which in 133 B.C. had become part of the Roman province of Asia. She is described as "a seller of purple," and was converted by St Paul when he lodged at her house on his first visit to Philippi.

This Lydia, never having been canonized, did not set a fashion with her name, and it was not until the seventeenth century that it emerged as a Christian name in this country, though at first it was more often found in romantic poetry than in parish registers. Unlike Damaris and Priscilla, also found in Acts, Lydia was not popular among the Puritans, and did not come into its own until the mid eighteenth century.

In fiction the most celebrated bearer of the name is Lydia Languish, the heroine of Sheridan's play *The Rivals*, who bases her behaviour on the sentimental characters she has read of in novels.

Much less well known, but real, was Lydia Dwight. Her father was a potter in Fulham, and in the Victoria and Albert Museum there are two delightful figures of his little daughter: one full of bouncing happiness, dancing; the other asleep, with a posy of flowers in her clasped hands.

MABEL Though it is sometimes claimed that Mabel comes from the French 'ma belle,' meaning 'my beautiful girl,' or from the Old Irish word 'meave,' meaning 'joy,' it is much more probably derived from the Latin word 'amabilis,' 'lovable,' which, in the form *Amabel*, was quite a common Christian name after about 1150. *Mabella*, *Mable*, and *Mably* are all very old variations, still occasionally used nowadays. But the form *Mabel*, which later became more popular than any of these, was also in use then; an early example was Mabel of Gatton, who lived in the thirteenth century and was a horse-woman.

The diminutive forms are *Mabs* and *Mab*. Queen Mab seems to be associated with an Irish heroine of romance who delighted in the name *Meadhbh*—which later developed into the Irish name *Meave*, 'joy'—and who was so highly esteemed by her compatriots that "Remember Meave!" became an Irish war-cry. Mab came to be regarded as Queen of the Fairies, who produced dreams by driving her chariot over sleepers.

Mabel was a favourite name in late Victorian times, but in the last forty years or so it has been much less common. Well-known examples are Mabel Constanduros, the radio character actress, and Mabel Lucie Attwell, the artist famous for draw-ings of chubby children.

MADELEINE The original form of this name, *Magdalene*, means simply '(woman) of Magdala'—the birthplace, situated on the Sea of Galilee, of St Mary Magdalene, whose story is told in Luke vii. After the Resurrection St Mary Magdalene is said to have been set adrift with her sister Martha and other companions of Jesus in a rudderless, oarless boat and cast ashore in the South of France, where they spread the Gospel. She is the patron saint of penitents, and the word 'maudlin' (*Maudlin* was an early variant, and, formerly, the usual pro-nunciation of the name), which now has the meaning of 'sickly-sentimental,' originally meant 'tearful.' Because of its modern connotation, however, the name Magdalene (preserved in the two colleges, *Magdalen* College, Oxford, and *Magdalene* College, Cambridge) lost favour and was supplanted by *Madeline*, an English variant made popular by Ludwig Bemelmans, and *Madeleine*, the French version. In Wales it is found as *Madlen*. Magdalene is now rare, as also is the later form *Magdalena*, though the shortened German form, *Magda*, is sometimes given in this country.

The most popular form of the name to-day is Madeleine, which has long been a favourite in France. *Madalene* and *Madelina* are less common. The usual pet form is *Maddie* or *Maddy*.

MARGARET Though this name is often regarded as a flower-name, connected with the marguerite, or as a jewel-name, connected with the Greek word 'margaretes,' 'a pearl,' it is, in fact, derived ultimately from the Persian, and means 'a child of light.'

The ancient Persians believed that oysters rose from their beds at night to worship the moon and that as they reached the surface of the water they opened their shells and took in one drop of congealed dew, which was transformed by the moonbeams into a pearl.

The flower-name *Daisy* and the jewel-name *Pearl* are treated separately on pp. 75 and 180.

The name appears to have originated in Antioch, capital of the Greek kingdom of Syria and one of the earliest strongholds of the Christian faith. It was there that "Mild Margarete that was God's Maid" was martyred in the third century. She was looked upon as the chosen type of female meekness and innocence.

In this country the first known historical bearer was the Hungarian-born grand-niece of Edward the Confessor; in 1069 she married the Scottish King, Malcolm III, and exercised

great influence on Scottish culture and the native church
She was canonized in 1251. The profound effect she had on
the national life of Scotland made her name an immediat
favourite there, and it is still a widespread Scottish name
having taken on a variety of pet forms, among them *Maisie*
Mysie, and *Maggie*.

It was not long before the name spread in England too. In
the Middle Ages it was among the commonest of girls' names
together with Elizabeth, Joan, Agnes, Maud, and Alice. It
quickly developed a large number of variations—some of them
such as *Margot*, *Marget*, and *Margery* (see p. 161), coming from
France, where the name established itself through *Marguerit*
de Navarre, mother of Henri IV, and *Marguerite* de Valois, hi
first wife.

The Welsh too like the name, which is often found among
them in the form *Margred*. *Megan* is a pet form developed from
Meg.

From the fourteenth to the sixteenth century the name wa
found in practically every royal house in Europe. Denmark
Sweden, and Norway were ruled by a Margaret; Margaret o
of Anjou was the Queen of Henry VI of England; Margare
of Austria was Regent of the Netherlands, as was Margaret o
Parma later. The name is still a royal one in this country, o
course, through the Queen's sister.

In the course of time other English forms evolved, of whicl
Madge (known already in the sixteenth century), *Gritty* (als
a diminutive of Griselda), *Greta*, *May* (sometimes *Mae)*
Maidie (another Scottish version), *Margaretta*, *Margareta*
Margarita, *Marghanita*, *Marguerite*, *Meta*, *Moggy*, *Peggoty*, *Peggy*
Peg, and *Meg* are still used.

Peg(gy) is said by some authorities to be a rhymed form o
Meg(gy), in the same way as *Moll(y)* became *Poll(y)*; othe

claim that it has no real original connexion with Margaret at all, but with an old Anglo-Saxon name, *Pega*, which became assimilated to Margaret when Pega went out of use. Regarding this, Robert Southey, in his *Letters From England* (1807), says:

> The probable solution is . . . that some person formerly bore both names [Pega and Margaret], who signed with the first and was called at home by the second—thus the diminutive of one became associated with the other: in the next generation one may have been dropt, yet the familiar diminutive preserved; and this would go on like other family names, in all the subsequent branchings from the original stock.

Peg was, at all events, a well-established pet form of Margaret in Shakespeare's time: in *Twelfth Night* he refers to an old song called *Peg-a-Ramsey*.

Greta, a Swedish abbreviated form of the name, became a favourite both here and in America during the 1920's on account of the great Swedish-born film star Greta Garbo. *Gretta* is also sometimes found.

May, besides being a pet form of Mary and associated with the month of May, is a diminutive of Margaret; its frequent use in Victorian times, however, was mainly as a pet form of Mary (see p. 165).

The Italian forms *Malgherita* and *Margherita* gave rise to the independent name *Rita*, which is really an abbreviated form of these Italian versions. It has been popularized in recent times by the Hollywood actress Rita Hayworth.

Being a saint's name, Margaret went out of fashion between 1500 and 1700; then it slowly began to regain the popularity it had enjoyed in medieval times. By the middle of the last century it had once again taken its place as one of the commonest girls' names in this country, and during the present century it has maintained that position—to such an extent that some of its pet forms have now become names in their own right.

It is not surprising, therefore, that there are many famous modern bearers of the name. Of these, only a few can be mentioned here: Margaret Mitchell, the American writer, was the author of the best-seller *Gone with the Wind* (1936), which took her ten years to write and by 1939 had sold over two million copies; another writer, Margaret Kennedy, is best remembered for *The Constant Nymph* (1924), which was later dramatized with success: Margaret Rutherford is known for her many funny rôles on stage and screen; Margaret Lockwood, also a film star; Margot Fonteyn, the prima ballerina; Dame Peggy Ashcroft, the actress; and Margaret Bondfield, who in 1929 became the first woman Cabinet Minister.

In literature there is the pitiful cry for "Margaret, Margaret," the sea-children's mortal mother in *The Forsaken Merman*, by Matthew Arnold; the fairy story of *Hansel and Gretel*, the broom-maker's children who, if the story had been written in English, would have been called Jack and Peg—*Gretel*, like *Gretchen*, being a German pet form of Margaret; and, finally, Keats's quaint Meg Merrilies,

> Brave as Margaret Queen
> And tall as Amazon.

The Lady Margaret who was a benefactress to both Oxford and Cambridge, and after whom the women's college Lady Margaret Hall was named, was Margaret Beaufort, a thrice-married fifteenth-century daughter of the Duke of Somerset.

MARION This form of *Mary* (or rather, of *Marie*, for i originated in France) was widespread on both sides of th Channel in medieval times. It was borne by Maid Marion who, besides being Robin Hood's sweetheart, was also a folklore figure in the old May-games and Morris dances.

The word 'marionette,' meaning a puppet moved by strings, is derived from the name, which later adopted another form, *Marian*. This, in turn, was extended to *Marianne*, a not-un-common form in England, though less favoured than on the Continent. To the French, *Marianne* has long been the French Republic personified.

Because this name was taken to be a combination of Mary and Anne, it gave rise to the use of *Mary Ann(e)* as a double name, one of the first to be used; its popularity dates from the eighteenth century. *Mariana* is the Spanish equivalent of Marian.

MARJORIE is a Scottish and *Margery* an English version of *Margaret*; both forms go back as far as the twelfth century and, like Margaret, reached England via France, where at that time *Margerie* was a pet form of *Marguerite*.

The liking for the name among the Scots may date from the late thirteenth century, when Robert Bruce, hero of the Scottish War of Independence, gave it to one of his daughters, who, by her marriage in 1315 to Walter the High Steward, became the ancestress of the Stewart (Stuart) royal dynasty, for their son became King Robert II, the first of the family to wear the crown of Scotland. The true Gaelic form is *Marsail*.

Marjory and *Marjery* are other spellings of this name, which has the pet forms *Marge* and *Margie*.

MARTHA The name Martha comes from an Aramaic word meaning 'lady.' It is usually associated with housewifely cares and hospitality, from Martha, the sister of Lazarus and Mary Magdalene, who, we are told in Luke and John, was

L

"careful and troubled about many things" while looking after the material comforts of Jesus when he was a guest at their house in Bethany. Martha is the patron saint of housewives.

In this country Martha was first used after the Reformation, but from the eighteenth century onwards it has not been common. *Mattie* and *Pattie* (or *Matty* and *Patty*) were the earliest pet forms, to which *Marta* and *Martita* have since been added.

The name was long a favourite one in France, as *Marthe*, because of the legend that, after the Crucifixion, Martha was among those who came by boat to the South of France (see under Madeleine, p. 156). It was also prevalent in Russia, where it was once a royal name in the shape *Marfa*.

The opera *Martha*, by Flotow, had great success in the middle of the last century, and may have helped to increase its popularity for a while in Victorian England. Since then, however, it has become rather rare in Britain, but is still popular in the U.S.A.

MARY In spite of the great deal of research which has been done to trace the origin of this name, no one can be sure when or where it was first used or what it means. The general belief is that it was first used by the ancient Jews, though it has been claimed by some as an ancient Egyptian name, 'mer Amon,' meaning 'beloved of Amon,' a divinity of Egypt who became their national god about 1700 B.C. Moses is also thought to be an Egyptian name. But it is much more likely that, in common with many of their early names (and this is among the earliest known of names used by the Jews), it was connected with the circumstances of the child's birth. This theory is supported by the historical background of the first known Mary, the sister of Moses and Aaron mentioned in the Book of Exodus as *Miriam* (see p. 170), the earliest form of Mary known to us. She was born during the Egyptian bondage, and the name might well signify 'bitterness,' from the Hebrew 'marah,' reflecting the feeling of frustration resulting from those hard, lean years.

These are two of the many meanings it is possible to attach to the name Mary; in fact, more than fifty have been attributed to it, most of them suggested by devotion to the Blessed Virgin Mary rather than supported by sound research. In the Middle Ages, it was generally supposed that the name was connected with the sea, and was variously interpreted as 'lady of the sea,' 'star of the sea,' etc. More convincing are the interpretations, based on old Hebrew words, 'wished-for child' and 'rebellion.' Whether its original meaning is included among the above suggestions, or whether it means something else, will probably never be known.

As the name of the Blessed Virgin, Mary was probably regarded in early times as too sacred for common use; at all events, in common with other biblical names, it was slow in being adopted. There is an apparently isolated example of a Spanish *Maria* in the ninth century, but as a Christian name Mary did not come into general use in western Europe until after 1100, when it was brought back from the East by Crusaders.

It established itself in France about this time as *Marie*, the form still common in France to-day. Soon afterwards, in the same form, it reached England where, during the next three centuries, its popularity increased considerably.

Marie remained one of the first half-dozen favourite girls' names up to the Reformation, when it fell sharply into disfavour. The reasons for this loss of favour were probably partly historical and partly religious.

Queen Mary I gained popular support on the death of

Edward VI in 1553 and was proclaimed Queen, in spite of Lady Jane Grey's rival claim to the throne. But the later persecutions of the Protestants, for which she was held partly responsible, earned her the nickname "Bloody Mary," and this must, to some extent, have weakened the popularity of the name in the mid sixteenth century.

Mary, Queen of Scots, was a Catholic ruling Scotland at a time when the Reformed religion was firmly establishing itself there. Her marriage to Lord Darnley, also a Catholic, caused much discontent, but it was only when her husband was murdered and she married his supposed assassin, the Earl of Bothwell, that the people rose against her. Soon she was obliged to throw herself on the mercy of Queen Elizabeth; but the presence of an influential Catholic minority in England made Elizabeth uneasy, and after several plots aiming at the restoration of the old faith she signed Mary's death-warrant. Mary was executed in 1587, and again the use of the name was adversely affected, both in Scotland and in England.

On the religious side, it is probable that the use of the name declined when Henry VIII rejected Papal authority; at the Reformation prayers to the Blessed Virgin were discontinued by the Protestants, who felt that they were not warranted by Holy Scripture. This attitude was later supported to a much larger degree by the Puritans.

However, by about 1650 the name began to reassert itself, both in this country and, for the first time, in Ireland, establishing itself firmly in its modern version, Mary. Mary I signed her name *Marye*, but it was Mary II (born 1662) who was, it seems, the first to use the modern English spelling and pronunciation. The Scots, on the whole, retained the spelling *Marie* until much later; they favoured the French -ie ending for their names, as can be seen also in Marjorie, Charlie, etc.

The Catholic Irish developed two forms of the name—
Maire, for common use, and *Muire*, reserved exclusively for
the Blessed Virgin.

The true Welsh form is *Mair*.

In the eighteenth century the Latinized form *Maria* was
adopted generally in England, though it was already known
in aristocratic circles in this country, and throughout Europe,
long before then.

Mary had by now outstripped every other girls' name in
popularity; roughly one girl in five in England and Ireland
was at this time being christened Mary or Maria. It had developed a large variety of elaborations, of which the main ones
—*Marion*, *Miriam*, *Moira*, and their variants—are treated
separately.

By the Victorian age Mary was still easily the commonest
girls' name in this country, followed by Eliza(beth), Sarah,
Ann(e), and Alice. The pet form *May*, which soon became a
popular independent name, dates from the last century; its
spread was largely due to the Victorians' affection for Princess
Mary of Teck, who was known in her family circle as May. She
became the wife of King George V.

Minnie, originally a Scottish pet form of Mary, became widespread in England in Victorian times. It is also a pet form of
Wilhelmina.

Among the oldest pet forms of Mary are *Moll(y)* and
Poll(y). It is generally supposed that Polly developed as a
rhyming nickname from Molly, in the same way that *Peg(gy)*
is said to have been formed from *Meg(gy)*. This may be true;
but it is equally possible that they were once distinct names
which, perhaps in medieval times, became associated with the
name Mary and were finally absorbed into it. Another theory
is that Polly developed from an old Walloon word, 'polle,'

meaning 'young girl'; this could also explain how parrots came to be called Poll(y), as they have been for hundreds of years. *Polly* was very popular in the eighteenth century, when John Gay named the heroine of his *Beggar's Opera* Polly Peachum. A modern invention is *Pollyanna*, the happy child who helps miserable people to see the sunny side of life, created by Eleanor Porter.

On the Continent, and to a lesser degree in this country, Mary has long been in use as a boys' name among Roman Catholics. It is usually bestowed as the second Christian name. In Catholic countries the Blessed Virgin Mary has many feast-days. The chief ones are December 8, March 25, and August 15: her Conception, her Annunciation, and her Assumption into Heaven. Some of these days have given rise to separate names, especially in Spanish-speaking countries— for instance, *Dolores*, in memory of her Sorrows (see p. 82); *Mercedes*, in memory of her Mercies; *Rosario*, alluding to the Catholic devotion of the rosary; and *Concepción*. The Mary (or Maria) part of these names has been discarded, as it has from Magdalene.

Nearly all the notable early writers for children had Mary as one of their names—Mary Wollstonecraft, Maria Edge-worth, Mary Lamb, Mrs Mary Martha Sherwood, Mrs Mary Howitt (first translator of Hans Christian Andersen), Charlotte Mary Yonge, and Mary Louisa Molesworth among them.

The Marie form has been particularly successful on the stage in the twentieth century, with Marie Lohr, Marie Tempest, Marie Lloyd, and Marie Ney.

The most famous Mary of modern times is Marie Curie, who discovered radium in 1898. She is the only person to have received two Nobel Prizes.

MATILDA The meaning of this name, which derives from Old German, is 'mighty battlemaid.' It soon became a favourite Christian name in Court circles here after the Norman invasion, for, in the Latinized form Matilda, it was borne by William the Conqueror's wife—to whom the Bayeux Tapestry is traditionally ascribed.

It was William's granddaughter, another Matilda, who fought so hard to oust her cousin Stephen from the English throne; she was more commonly known as *Maud*, a version which had developed from the Old French form *Mahault* or *Mahaud*.

The name remained popular in both forms for two or three hundred years afterwards, but then suffered an eclipse which lasted till the mid eighteenth century, when it was revived as *Matilda* or *Mathilda*.

It was not until about a hundred years later that the form Maud returned—in fact not until after the publication, in 1855, of Tennyson's famous poem, *Maud*:

> There has fallen a splendid tear
>   From the passion-flower at the gate.
> She is coming, my dove, my dear;
>   She is coming, my life, my fate;
> The red rose cries, 'She is near, she is near';
>   And the white rose weeps, 'She is late';
> The larkspur listens, 'I hear, I hear';
>   And the lily whispers, 'I wait.'

In Mrs Gaskell's *Cranford* there is a Miss *Matty*, who was so genteel that she would go upstairs to suck oranges behind a screen. Other pet forms of the name are *Patty*, *Tilly*, and *Tilda*, while *Maud*, sometimes found nowadays as *Maude*, has the diminutive *Maudie*.

Waltzing Matilda was a popular Australian song during the Second World War about a 'swagman' or wanderer.

MAVIS This is a 'bird-name' derived through French from an old English word for 'song-thrush.'

Its use as a Christian name dates from 1895, when Marie Corelli introduced a character called Mavis Clare into her novel *The Sorrows of Satan*. Since then it has become a popular name in this country.

Another 'bird-name' is *Merle*, the French word for 'black-bird.' This is an older name than Mavis; in Henry James's *Portrait of a Lady* there is a Madame Merle. Merle is not an un-common name in America, where its popularity has been enhanced by the film star Merle Oberon.

MELANIE Greek in origin, this name means 'black' or 'dark-complexioned.' Melanesia, the geographical region to the north-east of Australia, whose inhabitants are predomi-nantly dark-skinned, means literally 'black islands.'

Melania is an ancient name, known to the Greeks and Romans. In certain parts of Greece Demeter (known to the Romans as Ceres), goddess of all the fruits of the earth, was worshipped as *Melaina*, in mourning for her daughter Perse-phone, who had been carried off by Pluto to the Underworld (see Cora, p. 74).

The name reached this country from France, probably for the first time in the mid seventeenth century, and its earliest forms were *Melloney* (which, like *Mellony* and *Meloney*, is a popular version of the name to-day in America), and *Melania*, a Latinized shape rare nowadays. A character called *Melantha* appears in Dryden's play *Marriage à la Mode* (1672), but this form does not seem to have survived.

The most common English form now, *Melanie*, is a variant of the French *Mélanie*. *Melany* is another spelling, but one not often met with. The usual diminutives are *Mel* and *Melly*.

In fiction perhaps the best-known Melanie is the long-suffering friend of Scarlett O'Hara in *Gone with the Wind*.

MILDRED This, for once, is not a warlike but a gentle Northern name. The seventh-century King Merowald of Mercia christened his three daughters *Milburga* ('gentle defence') *Mildgyth* ('gentle gift'), and *Mildthryth* ('gentle power'). They all became saints, and St Mildred's ancient abbey in Thanet has recently been reoccupied, after four hundred years, by her own order of nuns. She is shown in art with a pet hart and an abbess's crozier.

Like many Anglo-Saxon names, Mildred was rescued from oblivion by the Victorians, and is now once again a not uncommon name. It is also found as *Mildrid* and *Mildreda*, and shares its pet form *Milly*, or *Millie*, with Millicent, Emily, and Amelia.

MILLICENT This ancient German name means 'strong worker' or 'energetic'; its first part is the same as that in *Emily* and *Amelia* (see p. 35), while the old form of the second was 'swintha.'

It became a favourite name in France about a thousand years ago, in the shape *Mélisande*, which is still known in that country through the romance of Pelléas and Mélisande, made into an opera by the French composer Debussy from the play by Maeterlinck. Like *Mélusine*, another French variant, *Melisande* is sometimes used as a font name in this country. Mélusine, by the way, is the most famous of all the fairies of French romance; she was a water-sprite who assumed human form six days a week, but every Saturday reverted to her mermaid-like form; when her husband discovered her secret

she was doomed to wander as a spectre till the Day of Judg-
ment. In English, Mélusine becomes *Melusina*.

Millicent was popular in England at the turn of the present
century, giving the pet form *Milly*, and was a natural choice
for Joyce Lankaster Brisley's child heroine *Milly-Molly-Mandy*,
whose full name is really Millicent Mary Amanda, first created
in 1928.

MIRIAM This is the earliest known form of the name *Mary*,
and mentioned in chapter xv of the Book of Exodus. After
the Israelites, under the leadership of Miriam's brother Moses,
had crossed the Red Sea they sang a Song of Triumph, and
"Miriam the prophetess, the sister of Aaron, took a timbrel in
her hand; and all the women went out after her with timbrels
and with dances."

Later the name assumed the form *Mariam*, which became
extended to *Mariamne*—the name of one of the ten wives of
Herod I, the tyrannical King of Judaea who died about the
year Jesus was born.

Miriam was not used in this country until the seventeenth
century, but has been in fairly steady use since then. It has
long been a favourite Jewish name.

MOIRA is an English rendering of the Irish name *Maire*,
which is pronounced exactly like Moira and is the Irish form
of *Mary*. *Moire* is another Irish form of the same name, which
in its diminutive form becomes *Mairin*, giving rise to the
popular name *Maureen*.

Both Moira and Maureen are common names in Ireland,
while in this country they have been increasing in popularity
throughout the present century. In America Moira is more

often found spelt as *Moyra*, but this is a less widespread name there than Maureen. *Maurine* is a variant.

Maura, likewise derived from the Irish form of Mary, has found less favour than either Moira or Maureen. Actually the name Maura existed in ancient Greece, though it has no connexion with the modern name; the Greek name meant 'dark' or 'black,' whence our word for the inhabitants of Morocco. There is a Greek St Maura; among the Greeks, too, was a Fate (goddess) called Moira, who hurried warriors to their appointed doom; but again here there is no connexion between the Greek and English names.

The Russian form of Maura is *Moura*, borne by the celebrated painist Moura Lympany, whose mother lived in Russia for several years.

Other well-known bearers of this name of many shapes are: Maureen Connolly ("Little Mo"), the tennis champion, who is an American of Irish descent; Moira Shearer, the prima ballerina; and Moira Lister, the actress.

MONICA St Monica, who lived in the fourth century, was a model of motherly and wifely patience that turned her son, the brilliant scholar Augustine of Hippo, into one of the greatest of Christian teachers. Probably her name is a Carthaginian one, with no known explanation; it has been suggested, however, that it may cast back to the Greek word 'monos,' meaning 'alone,' or to the Latin 'moneo,' 'I advise,' though it was more by her example than by words of advice that St Monica set her son on the road to saintliness.

In the Prayer Book this name is given as *Monnica*.

There is an Irish name, *Moncha*, which means 'a nun,' and there was a Welsh saint named *Monacella*, better known as *Melangell*, meaning 'sweet angel,' whose plot of ground around her hermitage in Montgomeryshire was granted to her as a wild-life sanctuary—probably the first; either or both of these names may have been assimilated to Monica.

Perhaps the best-known Monica of to-day is the witty writer Monica Dickens, granddaughter of Charles Dickens.

MORNA Both *Morna* and *Myrna* come from the ancient Irish name *Muirne*, which means either 'beloved' or 'affection.' Neither has been popular until recently; but Myrna Loy, the Hollywood actress, has made the name known in the U.S.A. and, to a lesser extent, in this country. Morna Rawlins has the rare distinction among women of being a Fellow of the Royal Society of Medicine.

MURIEL is an ancient Celtic name derived from 'myr,' meaning 'sea,' though later it became a happy simplifying of the Old Irish name *Muirgheal*, which has the poetical meaning of 'sea-sheen.' Like several other names of Celtic origin, it reached this country at the time of the Norman Conquest; William the Conqueror brought with him a large contingent of Celts from Brittany. It had probably been in use long before the Norman invasion among the Celts in the north and west of Britain, and some of William's companions must certainly have been descendants of theirs.

Soon after 1100 the form *Meriel* was vying with Muriel, but both fell into disuse about Chaucer's time, and remained out of favour until the late nineteenth century, when a sudden revival made Muriel widespread again. This revival was at least partly due to the pathetic character called Muriel who features in *John Halifax, Gentleman,* a novel by Mrs Craik, published in 1856, which was tremendously popular.

To-day there are Muriel Robertson, F.R.S., a leading bacteriologist, and Muriel Spark, the novelist. Most Meriels are still growing up.

MYFANWY, also spelt *Myvanwy*, is a popular Welsh name which means 'my rare one.' It occurs in a Welsh poem of the fourteenth century, but is undoubtedly older.

Formerly it was often turned into the English *Fanny*, but nowadays it is more likely to be borrowed by the Sassenach than changed by the Cymry.

MYRA The earliest known reference to this name is in a poem by the Elizabethan poet Fulke Greville, Lord Brooke, who appears to have invented it. Until quite recent times it was a name almost exclusively reserved for poets (George Crabbe has several poems addressed to a Myra) and romantic novelists.

Mira, sometimes regarded as another version of Myra, is more probably a short form of *Miranda* or *Mirabel*. Readers of Shakespeare will recall the charming character Miranda in *The Tempest*. Though still used as a font name, Miranda, which comes from a Latin word meaning 'a girl to be admired,' is not nearly as common as it was four hundred years ago. Mirabel (Latin 'mirabilis,' 'wonderful') is even less common, as are its other forms, *Mirabella* and *Mirabelle*.

Undoubtedly the most celebrated Myra is Dame Myra Hess, the pianist. Another distinguished bearer of the name is Dame Myra Curtis, former Principal of Newnham College, Cam-bridge.

NAOMI is a Hebrew word meaning 'pleasant.' In the Book of Ruth, whose mother-in-law Naomi was, the story is told of how Naomi, with her family, left Bethlehem in Judah, on account of the famine there, and went to live in the land of Moab. Because of her sufferings she said, "Call me not Naomi ('pleasant'); call me Mara ('bitter')."

Naomi was first used in this country in the seventeenth century by the Puritans, who delighted in OldTestament names. It has been in regular, though not common, use ever since.

Among the most famous examples of modern times are the writers Naomi Jacob and Naomi Mitchison.

NICOLA Nic(h)ola, the feminine equivalent of Nic(h)olas, is derived from Greek and means 'people's victory.' The Greek word for victory, 'nike,' appears in other names still used today —for example, *Ber(e)nice,* 'bringer of victory.'

Nicola, the Italian form, has long been used in this country. In King John's reign, there was a Nicola de Camville, who heroically resisted the French invaders when they attacked Lincoln. But in modern times the French forms *Nicole, Nicolette,* and *Colette* are gaining in popularity in England. *Nicolle* has also been noted. The usual pet form is *Nicky.*

Nicolette is a name well known to the French through the medieval romance *Aucassin et Nicolette.* This tells of the love of *Aucassin* for the Saracen captive Nicolette, who is really the daughter of the King of Carthage. In spite of many obstacles, the lovers are finally united.

There is a French St Colette, a fifteenthcentury Franciscan nun; but in England the name, which is a feminine equivalent of Colin, is better known through the French writer of the present century who used her surname, Colette, as a penname: her real name was Sidonie Gabrielle Claudine Colette, and her most famous character is a Claudine.

NOELLE 'Noël' is, of course, the French for 'Christmas,' and both it and *Nowel(l)*—the old English form, now no longer used except in carols—have been given ever since the Middle Ages to children of both sexes born at Christmas time. Nowadays some parents prefer to have their daughters christened *Noelle*, the unmistakably feminine shape of the name.

Christmas was also sometimes used as a baptismal name, but this is now uncommon as a boys' name and practically unknown as a girls'.

Noël Streatfeild, the children's writer, uses the mainly masculine form, and the feminine form is borne by the actress *Noëlle* Adam.

Closely related in origin is *Natalia* or *Natalie*, which comes from the Latin 'natale (Domini),' signifying 'birthday (of the Lord).' This name is used not only for Christmas children, but also to commemorate St Natalia. Unlike most female saints, she was neither a spinster nor a widow, but was martyred together with her husband, St Adrian. It has long been a favourite name in Russia, where it developed the familiar form *Natasha*, heroine of Tolstoy's *War and Peace*, but in England it is not common. The Portuguese version, *Natal*, is identical with the name of the South African province, discovered by Vasco da Gama on Christmas Day.

NORA In England during the Middle Ages, this name was widely used, but in its original form, *Honoria*, sometimes shortened to *Honora* or *Honor*. It was from the second of these three that the usual present-day form developed. Honoria was the feminine form of the Latin 'honorius,' 'man of honour.'

Though by no means uncommon in England, Nora is essentially an Irish name. It was introduced into Ireland by the Anglo-Normans, and in its abbreviated forms *Nora* and

Norah, as well as in its diminutive form, *Noreen,* has been popular there for hundreds of years. *Onora* is yet another Irish variation. Yet the most famous *Nora* in drama is the heroine of *The Doll's House* by the Norwegian playwright Ibsen.

Leonora, the Italian version of the name *Eleanor,* has also contributed to some extent to the spread of Nora.

NORMA Derived from Latin, this name means 'rule' or 'pattern,' and seems to owe its use as a Christian name to an opera—Bellini's *Norma,* first performed in 1831. In it the titular heroine is a Druidic priestess secretly married to a Roman proconsul.

Norma is sometimes bestowed as the feminine equivalent of Norman.

The most famous Norma of recent times is the Hollywood actress Norma Shearer. The name has been more popular in the U.S.A. than in this country during this century.

OLGA is an ancient Russian name, though it is probably of Scandinavian origin. Rurik, the reputed founder of the Russian monarchy in the ninth century, is said to have been a Scandinavian adventurer. The Norse word 'helga,' meaning 'holy,' gave rise to the masculine name Oleg, from which the girls' name Olga was evolved. *Helga* itself remains a popular name in Scandinavian countries, and is occasionally used in England.

Within a century of Rurik's settling in Russia there was a St Olga. She was the wife of the Duke of Kiev; during a visit to Constantinople she was baptized, and, returning to Russia, spread the Christian religion until her death in 968.

Like several other Russian names, such as *Nadine* ('hope'), *Sonia* (p. 195), and *Vera* (p. 203), Olga became popular in England during the last century.

OLIVE Used in this country in the thirteenth century, the earliest recorded form of this name is *Oliva*, which suggests that it may have been coined as a feminine equivalent of Oliver. But it may equally have been regarded then, as now, as a plant-name, all the more attractive for being a symbol of peace.

Olive trees mature slowly, so that in ancient Greece, where olive-oil was used for soap, lamp-fuel, and cooking-oil, if an invader destroyed the olive trees the region was impoverished for up to twenty years. Only in times of lasting peace could the trees produce their precious fruit; hence the olive branch as a symbol of peace. Legend also links the olive branch with Noah and the dove—a symbol of God's reconciliation with man.

The ancient Greeks worshipped Pallas Athene, who, on naming Athens, presented it with its first olive tree. An olive garland was carried by Athenian brides, in the same way that nowadays brides carry orange-blossom; and successful competitors in the Olympic Games of old were awarded olive wreaths.

St Oliva, from her name, came to be regarded as the protectress of olive crops in Italy. Her name-day falls on June 3, the time of the olive harvest.

Well-established at the time of the Renaissance, Olive had by then developed a variety of forms, the commonest of which were *Oliff* and *Olivet*, the latter suggested, no doubt, by the hill of that name near Jerusalem.

As *Olivia*, the name became popular for a time through Shakespeare's *Twelfth Night*, and again in the eighteenth century, when Goldsmith used it for the eldest daughter of Dr Primrose in *The Vicar of Wakefield*. This form is now more popular in America than here. Olivia Langdon was the maiden name of Mark Twain's American wife, whom he

M

married in 1870; and Olivia de Havilland is a well-known actress.

Ollie and *Livvy* are the usual pet forms.

OLWEN The original bearer of this Welsh name, the literal meaning of which is 'white footprint,' was a giant's daughter, wooed by a prince named Culhwch (pronounced 'Keel-hook'). He was set fantastic tasks, that needed the help of King Arthur and all his knights to accomplish, before he gained the lady's hand. Her story is told in the collection of Celtic legends of Britain called the *Mabinogion*. In this work it is stated that Olwen was so named because "white trefoils sprang up wherever she trod."

The appearance of Lady Charlotte Guest's translation of the *Mabinogion* in 1849 made the name very popular among the Welsh, from whom the English have occasionally borrowed it in this century.

PAMELA This name, a combination of the Greek 'pan,' meaning 'all,' and 'meli,' meaning 'honey,' was coined by Sir Philip Sidney for one of the main characters in his romance *Arcadia*, written about 1580. But it was not until the appearance, 160 years later, of Samuel Richardson's novel *Pamela* that it began to be used as a Christian name. It has enjoyed its greatest popularity during the present century.

Pam is a pet form of this name, which was originally pronounced 'Pameela' with a long second syllable; but though this may be more correct, the short e pronunciation is now universal.

PATRICIA is, in origin, an aristocratic name, for it comes from the Latin word 'patricius,' meaning 'nobleman.' Patricia was much less common than Patrick, its masculine counter/part, and, strangely enough, did not even evolve in Ireland, but in Scotland in the eighteenth century. That the Scots should have the credit for evolving the name is perhaps only fair, for St Patrick, the patron saint of Ireland, was, after all, probably born near Dumbarton.

The general popularity of the name began with Queen Victoria's granddaughter, Princess Patricia of Connaught, affectionately known as Princess *Pat*, a pet form now some/times used as an independent name. Other pet forms are *Patsy*, *Patty*, *Paddy*, *Tric*, and *Tricia*.

Among well/known Patricias of to/day are Patricia Went/worth, creator of that engaging old/maid detective, Miss Silver; Pat Smythe, who has won awards for show jumping all over the world; and Patricia Lynch, the best/known Irish writer for children to/day.

PAULINE *Paula*, *Paulina*, and *Pauline* are obvious feminines of Paul, the name taken by Saul of Tarsus as a Roman citizen before he became St Paul the Apostle and writer of the 'Pauline' Epistles. Common among the Romans as Paulina, the name comes from a Latin word meaning 'small.'

There was a fourth/century saint named Paula; she drew her spiritual guidance from St Jerome, translator of the Bible into Latin, and followed him in 385 to the Holy Land, where, at Bethlehem, she founded four convents. It is possibly on her account that the name came into use in England in medieval times, though it was not widespread.

More popular in England have always been the French forms *Pauline* and *Paulette*. Pauline was the name of the sister of Napoleon who became the Princess Borghese; Paulette is borne by the Hollywood actress Paulette Goddard, who has given it a certain currency both in the U.S.A and in this country. *Paulet* is also occasionally found.

In literature there is a Pauline in *A Winter's Tale*, by Shakespeare; a Pauline in *The Fortunes of Nigel*, by Sir Walter Scott; and a Paula in *The Second Mrs Tanqueray*, by Arthur Pinero.

PEARL Like most jewel-names, Pearl dates from the later part of the nineteenth century. It is one of many which became popular about the same time; others include *Beryl* (see p. 55), *Ruby* (p. 191), *Amber*, *Crystal*, *Diamond*, *Opal*, and *Amethyst*.

Pearl is also sometimes used as a pet name for *Margaret*, the Greek for 'pearl' being 'margaretes.' Pearl itself has the pet form *Pearlie*.

Perhaps the best-known Pearl of to-day is Pearl Buck, the American writer whose early life was spent in China; her first-hand knowledge of that country is reflected in such books as *The Good Earth* (1931) and her autobiography, *My Several Worlds*.

In America (and, more recently, in England too) Pearl is used both as a boys' and as a girls' name, as are *Marion*, *Lee*, *Beverl(e)y*, and *Lindsay*.

PENELOPE This was the name of the wife of Ulysses, ruler of Ithaca, who left his island to take part in the Trojan War. During his ten years' absence Penelope was pestered by many suitors, all of whom tried to persuade her that Ulysses would never return. Sure that he would, she told them that she would not remarry till she had completed the tapestry she was weaving. Every night she unravelled what she had woven during the day, and so deferred having to make a choice. Meanwhile the suitors had taken up residence in her palace, where they held riotous parties. When Ulysses finally did return he slew them and ruled Ithaca again with Queen Penelope.

The supposed origin of this name is the Greek word 'pene,' meaning 'a bobbin'; but William Camden, writing in the sixteenth century, suggests that the name was given to her, "for that she carefully loved and fed those birds with purpure necks, called Penelopes."

Not used before Camden's time as a Christian name in England, Penelope became widespread during the following century, when it developed the pet form *Pen*; this and *Penny* are the common pet forms used nowadays.

The name has long been known in Ireland, where it is taken as the equivalent of the native name *Fenella*. Also, according to old Welsh tales, it was a fairy name; gipsies use it in the form *Peneli*.

PHILIPPA A Greek name, Philippa means 'lover of horses,' like its masculine counterpart, Philip.

In 1328 Edward III married Philippa of Hainault, and it was she who gave the name its early vogue in England. Geoffrey Chaucer's wife was Philippa Roet of Hainault, a demoiselle of the Queen's chamber and, possibly, one of her goddaughters.

Records of the Middle Ages usually entered the name as Philippa, but its bearers were nearly always called *Philip*; Henry IV's daughter was known as Dame *Phelypp*.

The pet forms of Philippa are *Phil* and *Pippa*, the latter borrowed from Italian and familiar through Robert Browning's poem *Pippa Passes*, which ends with those supremely confident lines:

> God's in his heaven,
> All's right with the world.

PHOEBE, 'the shining one,' was one of the titles given by the ancient Greeks to the goddess of the moon, who was also known to them as *Cynthia*, *Selene*, and *Artemis*, and to the Romans as *Diana*. She was the female counterpart of Phoebus, the sun-god, and, according to ancient legend, was a Titaness, daughter of Heaven and Earth.

The earliest known historical reference to a Phoebe is in chapter xvi of St Paul's Epistle to the Romans (Authorized Version), where she is described as "a servant of the church that is at Cenchrea." It is not found as a Christian name in England until the sixteenth century, when it occurs also as *Phebe*, the form used in the Revised Version. In Shakespeare's *As You like It* there is a shepherdess of that name, beloved by the shepherd Silvius.

In Brighton during the Regency everybody knew of Phoebe Hessel. At the age of fifteen, she fell in love with a soldier and, in order to be near him, put on a soldier's uniform, enlisted, and followed him to the West Indies. When he died she went to live at Brighton, where she married a fisherman named Hessel. She died in Brighton in 1821 at the age of 108.

In J. M. Barrie's *Quality Street*, Phoebe Throssel is the heroine, known otherwise as "Phoebe of the ringlets."

Although not common since the seventeenth century, Phoebe, correctly pronounced 'fee-bee,' has remained in regular use.

PHYLLIS From the Greek 'phyllis' (genitive 'phyllidis'), meaning 'a green branch,' come the names *Phyllis* and *Phyllida*. The original bearer was an unfortunate girl who died for love and was changed, as Greek maidens in difficulties so often seem to have been, into a tree: in her case an almond tree.

It was a popular name in classical poetry, particularly for

country girls, and was used in this way by Virgil in his *Eclogues*. English poets from the Renaissance onwards adopted the name, sometimes also as *Phillis* and *Phillida*, in pastoral and lyric poems, imitated from Greek and Roman poetry, and in the sixteenth century it began to be used as a baptismal name.

Spenser speaks of "Phyllis, Charillis, and sweet Amaryllis . . ."—all type-names for rustic maidens—and William Drummond of Hawthornden, an early seventeenth-century Scottish poet, typifies in the following lines the settings in which nearly every Phyllis and Phyllida of that time were described:

> In petticoat of green
> With hair about her een [eyes],
> Phillis, beneath an oak,
> Sat milking her fair flock:
> 'Mongst that sweet-strained moisture (rare delight)
> Her hand seemed milk, in milk it was so white.

The name became so closely identified with country lasses of this kind, that by the eighteenth century it virtually ceased to be used as a font name. Its loss of favour continued through the greater part of the nineteenth century, but it was then revived, having meanwhile lost its rustic associations, and is now widespread, with the pet form *Phil*.

PRISCILLA Both *Prisca* and its diminutive form, *Priscilla*, are New-Testament names, appearing in chapter xviii of Acts and in St Paul's Second Epistle to Timothy.

In this country both names, which are derived from the Latin word 'priscus,' meaning 'ancient,' were adopted by the Puritans, who made use of many of the feminine names in the

New Testament. Nowadays Priscilla is not often met with, still less frequent is Prisca, but both forms are still in regular use in some families.

In literature Priscilla is the heroine of Longfellow's *Court-ship of Miles Standish*, and the name of a pretty little seamstress in Hawthorne's *Blithedale Romance*.

The pet forms are *Pris* and *Prissy*.

PRUDENCE This was one of the first 'abstract-virtue' names to be adopted by the Puritans, in the late sixteenth century. It was, however, in use long before then; Chaucer, for instance, speaks of a Mistress Prudence in his *Tale of Melibeus*, and other examples of it are found in records of the thirteenth century.

The most famous of all the 'abstract-virtue' names are, of course, *Faith*, *Hope*, and *Charity* (see pp. 106, 125, and 68), but there were many others in widespread use among the austere Puritans, such as *Abstinence*, *Temperance*, *Silence*, and *Obedience*. Few have survived; Prudence is one which has.

The usual pet forms of Prudence are *Pru*, *Prue*, *Prudie*, and *Prudy*. Herrick spells the name *Prewdence*, and refers to his maid called *Prew*.

QUEENIE, sometimes given as an independent name, is also a nickname for girls christened *Regina*.

Regina, the Latin word for 'queen,' was first used as a Christian name in this country in the Middle Ages, probably in reference to the Virgin Mary, "Queen of Heaven." In France it was given its native form, *Reine*, also found occasion-ally as a baptismal name in England; while in Germany Regina tended to be confused with the much older Germanic name *Ragin*, meaning 'advice.'

The nickname Queenie was also given to girls christened *Victoria* during the long reign of that Queen. In the present century the number of Queenies has diminished as this association has grown dimmer in people's minds.

In the U.S.A. the variant *Queena* is sometimes used.

RACHEL is a Hebrew name meaning 'ewe'—a symbol of innocence and gentleness. The Book of Genesis tells how Jacob served seven years for Rachel, younger sister of Leah, "and they seemed unto him but a few days, for the love he had to her."

Because of this Old-Testament story, Rachel became a very popular name among the Jews from very early times; but otherwise it was not used—in this country, at any rate—until the Puritans adopted it after the Reformation. Since the seventeenth century it has never gone out of use, though it has been infrequent during the last 150 years or so.

In the last century the name was known to theatregoers on both sides of the Channel on account of Mademoiselle Rachel, the great Swiss-Jewish actress celebrated for her tragic rôles. In literature it was something of a favourite name in the nineteenth century, and was borne by characters in Thackeray, Trollope, etc., as well as figuring in the poetry of the period—for instance, in the following lines by John Clare:

> O Rachel is fair as the dew pearls o' morning,
> And Rachel is sweet as the buds of sweet brere,
> Her dark jetty curls o'er her eyelashes dawning,
> The moss on the rose is nothing so dear.

The modern pet forms are *Rae*, or *Ray* (shared with *Raymonde*), and *Rachie*. The Gaelic equivalent is *Raonaid*.

REBECCA Originally this name was pronounced *Ribkah*, which in Hebrew means 'a knotted cord'; but just as a knotted cord should hold firm, so the name came to be interpreted as 'a faithful wife.'

The earliest bearer, noted for her great beauty, was the wife of Isaac and mother of Jacob and Esau. In the Authorized Version of the Bible her name is spelt *Rebekah*—a form still sometimes met with, though far less commonly now than in the seventeenth century, when the Puritans made it one of their favourite names. Through them it reached the New World. The American-Indian princess, Pocahontas, who lived in the early days of New England, adopted it at her baptism, which took place at Gravesend.

The two outstanding bearers of the name in literature are the beautiful Jewess in Scott's romance *Ivanhoe*, and the unprincipled Rebecca ('Becky') Sharp in Thackeray's *Vanity Fair*. Less usual pet forms than *Becky* are *Reba* and *Rebe*.

Another fictional Rebecca is the heroine of Ibsen's drama *Rosmersholm*, Rebecca West; to-day this name is much more famous as the pen-name of Cecily Isabel Fairfield, who had acted the part as a young woman and then adopted it when she became a novelist.

Rebecca is a well-known novel by Daphne du Maurier. The film of this book was made in Spain, where the word is still used to denote a woman's long-sleeved cardigan, like the one worn in the film by Joan Fontaine, who played the major rôle.

ROSALIND This name really has two histories: in its oldest known form, *Roslindis*, the meaning was 'horse-serpent,' a combination of two ancient German words. When, many hundreds of years ago, the Teuton hordes swept through Spain the name was adopted there, and at this point it more or less became an entirely new name, though similar in form, for to the Spaniards it was a combination of two different words—'rosa,' 'rose,' and 'linda,' 'pretty.' It is in the latter sense that Rosalind is universally interpreted nowadays.

Reaching England in the time of Elizabeth I, it quickly gained favour, especially after Shakespeare had written *As You like It*, in which the banished Duke's daughter is called Rosalind. Shakespeare used another version, *Rosaline*, in *Love's Labour's Lost* and in *Romeo and Juliet*.

Other forms of the name which have developed since then include *Rosalyne*, *Roseline*, and *Rhodalind*; but none of these, nor the Spanish form, *Rosalinda*, is nearly as common in England as Rosalind.

ROSAMUND Like Rosalind, this name has a surprising meaning, if traced back to its source: in Old German it meant 'horse-protection.' But it has long been more commonly associated with the Latin 'rosa munda,' 'pure rose,' or with 'rosa mundi,' Latin for 'rose of the world.' These meanings were attributed to it in the Middle Ages, when Latin was the language of scholars; this is probably why it survived the Renaissance, when Germanic names went largely out of favour. *Rosamond* is another form popular in England to-day.

The first historical bearer, known as *Rosmunda* or *Rosmonda*, was a daughter of Cunimond, warrior of a tribe called the Gepidae, who inhabited the Jura region. She lived in the sixth century A.D., but the name is undoubtedly older.

The first known English bearer was Rosamund Clifford, known as "Fair Rosamund," for whom Henry II built a house in the middle of a maze (so the story goes) so that "no man or woman might come to her"; the King thought that he alone might find the way to the house, but somehow his jealous wife, Elinor, found her way there too, and poisoned the Fair Rosamund.

She died about 1176, by which date the name had already been in use for over a hundred years among the Normans. It has never gone entirely out of use, and is nowadays among the commonest of the 'Rose' names.

ROSE The name Rose is used in nearly every country where roses grow, and is among the most popular of all flower-names. It is curious to note, therefore, that, in common with *Rosalind* and *Rosamund*, its original meaning was not 'rose' but 'horse'! Rose derives ultimately from the ancient German word 'hros.' The early Germanic tribes regarded the horse as a sacred animal, and worshipped it in its personified form, Hros, a god represented as a three-legged horse. The leaders of the first band of Teutonic invaders to Britain were named Hengist and Horsa, both of which mean 'horse.' The Anglo-Saxons, and also the Celts, held the horse in reverence; they put horse-figures on their coins and carved them on the chalk hillsides.

All these associations, however, belong to the remote past, and it is as a flower-name that Rose has survived and flourished. There is no doubt that the Greek form of the name, *Rhoda*, can mean nothing but 'rose,' just as Rhodes is the Island of Roses. The first Rhoda, mentioned in Acts, xii, 13, was the maid who answered the door to St Peter after he had escaped from Herod's prison.

Like Rosamund, Rose was brought over to this country by the Normans in the eleventh century, and it quickly took root here in various forms, which within a few generations settled down in the shape Rose. In the course of time other varieties evolved, such as *Rosalba* ('white rose'), *Rosetta* and *Rosette* ('little rose'), *Rosabel*, *Rosabella*, and *Rosabelle* ('beautiful rose'), and *Rosalie*. The Spanish *Rosita* and the Italian *Rosina* were also used in England, while the Latin form, *Rosa*, became popular here in Victorian times, together with the compound names *Rosanna* and *Rosanne*. The pet form of all these, as well as of *Rosalind*, *Rosamund*, and *Rosemary*, is *Rosie*.

Rosaleen, the Irish form, is sometimes used in this country too; the true Irish form is *Rois*, the pet form of which is *Roisin*.

Another form of the name is shown by St *Rosalia*, who lived in Palermo in the twelfth century. According to legend, she was carried by angels to the top of a mountain, where she spent her life on her knees, praying. After her death it was found that she had worn away part of the rock by her devotions, and the local inhabitants had a chapel erected there to commemorate her.

St Rose of Lima (capital of Peru) was born in 1586—the first saint born on American soil. Her real name was *Isabella*, but she was later called Rose. She sold the bouquets she made to help support her poverty-stricken family. After her death her name spread throughout the Spanish-speaking world, particularly in the pet form *Rosita*.

In literature there is a Rosa in Dickens's *Bleak House* and in his *Edwin Drood*, Rose Bradwardine in Scott's *Waverley*, Rhoda Fleming in the novel of that name by George Meredith (her sister's name was *Dahlia*, a far less common flower-name), and many others. Twentieth-century examples include Rose Macaulay, the novelist, and Rose Heilbron, Q.C.

The celebrated poem *Rose Aylmer*, by Walter Savage Landor was written in memory of a companion of his by that name, who had often accompanied him on his walks about Swansea, and who died in India in 1800:

> Rose Aylmer, whom these wakeful eyes
> May weep but never see,
> A night of memories and sighs
> I consecrate to thee.

Rosie is popular in American ballads, often represented as a source of torment and longing. Such a ballad is *I seen Little Rosie in my Midnight Dreams*:

> . . . Sometimes I plough the old grey mare,
> And then I plough the cuddy [donkey];
> When I make my fifteen cents, Lawd,
> I carry it home to Rosie.

ROSEMARY is sometimes bestowed as a combination of *Rose* and *Mary*, and sometimes as a plant-name.

The plant rosemary derives its name from the Latin words 'ros,' 'dew,' and 'marinus,' 'of the sea,' in allusion to the place where it naturally grows and to its greyish appearance. In olden times it was used as a medicine, and was believed to refresh the memory. Ophelia, in *Hamlet*, says: "There's Rosemary, that's for remembrance; pray, love, remember."

As a personal name, Rosemary is modern. The French form, *Rosemarie*, is also sometimes given in this country.

ROWENA This name, in spite of Sir Walter Scott, who gave it to his Saxon heroine in *Ivanhoe*, is Celtic; it seems originally to have been *Rhonwen*, which means 'slender (literally, 'lance') fair.'

The first celebrated bearer was the legendary daughter of the Jutish ruler Hengist and wife of the fifth-century British chief Vortigern. It was little used, however, until the appearance, in 1819, of *Ivanhoe*. Other related forms of the name are *Rhona* and *Rona*.

RUBY is one of the several jewel-names which became popular during the nineteenth century (see *Pearl*, p. 180). In the north of England and Scotland, however, it was long used as a pet form of *Roberta*, *Robina*, and *Ruperta*, feminine forms of Robert, meaning 'bright fame'; Ruby is nowadays found there as an independent name more often than any of these.

In the old English hunting song *John Peel* one of the hounds is called Ruby—perhaps the earliest record of Ruby being used as a name.

Ruby M. Ayres, the popular novelist, was born in 1883, when the name was very much in vogue.

The Latinized form, *Rubina*, is occasionally bestowed.

RUTH is the heroine of one of the most vivid Old-Testament stories, in the book named after her. It is a story of simple faith and love, finally rewarded by her marriage to Boaz, a leading citizen of the little town of Bethlehem in Judah, where she became the ancestress of King David and of Jesus. Her name can be interpreted as meaning either 'vision of beauty' or 'friend.'

When first used in this country, just after the Reformation, it was probably adopted less for its biblical associations than as an 'abstract-virtue' name, the word 'ruth' then being in common usage with the meaning of pity or sorrow. Though it has never regained the same popularity it enjoyed throughout the seventeenth century, it is still in steady use, occasionally with the pet form *Ruthie*.

Modern bearers include Ruth Draper, the American character impersonator; Ruth Fry, a tireless worker for world peace; Ruth Pitter, the poet; and Ruth Williams, the English girl who married the African chief Seretse Khama.

SARAH Abraham's wife was first called *Sarai*, 'the quarrel-some,' but by divine decree this was changed to Sarah, 'the princess.'

St *Sara* was the legendary handmaid of Sts Mary Magdalene and Martha (see p. 156). Her supposed tomb in Provence, at Les Saintes Marie, is visited by thousands of gipsies, who regard her as one of their race, every July, when they ride their horses into the sea.

The name was occasionally used in medieval times, but was never popular before the Reformation, when Old-Testament names largely took the place of saints' names. In the seventeenth and eighteenth centuries it was among the commonest of girls' names, and had already by then developed the pet form *Sally*, sometimes shortened to *Sal*. In America, especially, another form, *Sadie*, is found, though this is also a pet form of the Roman-Catholic name *Mercedes* (see p. 82).

Sara and its diminutive *Sarita* are variants of Sarah, and *Saranna*, a combination of Sara(h) and Anna, was in vogue in the eighteenth century.

In Ireland the native names *Sorcha*, meaning 'bright,' and *Saraid*, 'excellent,' have, to a large extent, been superseded by Sarah. The Gaelic form of Sarah, *Morag*, is extremely popular in Scotland.

The two most famous bearers are, perhaps, Sarah Siddons and Sarah Bernhardt, both leading actresses of their day. Sarah Siddons was known as "the tragic muse," partly because of her Shakespearean rôles, and partly on account of the portrait of her by Sir Joshua Reynolds so named. Sarah Bernhardt was also noted for her tragic rôles on the French stage—and for the pets she used to take around with her, which included a cheetah, a wolfhound, and, chained to her shoulder, a chameleon!

In literature too there are several famous Sarahs. Readers of Lamb will recall Sarah Battle, who regarded whist as the business of life and literature as one of its relaxations. Dickens's novel *Martin Chuzzlewit* contains one of his most comic characters, Sarah Gamp, famous for her bulky umbrella and her constant references to Mrs Harris, who exists only in her mind but who, conveniently, always confirms her opinions. Incidentally, she was known as *Sairey* Gamp, a pronunciation of the name which in the seventeenth century was normal. The best-known Sally is the one described in the popular eighteenth-century ballad *Sally in Our Alley*, by Henry Carey:

> Of all the girls that are so smart
> There's none like pretty Sally;
> She is the darling of my heart,
> And she lives in our alley.

A real-life Sally was Sally Lunn, who lived about 1800 at Bath, where she sold the tea-cakes named after her.

SELINA 'Selene,' the Greek word for 'moon,' was a title sometimes given to the moon-goddess Artemis, also known to the Greeks as *Cynthia* or *Phoebe*, and to the Romans as *Diana*. It is not unlikely that the similar-sounding, and commoner, name Selina developed from *Selene*. There is, however, another theory as to its origin. In the Middle Ages there was a girls' name *Ascelina*—possibly the feminine of the then common Askell—and this name, pronounced 'Asseleena,' may, by losing its first syllable, have given us *Selina* or *Celina*. Celina is found in medieval documents, and some say that this may have been taken from the French name *Céline*, with which the English *Celia*, common in England about 1600, is closely connected.

N

Celina is still sometimes bestowed as a font name; other versions are *Selena* and *Sillina*.

SHEILA In Ireland this name may be spelt in a variety of ways—*Sheelah, Sheilah, Shelagh, Sheelagh*—but in England it is most commonly found as Sheila.

All these forms are probably derived from two Old Irish names, *Sighile* and *Sile*, which in turn are phonetic renderings of *Cecilia* and *Celia*, both introduced into Ireland by the Anglo-Normans.

To Australians a sheila is simply a girl or woman.

SHIRLEY As a place-name, Shirley means 'shire meadow,' and from it developed the surname, not uncommon in Yorkshire.

The name was already in use, in Yorkshire, at any rate, before 1850 as a boys' name, but there are no records of it as a girls' name until the Yorkshire novelist Charlotte Brontë used it in her novel *Shirley* (1849). The heroine, Shirley Keeldar, is modelled on Charlotte's sister Emily.

By the turn of the century Shirley had spread beyond Yorkshire, and is now a common name everywhere. Another part of the world where it frequently occurs is in the Southern States of the U.S.A., home of Shirley Temple, the child film star of the thirties, who gave the name a vogue not only in America, but also in this country.

Shirl is a widely used pet form.

SIBYL In ancient Greece and Rome Sibyl was a title rather than a name; the Sibyls were women who claimed to be able to interpret the wishes of the gods through their oracles. Virgil describes how the Cumaean Sibyl helped Aeneas to reach the

Underworld to see the spirit of his father, by means of a Golden Bough. Livy relates the story of the Sibyl who offered precious books of prophecy to King Tarquin, foretelling the future of Rome; each time he refused them she returned with fewer, at a higher price, until his curiosity got the better of him and he bought the three which remained. These Sybilline Books were treasured for long afterwards (till they were destroyed in a fire) and were consulted in times of national emergency. Some of their predictions alluded to the coming of a wonderful child who would change the face of the world. Consequently the Sibyls came to be regarded as pagan prophetesses of Christ, and seven of them are depicted by Michelangelo on the ceiling of the Sistine Chapel in Rome.

As a Christian name, Sibyl was brought over to England by the Normans, and quickly gained in popularity. Several forms then in use have survived, among them *Sybil*—still a common spelling—*Sibylla*, *Sibyllina*, *Sibille*, and *Sibley*, a form still found in Scotland. The pet forms are *Sib* and *Sibbie*. Sibyl has been used as a substitute for the Gaelic name *Selbh-flaith*, meaning 'wealthy woman.'

Benjamin Disraeli wrote an important political novel en-titled *Sybil*, which increased the popularity of the name in Victorian times. Among the Sybils of this century are: Dame Sybil Thorndike, one of our greatest actresses; Sybil Campbell, one of the first women called to the Bar; and Sibyl Hathaway, Dame of Sark.

SONIA is the Russian form of *Sophia*; it was not used in England as a personal name before this century, but is now quite common.

Among the best-known bearers of the name are Sonia Dresdel, the actress, and *Sonja* Henie, from Norway, who skated her way to victory in the 1928, 1932, and 1936 Olympic Games.

Another version is *Sonya*.

SOPHIA 'Sophia' is the Greek word for 'wisdom' and, according to the *Book of Wisdom*, "the mother of fair love and of holy hope." St Sophia was the mother of three daughters named *Faith*, *Hope*, and *Charity* (see pp. 106, 125, 68).

When the Emperor Justinian dedicated his great cathedral in Constantinople to 'Hagia Sophia' in the sixth century it was probably to Divine Wisdom rather than to the early Christian martyr. This magnificent building, a mosque from 1453 till 1935, when it became a museum, still stands in all the glory of its mosaic domes.

Because Constantinople was in those early days the centre of culture, the name naturally became a favourite one in the East, where it was often bestowed on members of royal families. From there it reached Germany, probably by way of Hungary, and when George I inaugurated the Hanoverian dynasty in England in 1714 it became familiar here, at first chiefly in aristocratic circles, then generally. It was the name both of his mother and his wife.

Popular throughout the eighteenth century, together with its pet form *Sophy*, or *Sophie*, the name continued to be used until about the middle of the last century, when its popularity waned; since then it has never regained the same degree of favour.

The film star Sophia Loren, and Sophie Tucker, the original "red-hot mama," are well-known examples of modern times.

A near relative, still occasionally found, is *Sophronia* (Greek, 'prudence'), which dates back to at least the fourteenth century, for it is the name borne by one of Boccaccio's heroines in his *Decameron*.

There is an odd epitaph in Old Brighton churchyard, to a Miss Church:

> This Church, she perished by the fire,
> Her Christian name it was Sophier.
> Likewise her sister Mary Ann:
> Their father was a fisherman.

STELLA 'Stella' is the Latin for 'star,' and Catholics have long associated this name with 'Stella Maris,' 'Star of the Sea,' a title of invocation of the Blessed Virgin Mary.

Esther Johnson and Esther Vanhomrigh, friends of Jonathan Swift, were renamed by him *Stella* and *Vanessa*. In the first case he gave the Latin equivalent of *Esther*, which means 'star' in Persian; in the second, he took the first three letters of the surname and added *Essa*, a pet form of Esther.

In 1718 Swift addressed these lines to Miss Johnson on her birthday:

> Stella this day is thirty-four
> (We shan't dispute a year or more):
> However, Stella, be not troubled,
> Although thy size and years are doubled
> Since first I saw thee at sixteen,
> The brightest virgin on the green. . . .

Vanessa was Swift's own creation, but the name Stella had already been coined, about 1590, by Sir Philip Sidney, who wooed Lady Penelope Devereux with a collection of sonnets and songs entitled *Astrophel and Stella*. Both Stella and Vanessa are now established font names, and the latter has given its name to the Red Admiral genus of butterflies.

Other forms of Stella are *Estelle* and *Estella*. In Dickens's *Great Expectations* Pip, the hero, falls in love with Estella

Havisham, but this proud, self-possessed young lady rejects him in favour of Bentley Drummle, who ill-treats her, but dies, and she then turns again to Pip, who sees "no shadow of another parting from her."

Stella, Dowager Marchioness of Reading, was created one of the first four life peeresses, in 1958.

SUSAN The Persian city of Shushan, frequently mentioned in the Books of Daniel and Esther, was the City of White Lilies, and the word 'shushannah' in Hebrew signifies 'lily.' As a personal name it occurs, in the form *Susanna*, in St Luke's Gospel, viii, 3. Much older is the History of Susanna (originally part of the Book of Daniel, but rejected by translators as spurious), in which the story is told of how the Elders surprised Susanna in her bath.

When the name first came to be used in England, in the Middle Ages, it was usually found in the form *Susanna* or *Susannah*; but it was not much favoured till after the Reformation. Shakespeare bestowed it on his younger daughter.

Its greatest popularity was in the eighteenth century, and it was still widespread during Victorian times, when the longer forms were being replaced more and more by Susan. *Sue* and *Susie* are its usual pet forms nowadays, but a couple of hundred years ago the commoner pet forms were *Suke*, *Sukey*, and *Suky*.

In this century the French forms *Suzanne* and *Suzette*—as in those delicious wafer-thin pancakes, crêpes Suzette—have often been given in this country.

Two famous novelists bear the name—Susan Ferrier, a friend and compatriot of Sir Walter Scott, and Susan Coolidge, an American best remembered for her books on and for girls, such as *What Katy Did*; she was born in 1845, just four years before the Californian gold rush, when Stephen Foster's song *Oh! Susannah* was tremendously popular.

SYLVIA, sometimes spelt *Silvia*, is a name of Latin origin, meaning 'wood-dweller,' and is the equivalent of the boys' names Silas, Sylvester, and Silvanus.

Rhea Silvia was the mother of Romulus and Remus who founded Rome. Having become a popular name in Italy during the Renaissance, Sylvia became widespread in England after the appearance of Shakespeare's *Two Gentlemen of Verona*, in which Silvia is the beloved of Valentine, one of the two Gentlemen; it is in this play that the famous lines, set to music by Schubert, occur:

> Who is Silvia? what is she,
>   That all our swains commend her?
> Holy, fair and wise is she;
>   The heaven such grace did lend her,
> That she might admired be.

After Shakespeare's time Sylvia was in frequent use among pastoral poets as the typical name of a woodland maid.

Sylvia Pankhurst was a pioneer for women's rights early in this century. In fiction, there is Lewis Carroll's *Sylvie and Bruno* (showing the pet form), which, though far inferior to *Alice in Wonderland*, contains some of his most amusing and ingenious verses.

TERESA This is a name of uncertain origin; it may be derived from a Greek word meaning 'reaper,' or it may mean 'a woman from Therasia'—the name of two islands off the coast of Greece.

It seems first to have been used in Spain, as early as the sixth century, when a lady of this name corresponded with St Jerome, the translator of the Bible into Latin. It continued to be used exclusively in Spain until the sixteenth century, when the Spanish St *Theresia*, or *Teresa*, of Avila made it famous throughout the Roman-Catholic world.

This saint was a Carmelite nun, celebrated for her visions, her organizing ability, and for the two books she wrote, *The Way of Perfection*, and *The Castle of the Soul*, both of which were published in 1587, five years after her death.

Protestant England was slow to adopt the name, and it was little in evidence until about the middle of the eighteenth century. Having established itself, it borrowed from other countries a variety of forms, including the Latin *Theresia*, the German *Theresa*, the Italian and Spanish *Teresa*, and the French *Thérèse*. A typically English variant is *Tracey* or *Tracy*. The early English pet forms *Tess* and *Tessa* have now become names in their own right; *Terry* is another pet form. In Ireland, the old name *Treasa*, meaning 'strength,' was adopted as the equivalent of the English name.

One of the outstanding political figures of the eighteenth century was the Empress Maria Theres(i)a, Archduchess of Austria and Queen of Hungary and Bohemia. Marie-Antoinette was one of her many children.

The popularity of the name was enhanced through St Thérèse of Lisieux (a town in Normandy), who died in 1897 at the age of twenty-four. Like her Spanish namesake, she entered a Carmelite convent. Normally one is not received into a Carmel until the age of twenty-one, but she had asked Pope Leo XIII to allow her to do so at the age of fifteen in honour of his Jubilee, and he agreed. Known as "the little flower," she was canonized in 1925.

The most celebrated representative in fiction is the tragic

titular heroine of Thomas Hardy's novel *Tess of the D'Urbervilles*.

THELMA Like *Mavis* (see p. 168), Thelma is an invention of Marie Corelli's; it is the name of the titular heroine of her novel *Thelma, A Norwegian Princess*, which appeared in 1887. The choice of this name may have been influenced by the Greek word 'thelema,' which means 'will.'

It very quickly became a popular girls' name in this country, some pronouncing it 'Thelma' and others 'Telma,' and it is still not uncommon.

UNA The origin of this old Irish name is obscure, though it may be associated with the Irish word 'uan,' meaning 'a lamb.' The true Irish form is *Oonagh* or *Oona*, as in the name of Charles Chaplin's wife; another Irish form is *Juno*, famous through Sean O'Casey's play *Juno and the Paycock*, dealing with the poor of Dublin. There is apparently no real connexion between the Irish name Juno and Juno, wife of Jupiter and Queen of heaven in Roman mythology. The name Una is still in use in Ireland, though it is sometimes anglicized as *Winnie* or *Winifred*.

Edmund Spenser is responsible for another, entirely different interpretation of the name. In his *Faërie Queene*, Una (Latin for 'the One') is the symbol of Truth, in contrast to the double-dealing *Duessa*. It is on Una's behalf that St George, the Red Cross Knight, slays the dragon.

Closely related is the name *Unity*, an 'abstract-virtue' name which became popular, together with many other such names, at the time of the Reformation.

A popular Una in fiction appears in Rudyard Kipling's *Puck of Pook's Hill*; the children Dan and Una are taken by Puck through a series of adventures, meeting historical persons, and listening to their stories.

Distinguished bearers of the name to-day include Una Silberrad, the writer; Una Ellis-Fermor, Professor of English at London University; and Una Ledingham, Fellow of the Royal College of Physicians.

URSULA is derived from a Latin word meaning 'little she-bear.' The first known Ursula is said to have been a fifth-century Cornish princess, sent off to marry a chieftain on the Continent; but, according to legend, she was shipwrecked and shot to death with arrows at Cologne, together with 11,000 companions! To explain this obvious impossibility, it has been suggested that an entry in the old list of saints in which she is first mentioned for her name-day, October 21, "S. Ursula et XI M.," intended to mean 'St Ursula and Eleven Martyrs,' was misinterpreted as 'St Ursula and Eleven Thousand (Martyrs),' M being the Roman symbol for 1000.

At Bruges is preserved a beautiful coffer, said to contain some relics of the saint and painted by Jan van Eyck with scenes of her life and martyrdom. There is also to-day an Order of teaching nuns, the Ursulines, named after her.

Because of the legend attaching to St Ursula, the name was quite commonly bestowed in medieval times, also as *Ursa* and *Ursel*, and it has continued to be used, though not so frequently, ever since. It occurs once in Shakespeare—in *Much Ado about Nothing*, where Ursula is a gentlewoman attending on Leonato's daughter, Hero. In the eighteenth century it was commonly pronounced, and sometimes spelt, *Usly*.

Ursula March is the heroine of Mrs Craik's immensely popular novel *John Halifax, Gentleman*. Because of this book, written just over a hundred years ago, the then obsolescent names Ursula and Muriel (another important character) were revived as font names. Dame Ursula Suddlechop is a milliner and secret agent in Scott's *Fortunes of Nigel*.

The usual pet forms are *Urse* and *Ursie*. *Ursulina* is a variant.

Famous Ursulas of to-day include Ursula Bloom, the author, whose first book, *Tiger*, was published privately when she was just seven years old.

VALERIE This name comes from the Latin family-name of the Valerian clan, itself probably derived from the word 'valere,' 'to be in good health.' Its members were so distin-guished for their public services that special seats were per-manently reserved for them at the Colosseum at Rome.

The Latin shape of the name is seen in St *Valeria*, mother of two martyr sons, Gervase and Protase, who lived in the first century; and two French towns bear her name, Sainte-*Valérie*. But the introduction of the name into England, nearly always in the French-derived form Valerie, seldom as *Valery*, only dates from the late nineteenth century.

Valentine, meaning much the same as Valerie, is really a boys' name, but is occasionally given to girls, especially those born on St Valentine's Day, February 14. *Valentina* is an exclusively feminine version.

Val is the usual pet form of both names.

VERA Though it has come to be associated with the Latin word for 'true' or 'sincere,' Vera is, in fact, derived from the Russian word 'viera,' meaning 'faith.' It has long been used in Russia as a Christian name, but in this country it was un-known until about a hundred years ago. It became popular at much the same time as a number of other Russian names, including *Olga*, *Nadine*, and *Sonia*.

In Gaelic the name is rendered by *Eamhair*.

During this century it has distinguished itself through several well-known bearers—for instance, Dame Vera Laughton Mathews, war-time head of the Women's Royal Naval Service (the "Wrens"); Dame Vera Anstey, the economist; and Vera Lynn, the singer.

VERONICA Legend tells how, when Our Lord was carrying His cross to Calvary, a woman stepped out of the crowd with a handkerchief and, pushing through the guards, wiped His bruised and bleeding face. When she looked at the cloth afterwards, she found that the marks upon it showed a true image of the face of Jesus. Her name is not known, but from this story she came to be known as St Veronica (late Latin 'veraiconica,' 'of a true image'), with a special day, February 4, to commemorate her. She is the patron saint of photographers.

Both the speedwell flower and a garden shrub have *Veronica* as their botanical name, as imaging the blue of the sky.

As a given name, Veronica has long been popular on the Continent, particularly in France in the form *Véronique*, and reached Scotland in the seventeenth century, since when it has been in fairly steady use there. In England, however, there are very few examples occurring before the late nineteenth century. In America, the name was made famous by the Hollywood film star Veronica Lake.

The usual pet form is *Nicky*. *Ronky* has also been noted.

VICTORIA is the Latin word for 'victory.' St Victoria was a third-century Roman martyr, put to death for refusing to marry a pagan suitor and worship his pagan gods. From her comes the Italian form, as in Vittoria Colonna, a famous beauty of the Italian Renaissance, and *Vittoria*, the name of the flagship of Magellan, first to sail round Cape Horn.

But to the British the name will always be principally associated with Queen Victoria, its first well-known bearer in this country. She was christened Alexandrina Victoria, the Tsar Alexander I of Russia being her godfather, and Victoria, daughter of the Duke of Saxe-Coburg, her mother.

Innumerable things have been called after her, such as an Australian State, a light carriage, a giant water-lily (*Victoria regia*), the Victoria Cross—the highest military award for valour—a large red plum, a minor planet, a pigeon, railway stations, Lake Victoria—the largest lake in Africa—the Victoria Falls in Rhodesia, and many towns, streets, etc., in various parts of the world.

Yet curiously enough, despite her long reign and the Victorians' love of new names, Victoria did not become fashionable in the nineteenth century, nor has it been much favoured since, though in the last few years there has been a revival. The pet forms are *Vick*, *Vicki*, and *Vicky* (sometimes *Vikki*).

To-day the Spanish contralto Victoria de los Angeles is in the top rank of singers; Vicki Baum, Austrian-born, but now a naturalized American, has a world-wide reputation as a novelist; and Victoria Sackville-West is well known as a novelist, poet, and critic.

Victorine is a French variation, actually the feminine of Victor, meaning not 'victory' but 'conqueror.'

VIOLET is the English version of the older Italian name *Viola*, Latin for 'a violet.' Viola, one of the oldest European genuine flower-names, is symbolically associated with modesty. The poet Gower, a friend and contemporary of Chaucer, used

it as a woman's name in his *Lover's Confession*, and Shakespeare
adopted it for his heroine in *Twelfth Night*.

Other old forms of the name, still occasionally given, are
Violette and *Violetta*, common in France and Italy respectively
during the Middle Ages. More common than either at that
time in both countries was *Violante*, brought to England in
1362 by the Duke of Milan's daughter, who married Edward
III's son. An alternative French form of Violante dating from
much the same period was *Yolande*, still popular in America—
probably through the influence of Hollywood—and also found
as *Yolanda*. *Iolanthe* is yet another variation of this name
revived when Gilbert and Sullivan's operetta of that name
was first performed in 1884.

In this country the commonest of all these forms to-day is undoubtedly *Violet*, though its use as a Christian name dates only
from the later part of the nineteenth century, when many flower
names came into use. In Scotland, on the other hand, where
French influence has long been more marked than in England,
it has been in regular use, at least since the days of Mary, Queen
of Scots, who had a devoted friend called Violet Forbes.

Viola and Violet share the pet forms *Vi* and *Vye*.

In the earlier years of this century Violet Meynell was regarded as a poet of the first rank; and to-day we have Viola
Tree, the actress; Violette Szabo, the French Resistance
heroine; Violetta Thurstan, the explorer; and Lady Violet
Bonham-Carter, the celebrated Liberal.

VIRGINIA Virginius, which probably means 'manly race,'
was the name of a Roman clan, and it is from this rather than
from 'virgo,' the Latin word for 'maiden,' that this Christian
name is derived.

The first known bearer was the beautiful daughter of a

Roman centurion living in the fifth century B.C. She changed the course of Roman history, When she was seized by one of the decemvirs (officials of the city, ten in number) to be his slave, her father snatched up a butcher's knife and stabbed her to death, exclaiming: "There is no way but this to keep thee free." He then rushed to the Forum, where he raised a revolt, as a result of which the decemvirs were deprived of their powers and were replaced by tribunes, who protected the rights of the common people.

In America the name has a different history, connected with Elizabeth, the "Virgin Queen." The State of Virginia was named in her honour by Sir Walter Raleigh in 1584. Three years later the first British child born in America was christened Virginia, and the name has been popular in America, especially in New England, ever since.

As *Virginie*, the name became widespread in France during the second half of the eighteenth century after the publication, in 1787, of Bernardin de St Pierre's story *Paul et Virginie*, glorifying the simple life.

Four years earlier the Marquis de Lafayette had written to Benjamin Franklin: "They ask me what name my daughter is to have, and as there is a good saint by the name of Virginie, I was thinking if it would not be presuming too much to let her bear a name similar to that of one of the United States." Franklin, who thought this an excellent idea, commented: "Miss Virginia, Miss Carolina, and Miss Georgia will sound prettily enough for the girls; but," he added, "Massachusetts and Connecticut are too harsh even for the boys, unless they were to be savages."

Virginia was not adopted in England until about a hundred years ago. In the present century it has been in regular, though not frequent, use. It has the pet forms *Ginny* and *Virgie*.

Virginia Woolf was among the most important novelists of the last half-century.

VIVIEN is the usual spelling nowadays when this name is given to girls, while Vivian is the spelling usually reserved for boys. More common in the Middle Ages were the forms *Bibiana*, the name of a martyr of the early church, and *Viviana*, still occasionally used in England, as is the modern French form *Vivienne*. All these versions trace their origin to the Latin word 'vivus,' meaning 'alive.'

The name came into vogue in the latter part of the nineteenth century, chiefly because of Tennyson's poem *Vivien and Merlin*, based on the Arthurian romances. In these, Vivien is an enchantress who outwitted even the wizard Merlin himself by trapping him in a hawthorn bush, from which she was afterwards unable to release him and he was unable to extricate himself!

An enchanting contemporary is Vivien Leigh, the actress.

WENDY seems to be essentially a theatre name. Even its origin is said to have been the baby-word 'Fwendie' used by a very young girl friend of Sir James Barrie, the playwright, as a pet name for the great man; he changed it slightly for the Wendy Darling of his *Peter Pan*.

To-day there are the actresses Wendy Craig and Wendy Hillier; and Wendy Toye is a theatrical and television producer and film director.

WINIFRED The lady known to-day as St Winifred was called by the Welsh *Gwenfrewi*, 'blessed reconciliation,' a name which later became confused with *Guinevere* and several other names. But the Anglo-Saxons, unable then as now to pronounce Welsh with comfort, called her by the nearest sounding Anglo-Saxon name, which meant 'friend of peace.'

St Winifred was beheaded in the first century A.D. by Prince Caractacus for refusing to marry him. From very early days pilgrimages have been made to Holywell, in Flintshire, where the spring marking the site of her martyrdom still bubbles out of the earth. The English were so devoted to this Welsh martyr that eventually they carried off her bones to Shrewsbury Abbey. But pilgrimages are still made to Holywell, mostly in the summer, though St Winifred's name-day is November 3.

It was not until the sixteenth century that the name was adopted in England, in a variety of forms of which *Winefred* and *Winnifred* have survived to the present day.

The usual pet forms are *Win*, *Winnie*, and *Freda*. The last of these, sometimes bestowed as an independent name in this country, is common in Austria and Germany in the form *Frieda*. There it has no connexion with Winifred, unknown on the Continent, but serves as a feminine version of Frederick (in German, Friedrich), which means 'peace-rule.' Other forms used in England are *Frida* and *Freyda*, as well as *Frederika*, common in the Netherlands, and *Fredrica*. Freda is therefore the German equivalent of the Greek-derived name *Irene*, for both mean 'peace.'

YVONNE is a feminine diminutive of the French boys' name Yves, which has its equivalent in the Welsh name Evan, itself a form of John.

Hardly used before this century, Yvonne has become very popular in recent years. Another version, *Yvette*, the name of a French saint, is also sometimes given as a font name in this country.

Its best-known bearer, the actress Yvonne Arnaud, was French-born.

ZOË The history of the name Zoë begins in the third century A.D., when the Alexandrian Jews translated the Old Testament. *Eve's* name in Hebrew scripture is *Hawwah*, and this was rendered in Greek as Zoë, which means 'life'—Eve being "the mother of all living."

It was at once adopted as a Christian name in the eastern Roman Empire, where it seems to have been used in all classes, for it was borne not only by at least three empresses, but also by a humble martyr.

Its use in England dates only from the middle of the last century, and has not been much used at any time since. More popular in America (also as *Zoa*), it has been given prominence there through Zoë Akins, the playwright whose comedy *The Greeks had a Word for It* has a peculiar aptness as regards the origin of her Christian name!

MAIN INDEX

The names printed in italic are the head-names of the text

P

SUPPLEMENTARY INDEX

The following list contains only names not included in the Main Index, though some less common forms of names figuring in the main body of the text are given; in such cases reference is made to the page on which the original name is dealt with.

It is, of course, impossible to compile a complete list of names, partly because it is hard to know where to draw the line between those which may be regarded as obsolete and those still in use—however little—and partly because new names and new variations of existing names are being invented daily, not only by personalities in the world of entertainment, but also by imaginative parents who feel that they would like their child to have a name no one else has ever borne.

Nevertheless, this list has been made as comprehensive as possible, and while the great majority of names given here are provided with their meanings, a small number defy interpretation, and whatever meaning could be attached to them would, in most instances, be purely personal to those who launched them. Most of these coined names were doubtless inspired by their pleasant sound or by some personal association.

ADONIA (*Greek-Syrian*), festival of Adonis

ADORÉE (*French*), adored

ADRIANA ⎫
ADRIANNE ⎬ (*Latin*), feminine forms of *Adrian*, 'of the Adriatic'
ADRIENNE ⎭

AELWEN (*Welsh*), fair brow

AERONA (*Welsh*), like a berry

AERONWEN (*Welsh*), fair berry

AFFRICA (*Irish*), pleasant

AFRA (*Hebrew*), dust

AGRIPPINA (*Latin*), born feet foremost

AIMIL (*Gaelic*), an equivalent of *Amelia* (p. 35)

AISLINN (*Irish*), dream, vision

ALA (*Germanic*), holy

ALANA (*Irish*), my child

ALANDA, a coined feminine form of *Alan*, 'harmony'

ALARICA (*Germanic*), all-powerful

ALBA (*Spanish*), dawn; (*Latin*), white

ALBERGA ⎫
ALBERTA ⎪
ALBERTHA ⎬ (*Germanic*), noble-bright
ALBERTINE ⎭

ALBINA ⎫
ALBINIA ⎬ (*Latin*), white

ALCINA (*Greek*), sea-maiden

ALCYON (*Greek*), calm, peaceful

ALDA (*Germanic*), old

ALDEGONDA (*Germanic*), old war

ALDITH (*Germanic*), old battle

ALDONA

ALDORA

ALDWYTH (*Germanic*), old battle

ALEDWEN (*Welsh*), a feminine form of *Aled*, 'offspring,' 'young one'

ALETTA (*Latin*), winged

ALFREDA (*Germanic*), elf-counsel

ALIDA (*Greek*), place-name

ALISA, a form of *Alice* (p. 31)

ALITA, a contraction of *Amalita*, 'toiler'

ALLEGRA (*Latin*), cheerful

ALMEDA (*Italian*), a conventional name in romances

ALMERIA ⎫
ALMIRA ⎬ (*Spanish*), name of a province; or (*Arabic*) princess

ALMOND (*English*), tree-name

ALODIA ⎫
ALODIE ⎬ (*Latin-Germanic*), all-wealth

ALOHA (*Hawaiian*), greetings and farewell

ALPHA (*Greek*), first letter

ALPHONSINE (*Germanic*), noble-ready

ALVA ⎫
ALVINA ⎬ (*Spanish*), white

ALVIRA (*Germanic*), elf-counsel

ALVONA

ALWYN (*Anglo-Saxon*), noble friend

ALZENA (*Arabic*), woman

AMADEA (*Latin*), loving God

AMALINA, a diminutive of *Amalia* (p. 97)

AMANTA (*Latin*), loving

AMARANTHA (*Greek*), unfading

AMARYL ⎱ (*Greek*), refreshing
AMARYLLIS ⎰ stream

AMBROSINE (*Greek*), immortal

AMELINA ⎱ diminutive of *Amelia*
AMELITA ⎰ (p. 35)

AMIEL (*French*), friend

AMINTA (*Greek*), protection

AMITY (*English*), Puritan 'virtue' name

AMOR ⎱ (*Latin*), love
AMORET ⎰

AMYNTA (*Greek*), protection

ANCHORET (*English-Welsh*), much-loved

ANDA ⎱ (*Greek*), feminine
ANDRA ⎰ forms of *Andrew*,
ANDREANA ⎰ 'manly'

ANDROMEDA (*Greek*), man-ruler; Perseus' wife

ANEIRA (*Welsh*), very white *or* truly golden

ANELLA, Ann+Ella

ANGHARAD (*Welsh*), much-loved

ANGWEN (*Welsh*), very beautiful

ANHUN (*Welsh*), unselfish

ANIELA (*Italian*), angel

ANKARET (*English-Welsh*), much-loved

ANNIFER, a telescoping of *Ann* and *Jennifer*

ANNIKA ⎱ diminutives of *Ann*
ANNINA ⎰

ANNONA (*Latin*), harvest

ANNORA (*Greek*), light; (*Hebrew*), grace; *or* Ann+Nora

ANNWEN (*Welsh*), very beautiful

ANOUK

ANSELMA (*Germanic*), feminine form of Anselm, 'divine helmet'

ANTIOPE

ANWEN (*Welsh*), very beautiful

ANWYL (*Welsh*), dear

APHRA ⎱ (*Hebrew*), dust
APHRAH ⎰

APHRODITE (*Greek*), born from the foam of the sea

APOLLONIA (*Greek*), of Apollo

APRILANN, April+Ann

AQUILINA (*Latin*), little eagle

ARAMINTA, a Restoration-drama invention

ARDATH (*Hebrew*), flowering field

ARDDUN (*Welsh*), sublime

ARDELIA (*Latin*), zealous

ARETA (*Greek*), virtue

ARETHUSA (*Greek*), virtuous

ARIADNE
ARIANE ⎱ (*Greek*), very pure
ARIANNA ⎰

ARIANROD (*Welsh*), silver disk

ARIANWEN (*Welsh*), silver-white

ARIEL ⎱ (*Hebrew*), lion of
God *or* (sacrificial)
ARIELLA ⎰ hearth of God

ARLEEN ⎱ formed from *Aline*
ARLENE ⎰ (p. 26); *or* (*Celtic*), a
ARLINE ⎰ pledge

ARMINE ⎱ (*Anglo-Saxon*), uni-
ARMINEL ⎰ versal

ARMOREL (*Gaelic*), dweller by the sea

ARNHILDA (*Germanic*), eagle-battle(maid)

ARNOLDINE (*Germanic*), eagle-power

ARTEMA ⎱ (*Greek*), of Arte-
ARTEMIS ⎰ mis, moon-goddess
ARTEMISIA ⎰ (*see* pp. 80–81)

ARTHURINE (*Celtic*), a feminine form of *Arthur*, 'bear'

ASPASIA (*Greek*), welcome

ASTERIA (*Greek*), radiant as a star

ASTRA ⎱ (*Greek*), star
ASTREA ⎰

ASTRELLA ⎱ (*Greek*), little star
ASTRELLITA ⎰

ASTRID (*Scandinavian*), god-strength

ATHALIAH ⎱ (*Hebrew*), whom
God has tried *or*
ATHALIE ⎰ tested

ATHANASIA (*Greek*), immortal

ATHELA (*Germanic*), noble

ATHENA (*Greek*), of Athens *or* the goddess Athene

ATHENE (*Greek*), goddess of wisdom

AUREA
AURELIA
AUREOL ⎱ (*Latin*), golden
AURIOL
AURIOLE ⎰

AUSONIA (*Latin*), poetic name for Italy

AVONWY (*Welsh*), dweller by the river

AWEL (*Welsh*), wind, breeze, zephyr

AWENA (*Welsh*), poetry; prophecy

AYLWEN (*Welsh*), fair brow

AZALEA (*Greek*), plant-name

AZURA (*Arabic-Persian*), blue

BAMBALINA (*Italian*), little baby

BASILIA ⎱ (*Greek*), feminine
BASILLA ⎰ forms of *Basil*, 'kingly'

BATHILDA ⎱ (*Germanic*), com-
manding battle
BATHILDIS ⎰ (maid)

BATHSHEBA ⎱ (*Hebrew*),
BATHSHUA ⎰ voluptuous

BATISTA (*Greek*), baptized

BEATA (*Latin*), happy

BEDELIA (*Irish*), a genteel form of *Bridget* (p. 60)

BEGA ⎫
BEGGA ⎬ (*Gaelic*), small
BEGHA ⎭

BEITHIDH (*Gaelic*), an equivalent of *Betsy* (*Elizabeth*, p. 92)

BELINA

BELPHOEBE (*Latin + Greek*), beautiful shining one

BENEDICTA ⎱ (*Latin*), blessed
BENICE ⎰

BENITA (*Spanish*), blessed

BERA (*Germanic*), bear

BERENGARIA (*Germanic*), bear-spear

BERINTHIA, an artificial Restoration-drama name

BERNEEN (*Irish-Anglo-Saxon*), little *Bernarda* (p. 53)

BERRY, a pet form of *Berinthia*

BERTILIA ⎱ (*Germanic*), diminu-
BERTILLA ⎰ tives of *Bertha* (p.54)

BERTWINE ⎱ (*Anglo-Saxon*),
BERWINE ⎰ bright friend

BETA (*Hebrew*), a form of *Elizabeth* (p. 92)

BETHAN (*Welsh*), a diminutive of *Elizabeth* (p. 92)

BETHESDA (*Hebrew*), house of mercy

BEULAH (*Hebrew*), married

BILLEE (*Germanic*), a pet form of *Wilhelmina*, 'helmet of resolution'

BINA (*Latin*), a diminutive of *Colombina*, 'dove'

BIRDIE (*English*), little bird

BLENDA (*Germanic*), dazzling

BLISS (*English*), bliss

BLODEUWEDD (*Welsh*), formed like *or* of flowers

BLODEYN (*Welsh*), flower

BLODWEN (*Welsh*), flower-white

BLOSSOM (*English*), blossom

BLYTHE (*English*), happy

BOADICEA (*Latin-Welsh*), victorious

BONNIE (*English-Scottish*), good

BRIALLEN (*Welsh*), primrose

BRIANA ⎱ feminine forms of
BRIENNE ⎰ *Brian*

BRILLIANA (*English-Dutch*), from a place-name—the Brill, in Holland

BRITA (*English-Scandinavian*), a form of *Bridget* (p. 60)

BRITANNIA (*English-Latin*), Britain

BRITOMART ⎱ (*Celtic*), sweet
BRITOMARTIS ⎰ maid

BRONYA (*Russian*), armour

BRORA, place-name (in Scotland)

BRUNELLA ⎱ (*French*), brown
BRUNETTA ⎰

BRUNHILDA ⎫ (*Germanic*),
BRUNILLA ⎬ cuirass-battle
BRYNHILD ⎭ (maid)

BRYONY (*English*), plant-name

BUDDUG (*Welsh*), victorious
(=Latin, *Boadicea*)

BUENA (*Spanish*), good

BUFF (*English*), a pet form of
Elizabeth (p. 92)

BUNNY (*English*), a pet name

BUNTY (*English*), a pet name for a
lamb

BURNETTA (*Old French*), little
brown one

BUTTERCUP (*English*), flower-
name

CADENCE (*English*), rhythm

CADWEN (*Welsh*), fair battle

CAIA (*Latin*), the feminine form
of *Caius*, 'rejoicing'

CAIREEN ⎱ (*Gaelic*), equivalents
CAIRINE ⎰ of *Catharine* (p. 143)

CALANTHA (*Greek*), beautiful
flower

CALISTA (*Greek*), fairest

CALLIDORA (*Greek*), beauty's
gift

CALLIOPE (*Greek*), beautiful
face—the Muse of epic poetry

CALVINA (*Latin*), bald

CAMPASPE

CANDACE, title of Ethiopian
queens

CARA (*Italian*), dear

CARAGH (*Irish*), love

CAREY (*English*), from the surname

CARINA (*Italian*), nice, dear

CARITA (*Latin*), cherished

CARLEEN (*Irish*), a feminine form
of *Charles*, 'manly'

CARMEL ⎱ (*Hebrew*), garden,
CARMELA ⎰ vineyard

CARMEN ⎫ (*Hebrew*), garden,
⎬ vineyard; *or* (*Latin*)
CARMINE ⎭ song

CAROLANNE, Carol+Anne

CARONWEN (*Welsh*), little fair love

CARRYL (*Welsh*), love

CARWEN (*Welsh*), fair love

CARYL ⎫
CARYLL ⎬ (*Welsh*), love
CARYS ⎭

CASHEEN, a diminutive of *Cassandra*

CASSANDRA (*Greek*), prophetess
(literally, 'snarer of men')

CASSIE, a pet form of *Cassandra*
or of *Catharine* (p. 143)

CASSIOPEIA (*Greek*), mother of Andromeda

CASTA (*Latin*), chaste

CEARA (*Celtic*), ruddy

CEINDRYCH (*Welsh*), reflection of gems

CEINLYS (*Welsh*), sweet gems

CEINWEN (*Welsh*), beautiful gems

CEIT (*Gaelic*), an equivalent of *Kate* (p. 145)

CELANDINA (*Greek*), swallow; *or* plant-name

CERI ⎫
CERIAN ⎭ (*Welsh*), love

CERIDWEN (*Welsh*), fair poetry

CERIS ⎫
CERYS ⎭ (*Welsh*), love

CESCA, a diminutive of *Francesca* (p. 111)

CHALICE (*English*), (communion-) cup

CHARMAINE

CHASTINA (*Latin*), pure

CHERIE (*French*), darling

CHERYL (*Welsh*), love

CHIARA (*Italian*), bright, illustrious

CHLORIS (*Greek*), 'green one'—name of a flower-goddess

CHRISTA (*Latin*), Christian

CHRISTELLE (*Latin*), follower of Christ

CHRISTOPHERA ⎫
⎪
⎬ (*Greek*), feminine forms of *Christopher*, 'Christ-bearing'
⎪
CHRISTOPHINE ⎭

CHRYSOGON (*Greek*), gold-born

CHRYSTAL, a variation of Crystal (p. 180)

CINDERELLA, nursery tale heroine

CINDYLOU, Cinderella *or* Lucinda + Louise

CLARICE (*French*), a form of *Clara* (p. 71)

CLARONA (*Latin*), a form of *Clara* (p. 71)

CLEA ⎫
CLEONE ⎭ (*Greek*), fame, glory

CLELIA (*Latin*), illustrious

CLEOPATRA (*Greek*), fame of her father

CLODAGH (*Irish*), a river-name

CLORINDA (*Persian*), renowned

CLOVA, possibly used as a feminine of *Clovis*=Louis, 'famous battle'

CLOVANNIS, *Clovis* ('famous battle')+*Agnes* (p. 27) or *Anna* (p. 39)

CLOVER (*English*), plant-name

CLYDIA (*Greek*), glorious

CLYTIA (*Greek*), sunflower

COBA, a short form of *Jacoba* (p. 132)

COBINA, a short form of *Jacobina* (p. 132)

COLINA (*Latin*), a feminine form of *Colin* (*Nicholas*), 'people's victory'

COLINETTE (*French-Greek*), a diminutive of *Nicola* (p. 174)

COLLEEN (*Irish*), girl

COLUMBA
COLUMBINA } (*Latin*), dove
COLUMBINE

COMFORT (*English*), comfort

CONCETTA (*Italian*), an ingenious thought

CONCORDIA (*Latin*), harmony

CONRADINE (*Germanic*), a feminine form of *Conrad*, 'bold counsellor'

CONSUELA } (*Spanish*), (Our
CONSUELO } Lady of) Counsel

CORBETTA (*Old French*), raven

CORDELIA
CORDELLA } perhaps *Latin*,
CORDULA } 'warm-hearted'

CORINTHIA, (woman) of Corinth

CORISANDE

CORNELIA (*Latin*), Roman family name

CORNUBIA (*Late Latin*), (woman of) Cornwall

CORTINA (*Latin*), veil; *or* place-name (in Italy)

COSETTE (*French*), a pet form of *Nicole* (p. 174)

COSIMA (*Greek*), order

CRESCENTIA (*Latin*), increase

CRESSA, a pet form of *Cressida*

CRESSIDA (*Greek*), golden

CRISIANT (*Welsh*), crystal

CRISPINA (*Latin*), curly-haired

CUNEGONDE (*Germanic*), family-battle

CUTHBURGA (*Anglo-Saxon*), famous fortress

CYNARA (*Greek*), plant-name (artichoke)

CYNFERTH (*Welsh*), chief beauty

CYRENA (*Latin*), mistress of the bridle

CYRILLA (*Greek*), a feminine form of *Cyril*, 'lord'

CYTHEREA (*Phoenician*) goddess (=Aphrodite) of the island of Cythera

DAFFODIL (*English*), flower-name

DAGMAR (*Germanic*), day-famous

DALE (*English*), dweller in the dale

DAMITA (*Latin*), little doe

DANA (*Celtic*), goddess of fertility

DANAË (*Greek*), she who judges

DANETTE, a French feminine diminutive of *Jourdain* (= *Jordan*, Hebrew, 'flowing down')

DANICA (*Danish*), Dane

DANIELLA ⎤
DANIELLE ⎥ (*Hebrew*), feminine
DANUSIA ⎬ forms of *Daniel*,
DANUTA ⎦ 'God is Judge'

DARCIE ⎤ (*French*), place-name
DARCY ⎦ (Arcy)

DARIA (*Greek*), possessing wealth

DARLENE ⎤ (*Anglo-Saxon*), forms
DARLINE ⎦ of 'darling'

DAVIDA ⎤
DAVINA ⎥ (*Scottish*), feminine
DAVINIA ⎬ forms of *David*,
DAVITA ⎦ 'friend'

DEANNA ⎤ forms of *Diana*, *Diane*
DEANNE ⎦ (pp. 80, 81)

DEBONNAIRE (*French*), well-bred, gracious

DECIMA (*Latin*), tenth

DELICIA (*Latin*), delight

DELIGHT (*English*), delight

DELILAH (*Hebrew*) a temptress (literally, 'delight')

DELINDA

DELLA, a diminutive of *Adela* or *Delia*

DELMAR (*Anglo-Saxon*), dale-famous

DELORA, a form of *Dolores* (p. 82)

DELPHA ⎤ (*Greek*), plant-
DELPHINA ⎬ name (larkspur); *or*
DELPHINE ⎦ dolphin

DELWEN (*Welsh*), neat-fair

DELYTH (*Welsh*), neat, pretty

DEMETRIA (*Greek*), belonging to Demeter (*see* p. 69)

DENA (*Anglo-Saxon*), dweller in in the valley

DEODATA (*Latin*), God-given

DEONE (*Greek*), obligation

DEORIDH (*Gaelic*), an equivalent of *Dorcas*, 'gazelle'

DERINA (*Anglo-Saxon*), a feminine of *Derwin*, 'dear friend'

DERRYTH

DERWYN (*Welsh*), oak

DERYN (*Welsh*), a short form of *Alderyn*, 'bird'

DESDEMONA (*Greek*), misery

DÉSIRÉE (*French*), desired

DESMA (*Greek*), chain; *or* used as a feminine form of *Desmond* (*Irish*), 'man from South Munster'

DEVONA, (woman) of Devon

DEVORGILLA (*Gaelic*), true oath

DEXTRA (*Latin*), right-handed; dexterous

DIAMANTA (*Latin*), diamond

DIDO (*Latin-Greek*), Queen of Carthage

DILYS (*Welsh*), sincere, genuine

DINKIE (*English*), cute

DITTANY (*English*), plant-name

DIXIE (*American*), regional name

DIZZY, a pet form of *Désirée*

DJUNA

DOANDA (*Anglo-Saxon*), dweller on the downs

DOLINA (*Slavonic*), valley

DOMINA (*Latin*), great lady

DOMINICA (*Latin*), 'of the Lord'

DONALDA, a feminine form of *Donald* (*Gaelic*), 'world-ruler'

DONALDINA, a diminutive of *Donalda*

DONATA (*Latin*), given

DONNA (*Italian*), lady

DORALINDA, Dora+Linda

DORANNE, Dora+Anne

DORCAS (*Greek*), gazelle

DORÉE (*French*), gilded

DORELIA

DORIA ⎫ (*Latin-Greek*),
       ⎬ (woman) of Doris
DORICE ⎭ (p. 84)

DORITA, a diminutive of Dora (p. 83), *or* a combination of Dora and Rita (p. 159)

DORYL

DOVE (*English*), bird of peace

DREDA, short form of *Etheldreda* (p. 45)

DRINA, a pet form of *Alexandrina* (p. 31)

DRUSILLA (*Latin*), Roman family name

DUA (*Latin*), two, double

DUANA (*Gaelic*), poem, song

DUSCHA (*Russian*), soul

DYDDANWY (*Welsh*), consolation

DYMPHNA (*Irish*), eligible

DYNA (*Greek*), power

DYSIS (*Greek*), sunset

EARTHA (*Germanic*), earth

EASTER (*Anglo-Saxon*), of the goddess Eostre

EBBA (*Germanic*), a short form of *Ebergard*, 'boar-protection' *or* *Eberhild*, 'boar-battle(maid)'

EDBURGA (*Anglo-Saxon*), noble protection

EDELINA (*Anglo-Saxon*), a form of *Adela* (p. 25)

EDINA (*Anglo-Saxon*), a form of *Edwina* (p. 89)

EDMONDA (*Anglo-Saxon*), a feminine form of *Edmond*, 'guardian of property'

EDREA (*Hebrew*), mighty

EDREEN

EDWARDINE (*Anglo-Saxon*), a feminine form of *Edward*, 'guardian of property'

EGBERTA (*Anglo-Saxon*), a feminine form of *Egbert*, 'illustrious sword'

EGIDIA (*Latin*), a feminine form of *Giles*, 'wearer of the goatskin'

EGLANTYNE (*English*), plant-name

EIDDWEN (*Welsh*), fond-beautiful

EILWEN (*Welsh*), fair brow

EIRA (*Welsh*), snow

EIRIAN (*Welsh*), silver

EIRIOL (*Welsh*), snowdrop

EIRLYS (*Welsh*), gold-sweet

EIRWEN (*Welsh*), snow-white

ELA (*Hebrew*), exalted

ELATA (*Latin*), exultant

ELBERTA (*Germanic*), noble-bright

ELDA (*Hebrew*), God hath called

ELDORA (*Spanish*), the gilded one

ELDREDA (*Anglo-Saxon*), old counsel

ELECTA (*Latin*), chosen

ELECTRA (*Greek*), amber

ELERI (*Welsh*), place-name

ELFIN (*English*), little elf

ELFLEDA | (*Anglo-Saxon*), elf-
ELFLIDA | beautiful

ELFREDA |
ELFRIDA | (*Germanic*), elf-strength
ELFRIEDA |

ELGIVA (*Anglo-Saxon*), elf-gift

ELISSA (*Phoenician*), another name for Dido, Queen of Carthage

ELLINDA, a combination of *Ella* or *Ellen* and *Linda*

ELLIS, an old equivalent of *Alice* (p. 31)

ELMA | (*Anglo-Saxon*), noble-
ELMER | famous

ELMIRA (*Arabic*), princess

ELODIE (*Latin-Germanic*), all-wealth

ELONA, a form of *Eleanor* (p. 91)

ELRICA (*Germanic*), all-powerful

ELSTRID

ELSWYTH (*Anglo-Saxon*), noble strength

ELVA | (*Anglo-Saxon*),
ELVIE | elfin

ELVINA | (*Anglo-Saxon*), elf-
ELVINE | friend

ELVIRA (*Spanish-German*), elf-counsel

ELWY (*Welsh*), benefit

ELWYN (*Welsh*), white-browed

ELYSIA (*Latin-Greek*), paradise

EMBLA (*Scandinavian*), the first woman (in Norse mythology)

EMERALD (*English*), jewel-name

EMILIANA, a form of *Emily* (p. 96)

ENFYS (*Welsh*), rainbow

ENNEA (*Greek*), ninth

ENNIS (*Irish*), place-name

ENOLA (*American*), place-name (Carolina)

EPIFANIA ⎱ born at Epiphany
EPIPHANY ⎰

ERASMA (*Greek*), desired

ERINNA (*Irish*), peace

ERLINA (*Anglo-Saxon*), little elf

ERMENGARD (*Germanic*), universal dwelling-place

ERMENGILDA (*Germanic*), universal servant

ERMINIA (*Germanic*), universal

ERNA ⎱ (*Germanic*), earnestness
ERNESTINE ⎰

ERYL (*Welsh*), watcher

ESPERANCE (*French*), hope

ESTEREL, a diminutive of *Esther* (p. 101)

ESTRELDA, see *Estrild*

ESTRELLA (*Spanish*), star

ESTRILD (*Anglo-Saxon*), a combination of Eostre, goddess of the rising sun, and 'hild', 'battle(maid)' (*see* p. 119)

ESWEN (*Welsh*), strength

ETHELREDA (*Anglo-Saxon*), noble counsel

ETHELWYN (*Anglo-Saxon*), noble friend

EUCLEA (*Greek*), glorious

EUDORA (*Greek*), she of fine gifts (*see* Doris, p. 84)

EULA (*Greek*), a pet form of *Eulalia*

EULALIA ⎱ (*Greek*), sweet of
EULALIE ⎰ speech

EUPHRASIA (*Greek*), delight

EURLIW (*Welsh*), gold-colour

EUROPA (*Latin-Greek*) Europe; *or*, in mythology, mother by Zeus of Minos

EURWEN (*Welsh*), gold-fair

EUSEBIA (*Greek*), pious

EUSTACIA (*Greek*), fruitful

EVADNE (*Greek*), fortunate

EVANGELINA ⎱ (*Greek*), bringer
EVANGELINE ⎰ of good news

EVANTHE (*Greek*), lovely flower

EVERIL ⎱ (*Anglo-Saxon*),
⎰ forms of *Averil*
EVERILDA ⎰ (p. 47)

EWIG (*Welsh*), roe, deer

FABIA (*Latin*), Roman family name (='bean-grower')

FABIANA ⎱ (*Latin*), diminutives
FABIOLA ⎰ of *Fabia*

FAINE (*Anglo-Saxon*), joyful

FARRAN, from the surname (='traveller')

FAUSTA ⎫
FAUSTINA ⎬ (*Latin*), fortunate

FEDORA ⎫ forms of *Theodora*
FEODORA ⎬ (p. 85)

FELDA (*Germanic*), wise, inspired

FERN (*English*), plant-name

FERNANDA (*Spanish-Germanic*), a feminine form of *Ferdinand*, 'journey venture'

FIDELIA ⎫
FIDELIS ⎬ (*Latin*), faith

FIDUCIA (*Latin*), confidence

FIFINELLA, a diminutive of *Fifi*, the French pet form of *Josephine* (p. 139)

FINA, a pet form of *Rufina* or *Seraphina*

FLAVIA ⎫
FLAVILLA ⎬ (*Latin*), yellow

FLEURDELICE (*French*), flower-name (iris or lilies)

FLORANTHE (*Latin + Greek*), flower-blossom

FLORETTA ⎫
FLORETTE ⎬ (*Latin*), little flower

FLORIMEL (*Latin-Greek*), flower-honey

FORTUNE (*English*), good luck

FOSSETTA (*French*), dimpled

FRANCA (*Italian-Germanic*), a form of *Frances* (p. 111)

FREA (*Scandinavian*), lady

FREDELLA (*Germanic*), peace-elf

FREDICIA (*Germanic*), peace-ruler

FREYA (*Scandinavian*), lady

FRIDESWIDE (*Anglo-Saxon*), peace-strong

FROANNA

FRUSANNA(H), Frances + Susanna(h)

FULVIA (*Latin*), tawny

GABRIELLA ⎫ (*Hebrew*), strong
GABRIELLE ⎬ woman of God

GAERWEN (*Welsh*), a place-name (literally, 'white fort')

GAIA (*Greek*), earth

GALA (*Italian*), finery

GALATEA (*Greek*), milk-white

GALE (*Anglo-Saxon*), pleasant, merry; *or* a pet form of *Abigail* (p. 23)

GALFRIDA (*Latin-German*), a feminine form of *Geoffrey*, 'God-peace'

GAMBLE (*Scandinavian*), old

GARDENIA (*English*), flower-name

GARLAND (*English*), garland

GARNET (*English*), jewel-name

GAY ⎫ (*English*), gay; *or* from the surname; *or* from
GAYE ⎬ *Gabrielle*

GAYNA, a form of *Guinevere* (p. 136)

GEMMA (*Italian*), gem

GENEVRA, a form of *Guinevere* (p. 136)

GENISSA

GERDA (*Germanic*), protection

GERLINDA (*Germanic*), spear-serpent

GERMAINE (*Latin*), German

GILBERTA ⎱ (*German*), bright
GILBERTINE ⎰ pledge

GILDA (*Gaelic*), servants; *or* (*Anglo-Saxon*), golden

GINETTE (*French*), a pet form of *Geneviève*, formerly of *Eugénie*

GINEVRA, a form of *Guinevere* (p. 136)

GINGER (*English*), red-haired; *or* a pet form of *Virginia* (p. 206)

GISELA ⎱ (*Germanic*), pledge
GISELLE ⎰

GITHA (*Anglo-Saxon*), war

GLENDA (*Welsh*), holy-good

GLENIS (*Welsh*), holy

GLENNA (*Gaelic*), glen

GLENYS (*Welsh*), holy

GLINDA, a variant of *Glenda*

GLINYS (*Welsh*), little valley

GLORIA (*Latin*), glory

GLORY (*English-Latin*), glory

GLYNIS (*Welsh*), little valley

GOEWIN (*Welsh*), sprightly

GOLDIE ⎱ (*English*), from 'gold'
GOLDY ⎰ or Goldilocks

GONERIL

GRACIOSA (*Spanish*), attractive, graceful

GRANIA (*Irish*), love

GRACIA ⎱ (*Latin*), favour, grace
GRATIA ⎰

GRATIANA (*Latin*), thanks

GRAZINA (*Italian*), grace, charm

GREGORIA (*Greek*), a feminine form of *Gregory*, 'watchman'

GUELDA

GULIELMA (*Latin-French*), a feminine form of *William*, 'will-helmet'

GULLA (*Scandinavian*), yellow

GUNHILD ⎱
GUNHILDA ⎰ (*Germanic*), war-battle(maid)
GUNILLA ⎰

GUSTAVA (*Scandinavian*), a feminine form of *Gustavus*, 'staff of the Goths'

GWENDYDD (*Welsh*), morning-star

GWENNOL (*Welsh*), swallow

GWENOG (*Welsh*), smiling

GWLITHYN (*Welsh*), dew-drop

GWYLFAI (*Welsh*), May festival

GWYNIFOR (*Welsh*), a form of *Guinevere* (p. 136)

GYPSY (*English*), gypsy, wanderer

GYTHA (*Anglo-Saxon*), war

HADRIA (*Latin*), of the Adriatic

HAFWEN (*Welsh*), summer-beautiful

HAGAR (*Hebrew*), forsaken

HAIDEE (*Greek*), caressed

HALA

HALCYON (*Latin-Greek*), calm, peaceful

HARMONIA (*Greek*), unity

HAYLEY (*English*), from the surname

HEBE (*Greek*), youthfulness

HEDDA (*Germanic*), strife-battle

HEDDWEN (*Welsh*), blessed peace

HEDY (*Germanic*), a pet form of *Hedwig* (p. 47)

HEFINA

HELIANTHE (*Greek*), bright flower; sunflower

HELMA (*Germanic*), helmet

HEPHZIBAH ⎱ (*Hebrew*), my de-
HEPZIBAH ⎰ light is in her

HERA (*Greek*), lady

HERO (*Greek*), Leander's sweet-heart

HERTHA (*Germanic*), earth

HEULWEN (*Welsh*), sunshine

HIBERNIA (*Latin*), Ireland

HIPPOLYTA (*Greek*), letting horses loose

HOLDA (*Germanic*), charming, gracious

HOLLY (*English*), plant-name; (*Anglo-Saxon*), holy

HONESTA (*Latin*), full of honou

HONEY (*English*), honey, sweet

HONORINE, a form of *Hono* (p. 175)

HORATIA (*Latin*), Roman family name

HORTENSE ⎱ (*Latin*), Roman
HORTENSIA ⎰ family name

HUBERTA (*Germanic*), a feminine form of *Hubert*, 'mind-bright'

HUGUETTE (*Germanic*), a diminutive feminine form of *Hugh*, 'heart,' 'thought'

HULDA (*Scandinavian*), covered; (*Germanic*), grace, charm

HULDAH (*Hebrew*), weasel

HYACINTHA ⎱ (*Greek*), flower-
HYACINTHE ⎰ name

HYPATIA (*Greek*), highest

IANTHE (*Greek*), flower-name (violet)

IDINA (*Scandinavian*), work

IDONEA (*Scandinavian*), Norse spring goddess

IGNATIA (*Latin*), the fiery one

IGRAINE (*Old French*), King Arthur's mother

ILA (*Anglo-Saxon*), island-dweller

ILEANA, a form of *Eleanor* (p. 91)

ILLORA

ILMA, a form of *Wilhelmina*, 'helmet of resolution'

ILONA ⎫
ILONE ⎭ forms of *Helen* (p. 122)

IMELDA

IOLA (*Welsh*), a feminine of *Iolo*, 'lord-value'

IONA ⎫
⎬ (*Greek*), flower-name (violet); *or* place-name
IONE ⎭ (Ionia)

IORWEN (*Welsh*), lord-beautiful

IPHIGENIA (*Greek*), of royal stock

IRMENGARD (*Germanic*), universal dwelling-place

IRVA ⎫
IRVETTA ⎭ (*Anglo-Saxon*), sea-farer

ISADORA ⎫
ISIDORA ⎭ (*Egyptian* + *Greek*), gift of Isis

ISLA, a shortening of *Isabella* (p. 130)

ISMAY

ISMÉE

ISMENA (*Greek*), learned

IVA (*Russian*), willow

IVANNA (*Russian-Hebrew*), a form of *John*, 'the Lord is gracious'

IVERNA (*Late Latin*), an old name for Ireland

IVETTE, a form of *Yvette* (p. 209)

JACINA

Q

JACQUEMINE (*French*), a diminutive feminine form of *Jacques* (see *Jacqueline*, p. 131)

JACINTA ⎫
JACINTH ⎬ (*Greek*), flower-name (hyacinth); *or* a
JACYN ⎭ jewel-name

JAEL (*Hebrew*), wild she-goat

JANCIS, a combination of *Jane* and *Frances* or *Cicely*

JAVOTTE (*French*), a diminutive of *Geneviève* (p. 113)

JENNA, a form of *Jane* (p. 133) or *Jennifer* (p. 136)

JERONIMA (*Greek*), a feminine form of *Jerome*, 'holy name'

JERYL

JEWEL (*English*), jewel

JOCASTA (*Greek*), shining moon

JOCUNDA (*Latin*), pleasant

JOLANDA, a form of *Yolanda* (p. 206)

JONQUIL (*Latin*), flower-name

JOSETTE (*French*), a diminutive of *Joséphine* (p. 139)

JOSIANA, adapted from *Josiane*, a French diminutive of *Joséphine* (p. 139)

JOVITA (*Latin*), of Jove (Jupiter)

JUBILEE (*English*), jubilee

JULETTA ⎫
JULITTA ⎭ variations of *Juliet* (p. 143)

JUSTA
JUSTIA
JUSTINA
JUSTINE
⎫
⎬
⎭
(Latin), feminine forms of *Justus*, 'just'

KARINA, a variation of *Katharine* (p. 143)
KELDA *(Scandinavian)*, fountain
KENDRA *(Anglo-Saxon)*, having knowledge
KENTIGERNA *(Gaelic)*, a feminine form of *Kentigern*, 'chief-lord'
KERRY, a place-name (in Ireland)
KETURAH *(Hebrew)*, fragrance
KEZIAH *(Hebrew)*, cassia
KIARA *(Italian)*, bright, illustrious
KIM, from the surname *Kimball*
KINBOROUGH *(Anglo-Saxon)*, royal fortress

LALA, a pet form of *Helen* (p. 122)
LALAGE *(Greek)*, babbler
LALITA *(Sanskrit)*, pleasing
LALLA
LALLY
⎫
⎬
⎭
(Scottish), a dweller in the lowlands
LAMIA *(Greek)*, devourer
LAMORNA
LANA *(Greek)*, shining; or a short form of *Alana (Irish)*, 'my child'
LARAINE
LARENTIA, a variation of *Laurentia* (p. 147)

LARISSA *(Greek)*, place-name
LATONA *(Latin-Greek)*, mother of Apollo
LAURAINE
LAUREN
LAURINA
⎫
⎬
⎭
(Latin), forms of *Laura* (p. 147)
LEAH *(Hebrew)*, heifer
LEANNA, Lee + Anna
LEDA *(Lycian)*, woman
LEE
LEIGH
⎫
⎬
⎭
(Anglo-Saxon), dweller by the clearing or meadow
LEILANI *(Hawaiian)*, heavenly flower
LENI, a German diminutive of *Magdalene* (p. 156)
LENICE, a feminine form of *Leonard*, 'lion-hard'
LEOCADIA *(Spanish-Latin)*, a form of *Leona*
LEODA *(Germanic)*, woman of the people
LEONA *(French-Latin)*, a feminine form of *Leo(n)*, 'lion'
LEONARDA *(Germanic)*, a feminine form of *Leonard*, 'lion-hard'
LEONIE
LEONTYNE
⎫
⎬
⎭
(French-Latin), feminine forms of *Leo(n)*, 'lion'
LEOPOLDINE *(Germanic)*, people-bold
LERRYN

LESBIA (*Greek*), (woman) of the island of Lesbos

LETA (*Latin*), joyful

LEWANNA (*Hebrew*), the moon

LIA (*Latin*), Vulgate form of *Leah*

LIANA (*Latin*), plant-name

LIDA (*Slavonic*), people's love

LILAC (*English*), plant-name

LILITH (*Assyrian*), storm-goddess

LILYBELLE, Lily+Belle

LINDYBETH, Linda+Elizabeth

LINDYLOU, Linda+Louise

LINNEA (*Scandinavian*), linden-tree

LINTRUDE (*Germanic*), serpent-strength

LIRA (*Greek*), lyre

LITA, the diminutive of any name ending in -*lita*

LIUSAIDH (*Gaelic*), an equivalent of *Louise* (p. 152)

LIVIA (*Latin*), Roman family name

LIZETTA, a diminutive of *Liza* (p. 92)

LLAWELA (*Welsh*), a feminine form of *Llewellyn*, 'leader'

LLIAN (*Welsh*), linen

LLINOS (*Welsh*), linnet

LLYNETH (*Welsh*), a form of *Lynette* (p. 90)

LOBELIA, plant-name

LODES (*Welsh*), girl

LOMOND (*Scottish*), place-name

LONA (*Middle English*), lone

LORELLY

LORRAINE (*French*), place-name

LOTUS (*Latin-Greek*), plant-name

LOUELLA, Louise+Ella

LOUVAINE (*French*), she-wolf

LOVE (*English*), love

LOVEDAY (*English*), day for settling disputes

LOVEJOY (*English*), love+joy

LUANA, possibly Lucy+Anna, possibly a form of *Lewanna*

LUCIDA (*Latin*), shining

LUCIPPE (*Greek*), white horse

LUCRECE ⎱ (*Latin*), Roman
LUCRETIA ⎰ family name

LUDMILLA (*Slavonic*), beloved of the people

LULLAN

LUNETTA (*Latin*), little moon

LUZETTE (*French*), a diminutive of *Lucy* (p. 153)

LYONELLE, a made-up feminine form of *Lionel*, 'lion'

LYRA ⎱ (*Greek*), lyre
LYRIS ⎰

LYS (*French*), lily; *or* a pet form of *Elizabeth* (p. 92)

LYSANDRA (*Greek*), liberator of men

LYSANNE, a combination of *Elizabeth* and *Anne*

MABYN (*Welsh*), youthful

MADORA (*Greek*), ruler

MAGNOLIA, flower-name

MAHALAH ⎱ (*Hebrew*), tenderness
MAHALIA ⎰

MAIA (*Latin*), May, month sacred to Maia, mother of Mercury

MAIDA, place-name (Italy, Russia); *or* from English 'maid'

MAIRONA (*Irish*), a diminutive of *Maire* (p. 165)

MALCA, a made-up feminine form of *Malcolm*, 'servant of St Columba'

MALDWYN (*Welsh*), place-name (Montgomeryshire)

MALELE

MALINDI

MALVA (*Latin*), plant-name (mallow)

MALVINA ⎱ (*Latin*), diminutives of *Malva*; *or* (*Gaelic*),
MALVINE ⎰ 'smooth brow'

MAMIE, an American form of *Mary* (p. 162)

MANDALA

MANETTE ⎱ (*French*), diminutive forms of *Mary* (p.
MANON ⎰ 162)

MANSIL (*Welsh-Norman*), from the surname

MANUELA ⎱ (*Spanish-Hebrew*),
MANUELITA ⎰ God with us

MARCELIA, a combination of *Marcella* and *Celia*

MARCELLA ⎱ (*Latin*), Roman family name (*Marcellus*—derived
MARCELLE ⎰ from Mars)

MARCELLINA, a diminutive of *Marcella*

MARCIA ⎱ (*Latin*), Roman family name (*Marcius*—derived from
MARCIANA ⎰ Mars)

MARELDA (*Germanic*), famed battle(maid)

MARESA, a form of *Mary* (p. 162)

MARIABELLA ⎱ (*Latin*), beauti-
MARIABELLE ⎰ ful Mary

MARIEL, a German diminutive of *Mary* (p. 162)

MARIETTA, a diminutive of *Mary* (p. 162); *or* a place-name (in Ohio)

MARIETTE, a diminutive of *Mary* (p. 162)

MARIGOLD (*Engl sh*), flower-name

MARILYN, a combination of *Mary* (p. 162) and *Lynn* (p. 90) or *Lynda* (p. 152)

MARINA (*Latin*), of the sea

MARISSA, a diminutive of *Mary* (p. 162)

MARISTA

MARITA, a combination of *Mary* and *Rita*

MARLENE, a telescoping of *Mary Magdalene*

MARRIL ⎱ diminutives of *Mary*
MARRIOTT ⎰ (p. 162)

MARTINA ⎱ (*Latin*), of Mars, war-
MARTINE ⎰ like

MARYSIA, a coinage from *Mary* (p. 162)

MAUDERINA, a diminutive of *Maud(e)* (p. 167)

MAVORA

MAWDWEN (*Welsh*), see *Maldwyn*

MAXIMA (*Latin*), greatest

MAXINE (*French-Latin*), a feminine form of *Maximilian* (=greatest striver)

MAYA (*Latin*), a variant of *Maia*, 'May'; *or* (*Sanskrit*), 'illusion'

MEDEA ⎱ (*Greek*), ruler
MEDORA ⎰

MEDWENNA (*Welsh*), from a place-name; *or* from *Modwen*, 'maiden,' 'princess,' 'queen'

MEHETABEL ⎱ (*Hebrew*), God
MEHITABEL ⎰ benefits

MEINWEN (*Welsh*), slender-fair

MEIRION (*Welsh*), place-name (county)

MELBA, an adaptation of the place-name Melbourne

MELENA ⎱ derivatives of *Amelina*
⎰ —a diminutive of
MELINA ⎰ *Amelia* (p. 35)

MELINDA (*Greek and Latin*), sweet-soft

MELITTA (*Greek*), plant-name (balm)

MELODIE ⎱ (*English*), melody
MELODY ⎰

MELROSE (*Latin-Greek*), honey of roses

MELVA (*Celtic*), chief; *or* from Welsh 'melfa,' 'sweet place'

MELVINA, a diminutive of *Melva*

MENNA (*Welsh*), a form of *Mona* (=Anglesey *or* Isle of Man)

MERAUD (*Old French*), emerald

MERCIA (*Anglo-Saxon*), woman from the marches (border-country)

MEREDITH (*Welsh*), greatness-chief

MERIDA (*Spanish*), place-name

MERRILEES ⎱ (*Anglo-Saxon*),
⎰ dweller by St
MERRILIE ⎰ Mary's field

MERRILYN, a version of Marilyn (=Mary + Lynn or Lynda)

MERRION (*Welsh*), a form of *Meirion* (=Merionethshire)

MERULA (*Latin*), blackbird (*see Merle*, p. 168)

MERYL (*Welsh*), a form of *Muriel*, *Meriel* (p. 172)

MIA (*Italian-Spanish*), mine

MICHAELA (*Hebrew*), who is like God

MICHELE ⎫
MICHELINE ⎬ French versions of
MICHELLE ⎭ *Michaela*

MIGNON ⎫ (*French*), darling
MIGNONNE ⎭

MILBOROUGH (*Anglo-Saxon*), gentle defence

MILENA

MILICA (*Slavic*), a form of *Amelia* (p. 35)

MIMI (*French*), a pet form of *Marie* (p. 163)

MINA (*Germanic*), a pet form of *Wilhelmina*, 'helmet of resolution'

MINELLA, a diminutive of *Minna* (p. 59), *Minnie* (p. 165), or *Wilhelmina*, 'helmet of resolution'

MINERVA (*Latin*), goddess of wisdom (originally of handicrafts)

MISKA

MITZI (*German*), pet form of *Maria* (p. 165)

MODESTY (*English*), modesty

MODWEN ⎫ (*Welsh*), maiden,
MODWENNA ⎭ princess, queen

MONA (*Irish*), noble; *or* place-name (=Anglesey *or* Isle of Man)

MONESSA, a diminutive of *Mona*

MORA (*Gaelic*), sun

MORGAINE ⎫ (*Welsh*, great-fair;
MORGAN ⎪ Morgan le Fay was
MORGANA ⎬ King Arthur's
MORGWEN ⎭ sister

MORINA, an anglicized form of *Morwenna* (*Welsh*), 'maiden'

MORNAY

MORVYTH (*Welsh*), chieftainess

MORWEN ⎫ (*Welsh*), maiden
MORWENNA ⎭

MOYA

MOYNA (*Irish*), noble

MUSIDORA (*Greek*), gift of the Muses

MWYNEN (*Welsh*), gentle

MYFINA (*Welsh*), a form of *Myfanwy* (p. 173)

MYLENE

MYLITTA, see *Melitta*

MYLOU

MYOLA

MYRRH ⎫ (*Arabic*), plant-name
MYRRHA ⎭

NAIDA (*Greek*), water-nymph

NARCISSE (*French*), flower-name

NARDA (*Latin*), plant-name (spikenard)

NATHANIA, a feminine form of the Hebrew *Nathan*, 'gift'

NEAL
NEALE } (*Gaelic*), champion

NELDA (*Irish*), a feminine form of *Neil*, 'champion'

NELLIAN, Nellie + Ann

NERINE
NERISSA } (*Latin*), sea-nymph
NERITA

NERYS (*Welsh*), a feminine form of 'ner,' 'lord'

NEVA (*Spanish*), snow

NIGELLA (*Latin*), black; *or* plant-name

NOELEEN } diminutives of
NOELINE } *Noel(le)* (p. 175)

NOKOMIS (*American Indian*), moon daughter

NOLA, place-name (in Italy)

NONA (*Latin*), ninth

NONNA (*Latin*), nun; (*Italian*) grandmother

NORBERTA (*Germanic*), northern fame

NORINE, a variation of *Noreen* (p. 176)

NORITA (*Irish*), a diminutive of *Nora(h)* (p. 175)

NORNA (*Latin-Scandinavian*), a Norse Fate (goddess)

NOVA
NOVIA } (*Latin*), new

NYMPHA (*Latin-Greek*), bride, nymph

NYMPHODORA (*Greek*), bride-gift, nymph-gift

OBELIA (*Greek*), pillar

OCTAVIA (*Latin*), eighth

ODELIA, a Latinized form of *Odile*

ODETTE } (*French-German*), a
} diminutive of *Ottilia*,
ODILE } 'heritage'

OENONE

OLIEN (*Russian*), deer

OLINDA

OLYMPIA (*Greek*), paradise

ONA (*Anglo-Irish*), a form of *Una* (p. 201)

ONDINE (*Latin*), wave

ONYX (*Greek*), jewel-name

OPHELIA (*Greek*), help

ORIANA (*Latin*), risen

ORIEL (*French-Latin*), gilded chamber

ORINDA

ORSA (*Latin*), bear (*see Ursula*, p. 202)

OSBERTA (*Germanic*), god-bright

OSYTH (*Anglo-Saxon*), god-war
OTHA (*Germanic*), prosperous
OTTILIA ⎱ (*Germanic*), fatherland
OTTILIE ⎰
OTIS ⎱
OTYS ⎰
OWENA (*Welsh-Greek*), a feminine form of *Owen* = *Eugenius*, 'well-born'

PALLAS (*Greek*), maiden
PALMYRA (*Portuguese*), palm-tree; *or* place-name (Syria)
PALOMA (*Spanish*), dove
PAMELIA, Pamela + Amelia
PANDORA (*Greek*), all gifts
PANSY (*English*), flower-name
PARNEL(L) (*English-Latin-Greek*), a feminine form of *Peter*, 'rock'
PARTHENIA (*Greek*), maiden
PASCHA (*Hebrew*), Easter (Passover)
PEACE (*English*), peace
PELAGIA (*Greek*), sea-dweller
PENROSE (*Welsh*), a place-name (in Monmouthshire)
PENTECOST (*English-Greek*), Whitsuntide
PEONY (*English*), flower-name (literally, 'peacock-flower')
PEPITA (*Spanish*), a pet form of *Josephine* (p. 139)

PERDITA (*Latin*), lost
PERILLA (*Latin-Greek*), a feminine form of *Peter*, 'rock'
PERLE (*French*), pearl
PERLITA (*Italian*), little pearl
PERONEL (*French-Latin-Greek*), a feminine form of *Peter*, 'rock'
PERPETUA (*Latin*), perpetual
PERSIS (*Greek*), Persian woman
PETA (*Greek*), a feminine form of *Peter*, 'rock'
PETAL (*English*), petal
PETICA (*Latin*), a feminine form of *Patrick*, 'nobleman'
PETRA ⎫
PETRINA ⎪ (*Latin-Greek*),
PETRONELLA ⎬ feminine forms of
PETRONIA ⎪ *Peter*, 'rock'
PETRONILLA ⎭
PETULA (*Latin*), seeker
PHILADELPHIA (*Greek*), brotherly love
PHILANTHA (*Greek*), lover of flowers
PHILIPINA ⎱ (*Greek*),
PHILIPPINA ⎰ horse-lover
PHILOMEL ⎱ (*Greek*),
PHILOMENA ⎰ nightingale
PHILYRA (*Greek*), lime-tree
PHOTINA (*Greek*), light
PIA (*Latin*), pious

Pier (*English-French-Greek*), a feminine form of *Peter*, 'rock'

Piety (*English*), piety

Placida (*Latin*), calm

Plaxy (*Cornish*), a form of *Prassede* (*Greek*), active

Pleasance (*English*), pleasure

Pleasant (*English*), pleasant

Polonia (*Late Latin*), Poland

Polyxena (*Greek*), very hospitable

Poppy (*English*), flower-name

Portia (*Latin*), porcine

Prassede (*Greek*), active

Primrose (*English*), flower-name

Proserpine (*Greek*), awe-inspiring

Protasia (*Greek*), offering

Prunella (*Latin*), little plum

Psyche (*Greek*), soul; butterfly

Pulcheria (*Latin*), beauty

Quenburga (*Anglo-Saxon*), queen-fortress

Quendrida (*Anglo-Saxon*), queen-strength

Quintella
Quintilla   ⎫ (*Latin*), fifth
Quintina   ⎭
Quita

Radegund (*Germanic*), counsel-war

Rafaela   ⎫ (*French-Hebrew*),
Rafaelle ⎭ God's healing

Raine (*Germanic*), advice

Ramona, a feminine form of *Ramón*, the Spanish version of *Raymond* ('advice-protection')

Raphaela (*Hebrew*), God's healing

Raymonde (*Germanic*), advice-protection

Rena (*Latin*), a short form of *Regina*, 'queen'

Renata (*Latin*), reborn

Rhea (*Greek*), an ancient earth-goddess

Rhedyn (*Welsh*), fern

Rhelda

Rhiain (*Welsh*), maiden

Rhiaingar (*Welsh*), maiden-loved

Rhiannon (*Welsh*), nymph, goddess

Rhianwen (*Welsh*), blessed maiden

Rhianydd (*Welsh*), nymph, goddess

Rhodacella

Rhodeia (*Greek*), rosy-cheeked

Rhodope ⎫ (*Greek*), rosy-
Rhodopis ⎭ faced

Ricarda (*Latin-Germanic*), a feminine form of *Richard*, 'power-strong'

RICHARDYNE (*Germanic*), ruler-hard

RICHENDA (*Germanic*), ruling

RICHETTE (*Germanic*), a diminutive of *Richard*, 'ruler-hard'

RICHMAL (*Anglo-Saxon*), ruler-sign

RIVA

ROBERTINA ⎱ (*Germanic*), feminine diminutives
ROBINETTA ⎰ of *Robert*, 'fame-
ROBINETTE ⎰ bright'

ROBIN ⎱ (*Germanic*), feminine of
Robin (*Robert*), 'fame-
ROBYN ⎰ bright' (*see* p. 191)

RODERICA (*Germanic*), a feminine form of *Roderic(k)*, 'fame-king'

ROESIA ⎱ (*Old French-Germanic*),
ROHAISE ⎰ early forms of *Rose*
ROHESIA ⎰ (p. 188)

ROMA (*Latin*), place-name (Rome)

ROMAINE (*French-Latin*), (woman) of Rome

ROMAIRE

ROMANA (*Latin*), (woman) of Rome

ROMOLA ⎱ (*Italian-Latin*),
ROMULA ⎰ (woman) of Rome

RONA, place-name (in Hebrides)

RONALDA, a feminine form of *Ronald* (*Scottish-Germanic*), 'power-force'

ROSECLEAR (*English*), rose without blemish

ROSELLE (*English*), plant-name (hibiscus *or* little rose)

ROSENDA

ROSSLYN (*Welsh-Cornish*), moorland lake

ROZELLE, see *Roselle*

RUDOLPHINE (*Germanic*), fame-wolf

RUE (*English*), pity; *or* plant-name

RUFINA (*Latin*), rosy, reddish

SABINA (*Latin*), Sabine woman

SACHARISSA (*Greek*), sweet

SADELLA ⎱ forms of *Sadie* (p.192)
SADELLE ⎰

SAFFRON (*English*), flower-name *or* colour-name

SALENA, Sal (Sarah)+Lena

SALETTE, little Sal (see *Sarah*, p. 192); *or* place-name (France)

SALINA, Sal (Sarah)+Lina

SALOME (*Greek-Hebrew*), peace

SAMANTHA ⎱ (*Aramaic*), listener
SAMANTHY ⎰

SANCHA ⎱ (*Spanish*), holy
SANCHIA ⎰

SANDRIA, a short adapted form of *Alexandria* (p. 30)

SAPPHIRA ⎱ jewel-name
SAPPHIRE ⎰

SARABEL, Sara + Belle *or* Isabella
SARALINDA, Sara + Linda
SASKA
SAXON (*English*), of the Saxon race
SCARLET ⎱ (*English*), flaming
SCARLETT ⎰ red
SCIENTIA (*Latin*), knowledge
SCILLA (*Latin*), plant-name (squill); *or Greek*, 'she who rends'
SEBASTIANA ⎱ (*Greek*), vener-
SEBASTIENNE ⎰ able
SECUNDA (*Latin*), second
SEIRIAN (*Welsh*), sparkling
SEIRIOL (*Welsh*), bright
SELDA, a short form of *Griselda* (p. 118)
SELIMA ⎱
SELMA ⎰ (*Hebrew*), peace
SEPTIMA (*Latin*), seventh
SERAPHINA ⎱
SERAPHITA ⎰ (*Hebrew*), seraph
SERENA (*Latin*), serene
SERICA (*Latin*), silken
SHANI, a form of *Jane* (p. 133)
SHARON (*Hebrew*), the plain
SHAUNA (*Irish*), a form of *Jane* (p. 133)
SHELLEY, from the surname
SHEREE, an anglicized form of French 'chérie,' 'darling'

SHERIDAN (*English*), surname from place-name (Sheraton)
SHERRY, an adaptation of *Caesar*
SHERYL (*American*), a form of *Shirley* (p. 194)
SHIREEN
SHONA, a form of *Joan* (p. 137)
SIDONIA ⎤ (*Greek*), linen; *or*
SIDONIE ⎬ (*Latin*), (woman) of
SIDONY ⎦ Sidon
SIGMUNDA (*Germanic*), victory-protection
SIGRID (*Scandinavian*), victory-beautiful
SILIS (*Gaelic*), an equivalent of *Cecily* (p. 65)
SILVANA, see *Sylvaine*
SIMONA ⎱ (*Greek*), snub-nosed
SIMONE ⎰
SIMONETTA, a diminutive of *Simone*
SINA (*Gaelic*), a form of *Sheena* (p. 134)
SIRIOL (*Welsh*), bright
SOLANGE (*French*), a pet form of *Solemnia*, 'solemnity'
SOLITA (*Latin*), accustomed
SOPHONISBA (*Phoenician*), daughter of Hasdrubal
SPERANZA (*Italian*), hope
SPERATA (*Latin*), hoped-for
SPRING (*English*), spring

STAR (*English*), star

STEFANIE ⎤
STEPHANA ⎬ (*Greek*), feminine forms of *Stephen*, 'crown'
STEPHANIE ⎦

STORM (*English*), storm

SULA (*Icelandic*), gannet; *or* a short form of *Ursula* (p. 202)

SULWYN (*Welsh*), sun-fair

SUNITA

SWANHILD (*Germanic*), swan-battle(maid)

SYDNA, a feminine form of *Sydney*, 'St Denis'

SYDNEY, an Irish form of *Sidony*, '(woman) of Sidon'; *or* from St Denis

SYLVA (*Latin*), woodland

SYLVAINE (*French-Latin*), dedicated to the god of trees

TABITHA (*Aramaic*), gazelle

TACITA (*Latin*), silent

TALLULAH (*American Indian*), running water

TAMAR ⎤
TAMARA ⎦ (*Hebrew*), palm-tree

TAMSIN ⎤
TAMZEN ⎦ (*Aramaic*), twin—pet forms of *Thomasina*

TANGWYSTL (*Welsh*), peace-pledge

TANIA, a pet form of *Tatiana*

TANIT (*Phoenician*), goddess of love

TANSY (*English*), plant-name; *or* a pet form of *Athanasia*, 'immortality'

TANYA, a pet form of *Tatiana*

TARA, name of a hill in Ireland

TARN (*English-Scandinavian*), mountain-lake

TATIANA

TEGAN (*Welsh*), beautiful

TEGWEN (*Welsh*), beautiful-blessed

TERENTIA (*Latin*), Roman family name

THALASSA (*Greek*), sea

THEA (*Latin*), goddess

THECLA (*Greek*), God-famous

THEDA (*Greek*), a short form of *Theodora* (p. 85)

THEKLA (*Greek*), God-famous

THELDA

THEOBALDA (*Germanic*), people-bold

THEODATA (*Greek* + *Latin*), God-given

THEODOSIA (*Greek*), God-given

THEOPHANIA (*Greek*), manifestation of God

THEOPHILA (*Greek*), beloved of God

THESBA

THETIS (*Greek*), disposer

THIRZA (*Hebrew*), place-name

THISTLE (*English*), plant-name

THOMASINA ⎱ (*Aramaic*), twin
THOMASINE ⎰

THORA (*Scandinavian*), dedicated to Thor, god of Thunder

THYRA (*Scandinavian*), dedicated to Týr, god of war

THYRZA (*Greek*), wand, staff

TIBELDA, a form of *Theobalda*

TIFFANY, a pet form of *Theophania*, 'manifestation of God'

TIMOTHEA (*Greek*), honour-God

TIPHANIE, a pet form of *Theophania*, 'manifestation of God'

TITANIA, name (='giantess') used by Ovid for *Diana*

TOPAZE (*English*), jewel-name

TOPAZIA (*Latin*), jewel-name

TORA (*Scandinavian*), dedicated to Thor, god of thunder

TRESILLA, from a place-name (Tresillian, in Cornwall)

TREVENA, a place-name (in Cornwall)

TRINKY

TRYPHENA ⎱ (*Greek*), daintiness
TRYPHOSA ⎰

TULLIA (*Latin*), Roman family name

UILEMHIN (*Gaelic*), equivalent of *Wilhelmina*, 'helmet of resolution'

ULRICA (*Anglo-Saxon*), wolf-ruler *or* all-powerful

ULTIMA (*Latin*), last

ULVA (*Latin*), plant-name (sedge); *or* (*Scandinavian*), wolf

UNDINA ⎱ (*Latin*), wave (in Roman mythology, a
UNDINE ⎰ water-sprite)

UNNA (*Icelandic*), woman

URANIA (*Greek*), sky; the Muse of Astronomy

URITH (*Germanic*), deserving

VALDA (*Germanic*), power-strength

VALETTE

VALISSA, from the surname *Vallis*, 'of Valois'

VALMA

VALMAI (*Welsh*), May-flower

VANDA (*Germanic*), kindred

VANNA, a short form of *Vanora* (p. 136) *or* of Giovanna, the Italian form of Joan (p. 137)

VARENNA

VASHTI (*Persian*), best (*see* p. 101)

VASSY, a Cornish variant of *Vashti*

VAYNOR

VELDA (*Germanic*), inspired, wise

VELMA

VENUS (*Latin*), love

VERANIA

VERENA, place-name (in Switzerland)

VERNAL (*English*), spring-like

VERONA, place-name (in Italy)

VERRA, a variation of *Vera* (p. 203)

VESTA (*Latin*), Roman goddess of the hearth

VIANNA, Violet + Anna

VICTORIOLA (*Latin*), a diminutive of *Victoria* (p. 204)

VIDA (*Scottish-Hebrew*), a short form of *Davida*, 'friend'

VIDETTE (*Welsh-Hebrew*), a feminine form of *David*, 'friend'

VILLETTE, in C. Brontë's novel, her fictional name for the city of Brussels

VILMA (*Germanic*), a short form of *Wilhelmina*, 'helmet of resolution'

VINCENTIA (*Latin*), conquering

VIRA, a diminutive of Elvira, 'elf-counsel'

VIREEN

VIRGILIA (*Latin*), Roman family name

VITA (*Latin*), life

VIVA } (*Latin*), alive
VIVIA }

VOLETA } (*Old French*), veil
VOLETTA }

WALBURG } (*Germanic*), power-protection
WALBURGA }

WALLIS (*English*), from the surname

WANDA } (*Germanic*), kindred
WENDA }

WENDELA }
WENDELLA } (*Germanic*), wanderer
WENDELINE }

WENONA } (*Santee*), first-born
WENONAH }

WILFREDA (*Anglo-Saxon*), a feminine form of Wilfred, 'will-peace'

WILHELMINA }
WILLA } (*Germanic*), helmet of resolution
WILLIAMINA }
WILLIMA }

WILLOW (*English*), plant-name

WILMA } (*Germanic*), forms of
WILMET } *Wilhelmina*, 'helmet of
WILMOT } resolution'

WINEMA (*American Indian*), chieftainess

WINONA (*Santee*), first-born

WINSOME (*English*), pleasant, attractive

WISDOM (*English*), wisdom

WYLMA, see *Wilhelmina*

WYNNE (*Welsh*), fair, blessed

XANTHE (*Greek*), yellow

XANTHIPPE ⎤ (*Greek*),
         ⎬ yellow mare;
XANTIPPE ⎦ wife of Socrates
XENIA (*Greek*), guest, host
XIMENA

ZAMIRA (*Hebrew*), song
ZANA (*Persian*), woman
ZELDA, a short form of *Grizelda*
  (p. 118)
ZENA (*Persian*), woman

ZENDRA
ZENIA (*Greek*), guest, host
ZENOBIA (*Greek*), life from Zeus
ZIA
ZILLAH (*Hebrew*), shade
ZINNIA (*English*), flower-name
ZONA (*Greek*), girdle
ZORANA ⎤
       ⎬ (*Slavic*), golden
ZORINA ⎦
ZULEIKA (*Persian*), brilliant
  beauty

LIST OF REFERENCE BOOKS USED

BARING-GOULD, S.: *The Lives of the Saints* (London, 1897).

BENET, W. R.: *The Reader's Encyclopedia* (London, 3rd ed., 1956).

BLAKENEY, E. H. (ed.): *A Smaller Classical Dictionary* (London, 1920).

BUTLER, A.: *Lives of the Saints* (1756–59; rev. ed. by H. Thurston and D. Attwater, London, 1956).

CAMDEN, W.: *Remains Concerning Britain* (London, 7th ed., 1674).

DAUZAT, A.: *Les Noms de Personnes* (Paris, 1956).

DAVIES, T. R.: *A Book of Welsh Names* (London, 1952).

HARVEY, SIR P.: *Oxford Companion to English Literature* (Oxford, 1946).

HASTINGS, J. (ed.): *A Dictionary of the Bible* (Edinburgh, 1900).

LANGER, W. L.: *An Encyclopedia of World History* (London, 1956).

MENCKEN, H. L.: *The American Language* (New York, 1936).

PARTRIDGE, E.: *Name This Child* (London, 2nd ed., 1938).

SWAN, H.: *Girls' Christian Names* (London, 1900).

WEEKLEY, E.: *Jack and Jill* (London, 1939).

WELLS, E.: *What to name the Baby (A Treasury of Names)* (Garden City Books, New York, 1953).

WITHYCOMBE, E. G.: *The Oxford Dictionary of English Christian Names* (Oxford, 2nd ed., 1959).

WOULFE, P.: *Irish Names and Surnames* (Dublin, 1923).

YONGE, C. M.: *History of Christian Names* (London, 2nd ed., 1884).

The Bible: Authorized Version.

The Book of Common Prayer.

Chambers's Biographical Dictionary (Edinburgh, 1953).

The Larousse Encyclopedia of Mythology (London, 1959).

Missale Romanum (Authorized edition, 1951).

Notes and Queries, passim.

Who's Who.